The Life I've Lived:

The Formation, Career, and Retirement of an Historian

Shepard B. Clough
Professor Emeritus of Western European History
Columbia University

University Press of America, Inc.™

P.O. Box 19101, Washington, D.C. 20036

Printed in the United States of America

ISBN: 0-8191-1116-3 (Case)
0-8191-1117-1 (Perfect)

Library of Congress Catalog Card Number: 80-5503

Shepard B. Clough

To

Marion

Contents

Introduction

by

Peter Gay, Yale University

Autobiographies by professors are rare; lively specimens of the genre are rarer still. Most academic reminiscences focus on great teachers from whom the author has learned, distinguished colleagues with whom he has worked, promising students whom he has taught. The professional space engrosses the personal space. Shepard Clough's recollections of a long and productive life reach out beyond the academy to place one professional historian's labors, his own, into a broader context.This is most welcome, as are Shep Clough's candor and clarity of presentation. His book is, in the true sense of the word, a life.

An academic career is not all scholarship and committee meetings; it is rife with anxieties and conflicts. There is the struggle of the junior instructor to make ends meet and to balance the often incompatible demands that his employer makes on him: the task of preparing for his classes interferes with the need to complete his thesis or write his first book for the sake of professional advancement. University departments are often most illogical: they insist on good teaching and persistently fail to reward it; they demand scholarly productivity but allow little time for it.

Nor is this all. There are the intelligent wives, themselves well educated and professionally active—most academics have such wives—who want time for their work, may have to pursue their researches in places remote from their husbands, and find jobs in other cities. Beyond this, the legitimate demands of family life and university service are often irreconcilable; the academic charts his course as though his channel were mined, zigzagging by adopting a series of compromises that wholly satisfy no one, least of all himself. There are, too, the efforts to please one's professional seniors without selling one's professional soul, and the efforts to find fellowship aid to do one's own work—academics nearly always refer to the scholarly enterprises that will take them away from their place of employment as their "own" work, broadly hinting that their university chores amount to what the Marxists call alienated labor. And there are the tides of history—depression, war, student unrest—that sweep over the university with sublime disregard for the quiet of the class room or the blissful isolation of the study and drag professors along in their undertow. Shep Clough, who has experienced all of these vicissitudes, deals with them here, frankly and fully. He spends little time on introspection: he tells us, rather, what he did and what he thought, confident that the standards of ethical and professional judgment by which he has always lived are substantially sound. The tensions in this book are in the world, not in its author.

To write an autobiography is to make choices. At first reading, I had wanted more professional detail, more about the habits and the writing of historians and politicians that Shep Clough has known; this is the higher gossip that the most staid of professors enjoys, and thrives on. But on second reading, I have come to see that his fundamenal choices are right—for him. This autobiography represents its author fairly: his family and his farm and his travels have occupied much privileged space in his life, and deserve full representation in an account of that life. I was Shep Clough's colleague in his department from 1956 on, but had known him before. And for three summers, 1960 to 1962, my family and I were his tenants in Peacham, Vermont—an experience that moved us to look for, and enabled us to find, a summer house in a neighborhood we had come to love. Thus I have known Shep Clough in the two capacities to which he devotes most of the space in these pages: as an urban professor at Columbia and as a rural householder in Peacham. And this enables me to testify to the accuracy of his self-portrait, both in its general balance and its specific detail. I do not remember or judge everything precisely as he remembers or judges them—his treatment of the student uprisings at Columbia in 1968 strikes me as rather more jaundiced than I would treat the same events: I do not think that so much of the faculty was as feeble, as eager to surrender, as he suggests. But whatever my cavils. I recognize his account and respect his feelings; the sentence with which the chapter of 1968 ends—"Retirement came, unfortunately, as a great relief"—is poignant in its simple resignation.

Yet in the years that Shep has been retired, years to which he devotes a lively concluding chapter, have been far from resigned. They squarely confront another issue that academics like to evade: what to do with oneself after one's regular routine—the class taught, the office hour, the departmental meeting—has been abruptly, cruelly, irreversibly destroyed by the logic of the calendar. Here too, cultivating his garden like a latter-day Candide, as in the earlier chapters, Shep Clough has much to tell us and invites us to listen.

The Life I Have Led

Chapter I

The Formative Years

To write about oneself is not precisely an immodest act. So, I apologize at the outset for what on this occasion is a lack of modesty.

I take pen in hand in the hope that at my advanced years (seventy-nine at the end of 1980) I have something to say about my life that will serve as a guide to those who come after me and that may be of interest to those who have known me. I must admit, however, that I enjoy writing and that the subject being dealt with here can be treated with reliance only on my memory. No library or archival research was required, thank God, for what follows.

From the beginning one should realize that my story is that of a country boy of a middle income family who rose on the stepping stones of education to the rank of full professor in the field of Western European history in one of our leading urban universities. This fact does not make my life unique, but the process by which I have gone through the maze of life is rare enough.

The account of my life, which I herewith give you, begins with such matters as the formation at an early age of my personality traits, of the establishment of my hierarchy of values, of my habits, and of the pains and pleasures of family life. Then, it goes on to treat of the selection of a profession, to the vicissitudes and rewards of an academic career, and to problems of teaching and research. It concludes with how one winds down one's life in old age "sans teeth, sans eyes, sans taste, sans everything"—to coin a phrase.

In the process of telling my story, I shall place especial stress upon my conviction that one cannot really live one's life by a trial and error method. At every moment—at every step—one is playing for keeps.

If this prologue, dear reader, intrigues you, carry on. If it does not, please place the book in the hands of someone who is more curious about life than you and has sympathy for poor professors.

I suppose that, logically speaking, the most important day of my life was December 6, 1901, for on that day I was born. The place of this happy event was Bloomington, Indiana. Inasmuch as my formative years were spent in New Hampshire, I have always been regarded as a New Englander; and as my English accent places me unmistakably in the northeast, a word of explanation concerning my birthplace is in order.

My birth occurred while my father was the preacher in the First Baptist Church of Bloomington, Indiana. That fact also requires an explanation. Father was the only child of a tanner of Wilmot Flat, New Hampshire, population 300, a thoughtful man, who, as a Unitarian, had a real addiction to Robert Ingersoll, the Roycrofters, and Elbert Hubbard. He read widely in English literature and was very fond of Dickens. He imbued my father with a love for reading and he encouraged him in his elementary schooling, obtained in a one-room schoolhouse. Then my grandfather made it possible for father to go on to a secondary education at Colby Academy (now Colby-Sawyer College) in the neighboring town of New London. Here my father became interested in religion and got the notion of becoming a minister. It was here, also, that he met my mother, a *petite* young lady, whose father was a successful farmer (his farm is now The Lake Sunapee Golf Course). My grandfather Shepard was a state Democratic leader and is said to have provided the American novelist, Winston Churchill, with much of the material for his novel *Coniston*, which is about rural politics in New

Hampshire. My parents seem to have been drawn togther by similar interests and goals and while still teenagers had at least a tacit understanding that some day they would be married.

At Colby, my parents did well in their studies. In addition, my father made a reputation for himself in public speaking and my mother, for herself, in writing poetry. They did so well, in fact, that their teachers urged them to continue their education in college. This they did. My father went to Yale, and my mother to Smith. How those two managed financially is somewhat of a mystery to me, for they received very little money from home. To be sure, tuition in those days of "education without frills" was low, but one did have to have some money for eating and sleeping. For these expenses, my father tutored rich boys and kept furnaces; my mother received food packages from home and cooked her own meals.

In spite of hardships, however, they found time for extracurricular activities. My father acquired some renown as a member of a debating team that defeated Harvard, and my mother continued to produce poetry, some of which was published in the college literary magazine. Best of all, however, they continued to see each other and to have their affections deepen.

Their futures remained vague, however, until one day, one of my father's professors, William Rainey Harper, entered upon the scene. My father was a student in a course given by Professor Harper and had come to the Professor's attention by his sincerity and his good work. One day he asked my father to stop by his office after class and when my father did so, Harper spoke as follows: "Clarence, I understand that you intend to become a minister. If this is so, I may be able to help you." He then went on to explain that John D. Rockefeller had decided to create a great university at Chicago, had selected him to be its president, and had begun to construct buildings. "Now," said the future President of Chicago University, "we need some students. Clarence, would you be interested in being one of them? I propose that you come to our divinity school; we'll be in a position to help you financially." My father accepted this offer with alacrity, for here was a chance to prepare for the very calling he wanted.

Thus did my father take the first definite step toward becoming a Baptist minister. He married my mother soon after the above incident, and they went to Chicago. Once there he obtained a "mission" church in a very tough neighborhood, which added enough to his fellowship to keep his grocery bills paid.

I have never known much about his three years in the theological seminary, but I did inherit books in Hebrew and Greek which date from the years he was there, to say nothing of a slew of volumes on homiletics, on the history of the Christian religion, and sermons for use when one has not prepared one's own! These tomes suggest that the training was rigorous; and that father did well is evidenced by the fact that he received glowing recommendations to the First Baptist Church of Bloomington, Indiana and received a "call" to it.

At Bloomington things seem to have gone well, at least at first. He raised enough money to build an imposing stone church (since demolished); he doubled the membership of the church; he taught courses on religion at the University of Indiana; and he made many good friends, including Elmer Burritt Bryan, subsequently President of Colgate University.

The life of a minister in the "Bible Belt" was not, however, an easy one in those days, or, for that matter, in ours. Preachers' salaries were low and parts of them were paid in potatoes, "nubbin' ears" (little ears of corn), and wood that was green or rotten. Such an income seemed demeaning to my father, but this was not the heaviest cross he bore. That was the criticism which he received from some of the prigs in his congregation. They complained that he played cards, condoned dancing, enjoyed harness racing, and did not believe in the literal interpretation of all the tales of the Bible

Such faultfinding was hard to take, especially by my father, who was not a patient man. Indeed, he was an irascible person and when he blew a fuse, the lights went out for miles around. Gradually he became disenchanted with the ministry and toyed with the idea of seeking something else to do.

What brought matters to a head seems to have been a financial crunch when children began to arrive. My elder sister was born in 1898 and I in 1901. Furthermore, the story goes that when he had taken a good look at me, his faith in an all-loving Heavenly Father was badly shaken.

Finally, in 1902 my father decided to leave Bloomington and go back to Chicago to do social work rather than to preach; and my mother concurred in his resolution. At this point, however, my grandfather Clough, the tanner, heard of the intended move and intervened. He invited my father to return to New Hampshire and to go into business with him. The development of a method of producing tannic acid synthetically had rendered obsolete tanning from the bark of trees. So my grandfather closed his tannery and bought a small-town coal, wood, ice and building material business. He was progressing in years and wanted his son to run the new business with him. This invitation was, I am sure, motivated, in part, by the desire of both my grandparents to have their only son with them.

Here was a solution to some of the problems which had been bothering my father, but to accept the proposal would mean a drastic change in his life and the sacrificing of a long desire and protracted preparation for the ministry. Accept it he did, however, but I know that he was never very happy in his business life and sought consolation in forms of public service that stretched from membership on the local school board through a stage in the state legislature and from serving as a substitute minister to membership on the boards of trustees of several institutions.

The story which I have just recounted, I hope in not too much detail, explains why from infancy I was reared in the small town of Lebanon, New Hampshire. Like so many other villages of New England the economy of this place was based primarily upon textiles. A small river provided needed power for the factories and French Canadians furnished relatively cheap labor. Fortunately for me, Lebanon is situated near Dartmouth College and this proximity furnished a certain cultural atmosphere, which was to have a bearing on my future development.

As a child, I did not enjoy robust health. I had not only the usual children's diseases but also every winter a bad case of the grippe, and I nearly died of diphtheria—I was the first in town to be given an anti-toxin for it. I think that my frequent illnesses had much to do with forming my penchant for reading, study, and reflection. As soon as I was able, I delved into the history of America—a habit which was encouraged by the fact that I was distantly related to George Bancroft and, because of this fact, had Bancroft as a middle name.

As I went along in school, I did very well, although I usually fell sick at the moment of crucial examinations. These crises so disturbed me that even now I have nightmares about getting behind in whatever work I am doing. I still fret when some task hangs over my head and I do not see ahead to its conclusion. Also, I think that I learned, when I did not reach the top, how important it is to keep on plugging if one wants to be a success. I remember once that my father told me, in a rare heart-to-heart talk, and not very flatteringly, that one can compensate for a lack of innate brilliance by working a little harder and especially more steadily than one's closest competitors. I never forgot his words.

As I look back upon my grammar school days in Lebanon, I realize that much of the instruction which I received was from excellent and devoted teachers. Even at the time I thought that this was the case. Contrary to the experience of John Dewey, whom I came to know at Columbia, I enjoyed my work. To be sure, we were drilled in many details, such as spelling, diagramming sentences, the multiplication tables, and the theorems in geometry, but we enjoyed *knowing*. I am appalled by the lack of attention given nowadays to fundamentals in modern education. Either teachers are so ignorant that they do not know what to teach or they are too lazy to drill their students. They hide their lack of knowledge and their sloth behind theories of education perpetrated as gospel. For example, they preach that children should be allowed to *communicate*, and that communication should not be impeded by the rules of spelling, grammar, or composition. They are unwilling to realize that illiteracy is itself a severe obstacle to communication.

In my day, we devoted considerable time to public

speaking. I am frequently stunned by the performances of college graduates when they appear on public platforms. Their reliance on "Ya Know" is pitiful. Their ability to get their message, if any, across is dismal. Oh, for the return of spelling bees and forensic competitions, especially debates. I remember so well the aphorism of my economics teacher at college, Lionel Edie, later a successful investment counsellor, that the group in college which has succeeded most in life was composed of former members of debating teams.

My taste for public speaking was surely whetted by the fact that my father had been successful at debating and was often called upon for "orations" on Fourth of July celebrations or to speak at political rallies. I had the notion that debating was something at which I would be good. So when I was in the eighth grade, I connived a challenge to the seventh grade to debate the question: "Be it resolved that Abraham Lincoln was a greater President of the United States than George Washington." We drew lots for sides and my team had the affirmative. We practiced diligently, but on the appointed day went down in ignominious defeat. The one who did us in was Louise Bryant. How I hated her pigtails for that, but I came to love them later on, as we shall see.

Before leaving the subject of teachers and schools, I would say one more word about the devotion of my teachers to their tasks. They were disciplinarians. They stood for no non-social permissiveness. Mr. Smith, my teacher in the eighth grade, had an isolation ward for the mischievous, which was in an empty room adjoining his classroom and within ear-shot of what was going on. I shuttled back and forth between these two locations, although I admired him very much and he liked me. I am sure that I was a bothersome kid and made a nuisance of myself. I thought at the time that the trouble was that I did not have enough to do to keep me interested in school work. This rationale was enforced by the fact that when I visited a one-room school house, I was so wrapped up in what the more advanced students were doing that I got into no trouble at all. I might add that much can be said for combining grades, as was done in one-room schools, and much can also be said against centralized institutions with their bus rides of two or three hours a day. What a waste of time!

My youth, although heavily oriented toward books and learning, had its other aspects. There was the family, which in my case was a tremendous influence upon me. My parents had struggled hard to "make something of themselves" and they imparted to their children the desirability of doing likewise. In fact, four of the five Clough children were at one time in one or another of the various *Who's Who*—three of us from teaching and the fourth from magazine writing. The fifth had an excellent reputation in the decoration of antiques. We were a close group and did much together. We had family sings around the piano, especially at Christmas, and I can remember that my mother reported once that Miss Morris, the town librarian, a maiden lady of a certain age, told her that after having passed by our house and having seen us singing together, she went home and cried her heart out because she had no family.

My father was a hard working man, but, as I have already reported, was thwarted in what he had hoped to do with his life. Yet he was successful in business within the limits of the possibilities of his local environment. My mother was, however, the one who comforted us when we were in trouble and exercised patience in her efforts to have us make good. She would help us with our lessons, when we faltered, and she would pick us up, when we stumbled.

Our most enjoyable family holidays were Thanksgiving and Christmas. The former we usually spent with our Mother's family at New London, twenty miles away, and I have a vivid recollection of the time fifty-three children and grandchildren of Eli and Lucia Shepard sat down to dinner in the spacious living room of their house. This was a big event and we were usually prepared for it by reading stories of the Pilgrims or poems by Whittier.

Christmas was, however, the high spot of the festive year. It was always spent with grandfather and grandmother Clough at our house. We had a strict ritual regarding it. We always had a tree from our own woods. We always went to Church on Christmas Eve, where we sang carols and received a present of an orange from a local grocer. We always put out a sandwich for Santa Claus in case he might be hungry and he always took one bite to prove his physical existence. And we always got the same rationale for his not eating all the sandwich—he was in such a hurry to visit other children that he could not stop to eat it all. Also, we always read aloud at some time of the season U. H. H. Murray's *How John Norton the Trapper Kept His Christmas*, which is one of the most beautiful Christmas stories ever written. It brought tears to our eyes and at crucial parts made my father choke with emotion. Whenever a substitute was tried, like Dicken's *Christmas Carol*, we children always felt let down.

The high spot of Christmas Day consisted of "having the tree." We placed our presents for one another under the tree on Christmas eve and then distributed them on Christmas morning, but only *after* the dishes had been done,and *after* our grandparents had arrived. Presents were taken from the tree in such a sequence that no one was slighted and each present was opened and commented upon before the next one was taken.

After the tree we would usually take our outdoor toys, like sleds or skates or skis, for trial runs and to get up an appetite for the dinner. And what dinners we had. The *pièce de résistance* was roast turkey with wonderful sage dressing, cranberry sauce, baked squash, boiled onions, and then celery and olives—celery the only fresh vegetable that I can remember we had from late summer until dandelions or parsnips were dug in the spring. And how we loved it. For dessert there were pumpkin and mince pies and a custard pudding that my grandmother Clough made which was a work of genius. It came out in layers of different custards—an effect achieved I think, by different finenesses of bread crumbs and raisins and letting the whole settle for an hour or so. Try as I have, I have never been able to duplicate this dish.

Following the dinner, we went outside again, to slide with our sleds or double runners on the hill behind our house. We also skied or skated, depending on snow and weather conditions. Skiing was introduced in our town by Finns and Norwegians who came to the mills of the town. I can hardly remember when I could not ski. Why I did not break my neck is something I shall never know. I have recently returned to places where I used to jump, and they now scare me to death.

Skating was, however, my great forte and in our area skating meant playing hockey. It was brought to us by French Canadians who came to the town either as lumberjacks or mill hands. Some of them were excellent players and raised the level of our game to a high enough standard so that our "town team" could play the Dartmouth varsity without disgrace.

I skated well and in the sixth grade was able to beat Mr. Smith, my future eighth grade teacher, who was reputed to be a Hans Brinker. Inasmuch as I was small and not very rugged, I had my tormentors of the bully type. Several of them were of the minority group of our town—descendants of French Canadians. They would rough me up on the playground and "get me" in football. But I kept track of the injuries that they did me and when it came to hockey, I'd get my revenge. We played without the protective devices now used and shins were a vulnerable spot. Mine were usually raw from early winter to late spring, but certainly no rawer than those of my sworn enemies.

Although Thanksgiving and Christmas were the highlights of our family life during my youth, we did many other things as a group. One of those was to go away on automobile trips. One of the most memorable, but also the most miserable, was a camping trip to the White Mountains together with another family from Bloomington, Indiana, that my parents had been friendly with when my father was a minister there. My father's car was a Stanley Steamer, which was not the most trouble-free vehicle ever invented. It had a habit of going into a loud hum when it saw high-brows, a noise that was something like a low-key siren. At Bretton Woods, before all the social brass of the area, it put on the best performance of its career. My sister and I were completely mortified! This was nothing, however, to the discomfort we had on the trip. It rained hard every day, and especially at the time we had to pitch tent or build a fire to cook the trout that my father was always providing. I never became so water-logged in my life.

Another trip of fond memory was when we children were taken for a week to visit "historical Boston." Boston, not New York, was the hub of our universe. We went down in our trusty Stanley Steamer which was always an event. In those days tires were good for only five or six thousand miles, and were so expensive that every effort was made to stretch their lives with inner-tube patches, "boots" that went over the outside of the tire, and liners inside the shoes. Going to historical sites involved driving over cobblestone streets that were murder on tires. On one hot day our tires popped like pop-corn and I decided that I could put up with anything that hell might furnish so long as it was not changing tires and pumping them up by hand.

I recall very distinctly that in those days I was very sensitive to city smells. We stayed in the home of a distant relative, who turned over his house to us, for putting up so many bodies at the Copley Square was more than the family budget could stand. The house had a musty odor that had a peculiar effect on my stomach. So, too, did the Peabody Museum, Faneuil Hall, and the Mother Church. But when we hit T wharf, that did it. In those days this area of the city was dominated by a stench that combined roasting coffee, horse manure, dried cod, and rotting fish and fowl.

The trip was, however, wonderful. I landed all over again at Plymouth Rock; I threw tea into the harbor; I went up in the tower of the Old North Church, for which I had to memorize the *Ride of Paul Revere*; I saw Harvard; I visited Lexington; and I walked over Concord Bridge where the shot that was heard around the world was fired. It was an amazing experience and one that did much to increase my appetite for history.

Some years the family went to the beach for our vacation and on most such occasions we headed for York Beach, up on the bluff, where the waves pounded most magnificently and where the fishing was good. The trip down stands out, however, most vividly in my memory. The Stanley Steamer was, like all other cars at the time, an open car with a top that could be pulled up in case of need. When the roof was folded down, the folds were a wonderful place in which to store things. Because we needed space in the car in which to put *humans*, my Mother put *things* in the folds of the cover—things like food, and among the food a bag of flour. On the way to York Beach the rains came. Father stopped the car and in a hurry stretched the folded top over the occupants of the car. As he did so the bag of flour came forth as though shot from a gun and made a direct hit on the head of the wife of the superintendent of schools, who, for reasons I do not recall, was with us. I've never seen a better job of marksmanship in my life.

When we did not go as a family on our summer vacations, my elder sister and I were invited to a camp owned by an aunt on Lake Sunapee—a place which we adored. I never was sent off to summer camps, nor were the rest of us, but I did go to Camp Abnaki on Lake Champlain as a counsellor the year before I went to college. This was largely to see new country and to recover from an operation. At about this time, or a year later, my father bought a lot on the shores of Mascoma Lake, near Lebanon, and built a cottage on it which I did much to design. It was not very beautiful, but it was very livable. It kept the family together and became a rendez-vous for my generation and for my children, nieces, and nephews. It is great to have a place like this to give people roots.

In that period of my youth I engaged in most of the sports that were then in vogue. I played baseball and football, but I was not good at either, for I was small and somewhat frail. I could field a ball and also hit, but my throws were slow and my hits were short. About all I have to show from football is a broken nose, which still bothers me, and a knee that tells me the approach of a storm.

I did not hunt, as many other boys of my town did, but I did fish for brook trout. This was my father's favorite diversion and he used to take me with him when he went off to try his luck on the brooks of our area. These junkets usually took place in May or June when the black flies were at their most vicious, and how I became a devotee of fishing is difficult to explain. To be eaten alive by pesky flies and mosquitoes, to spend hours untangling one's line from bushes, and to tramp miles through swamp and brush, and to have fun is something that no modern t.v. addict will ever understand. Yet it *was* fun. To outwit a speckled beauty and then to bring it home to the applause of the potential consumers provided recompense in abundant measure.

Finally, I should add three other "sports" to my list. One, which was a favorite, was the gathering of spring flowers. No one who has never done it can imagine the thrill which comes from going into the fields and forests in early spring when the earth awakes from its long winter's sleep; to discover where the hepaticas bloom the first, where trilliums with their pungent odor may be found, or best of all, to find the first trailing arbutus of the year. These are joys the city dweller can never appreciate. I knew all the places within walking distance, and later bicycle distance, from my house where the flowers could be found. And after the first ones, there were violets and lilacs and wild cherry blossoms to be had. Even to the present day I go out in the spring in search of these springtime wonders and the thrill I get from finding them never ceases. When I lived in New York and was full professor of history at Columbia University, I kept up my childhood habit. I knew places within a radius of thirty miles where I could find all the treasures of my youth.

Another recreation which I enjoyed was camping out. This consisted, at the beginning, of having "camps" in the woods behind the house, made from branches and boughs in Indian style, and later shacks made from slabs from local sawmills or waste lumber which we found around the house. Sometimes we would even be so bold as to take over a shack built by tramps and sometimes we'd encounter the builders. They taught us all manner of tricks about making coffee in coffee cans and concocting stews in which the "juices swapped around." They showed us how to fry fish, and we showed them where we got frogs and how we cooked the legs—a great delicacy, I assure you. Later on, there was "sleeping out," which involved a tent, set up in the back yard, but between mosquitoes and rain, little sleeping was actually done in them.

Finally, there was tennis. While I was still in grammar school my father built a court in the backyard in the hope, I think,that tennis would build me up. I played a lot and became reasonably good, but not good enough to be champion of the town. Bigger boys than I had this honor. Tennis was something, however, that was very good to know, for, when I later lived in cities, I found it to be one of the few sports which I could afford and which required a minimum of involvement with others.

From what has just preceded one might have the impression that my youth consisted of being sick, of going to school, and of play, but such was by no means the case. There was work. One of my earliest memories was of going to my father's "office" and having the task of emptying the waste baskets. I don't believe that I was more than five years of age. For this responsible task I received twenty-five cents a week. But I loved it. Besides, my father had a bookkeeper and jack-of-all office trades who was very kind to me and spoiled me within limits— something that I confess I enjoyed immensely. As I grew older, I could do odd jobs around the coal, wood, and ice yard, the lumber yard, or the grist mill. Among the things which were sold at the grist mill was a poultry mash called *Lay or Bust*, and I can still remember watching for hens, which were molting and hence not laying, to blow up. When they never did, I concluded that the mash was a big hoax.

As I entered my teens, I was given more difficult jobs to do, presumably commensurate with my strength. I washed cakes of ice, for example, which were covered with sawdust in which they were packed to keep them from melting in the heat of summer. Once I intentionally spattered a man whom I did not like and he grabbed me and turned the hose down my neck. Inasmuch as the day was cold, the experience was most umpleasant, but I never splattered anyone after that. I was also given the task of piling stove wood, and later on of splitting it on a mechanical splitter. I shoveled coal into bags, when it had to be delivered upstairs— and then I delivered it. Sometimes I was kept at home to shovel snow, to mow the lawn, to weed and hoe the garden, or to rake leaves and pick apples, according to the season. I balked at some of these tasks, especially when my brothers were big enough to share a part of the burden and when I thought that they were not doing a fair amount of the work.

My most responsible job was to "tally lumber," which meant that I had to keep account of the lumber being loaded. This was boys' work, but it was not very exciting. It was a hot job in summer and a cold one in winter, but upon it depended the amount that my father was paid. One time a discrepancy arose between my account and the tally of a buyer, but the buyer agreed to take my tally because it was so neatly kept. When my father reported this to me, I was set up for weeks.

One of my regular duties was to make simple household repairs, particularly electrical ones. Sometimes I became somewhat over-ambitious in my undertakings, as on the occasion when I tried to take electrical power out of a light socket after my one-cell battery ran down. Then there were jobs which my mother put me to in order to cure me of making work for her. I had the habit of swinging myself around every turn in our large house by grabbing hold of the door casings and giving a tug. Inevitably I left my finger prints behind in a good black smudge. Periodically I had to wash off these finger prints and after the hundredth time, I got the message. The fewer soiled spots I put on, the fewer I had to take off. My mother's technique is one that should be widely emulated.

Then, I also had such tasks as keeping the coal fire in the furnace and cleaning out the flues as need arose—a good profession to have. This led me to furnace-tending in my high school years and allowed me to earn my pocket money. The one thing which I did not learn and which I wish I had acquired was how to cook. That I mastered much later, but cooking ought to be part of every male's education, in this age of "woman's lib."

The work which I did as a child and youth resulted in associating with people from all walks of life and some pretty rough ones. I certainly learned a lot from them, both good and bad. In later years my colleagues often wondered at the language which I sometimes employed, and at the extent of my vocabulary. They also wondered at my readiness to do menial tasks.

I recall an episode which occurred one year when I taught at the "Sciences Po," a school in Paris for elitists who planned to enter the foreign service. I was washing my car in a Parisian street when some of my students walked by and when I greeted them, they were so stunned that I should be doing such a thing that they took a long time even to recognize me. To be willing to undertake anything has always been an asset to me.

On the negative side, however, I believe that because I had so many and such varied tasks to do, I got into the habit of rushing through them. If I had not, I would have had them hanging over my head interminably. In fact, I did little which required perfection and in which I could take pride from extremely good craftsmanship. Even when I became a professional historian, one of the most difficult things for me to learn was to take the time and have the patience to have my work as finished as it should be. Here was a handicap which one should try to avoid during the process of growing up.

I learned, however, to have respect for people in all strata of society. My mother used to quote President Seeley of Smith College as having told the girls of her day that the sign of a well educated person was one who could be at ease at any level of society and who never embarrassed anyone. My early training made such behavior easy for me.

As I grew still older, my father had me assume more responsibilities in his business. I did almost everything from the lowest to the highest—bookkeeping, selling, and making suggestions for the future. I saw the ice business going to pot as the electric refrigerator began to take over and urged my father to get out of it before it was too late. This he did. I thought also that the coal business would give way to oil, and my father briefly flirted with the idea of taking on oil, but finally decided against it. He put his risk capital into lumber and did reasonably well in that field. In general, however, I did not take to business. But more of that later.

Another aspect of growing up, which should not be ignored in any serious biography, has to do with sex. I can remember even now that I was interested in the differences between boys and girls well before I went to school. Living in even a semi-rural enviroment gives one plenty of opportunities to know about sex by observing animals, especially domesticated ones. Moreover, I spent long vacations on the farm of my maternal grandfather at New London, New Hampshire and had a very liberal education in the reproductive life of animals of the bovine family.

By the time I was in the sixth or seventh grade I stopped detesting girls and began to find pleasure in their company. One of my first *amours* was Grace C . . . We used to meet by going to prayer meetings on Friday nights and then taking a very long time getting home. For reasons that I shall never understand, we would simply stand on a street corner (it was possible in those days) looking at each other and saying and doing absolutely nothing. This kind of wooing came to an end when a playmate, Geraldine F . . . went sliding with me one beautiful day on my double runner and taught me how to kiss . . . passionately. Although my town had unmistakable similarities to Peyton Place, which was not far away, and to Thornton Wilder's *Our Town*, my experience with girls stopped at this stage. But the girls changed. After Geraldine, it was Louise B . . . and with her I had a protracted and deep affair. She was highly intelligent, talented (she had licked me in debating), strong (she could put me down), beautiful, and passionate. We went often to dances together and to parties. Except for developments to be related further on, I might well have married her. We enjoyed each other, but our relations were restricted to what was considered proper.

One last reminiscence of the first years of my life belongs in this place. It concerns narrow escapes which I had. I was snapped from the very jaws of death enough times so that I came to believe (encouraged by my mother) that I was in some sense a chosen individual, or at least that I was extremely lucky. There was the time when I had diphtheria, which I have already mentioned, but was saved by the new anti-toxin. Then there was a big bout with pneumonia, during which I ran such high fevers that I had convulsions. Thirdly, there was the episode when I walked barefoot into the red-hot coals of a fire and had my feet badly burned and infected. Fourthly, there was the horrible experience of getting caught in an endless chain, which took sawdust away from the saw in one of my father's sawmills, in such a way that I was carried toward the saw. I still have nightmares about being cut to pieces. Fifthly, there was the case of being gored by a cow right over the right eye, which was all my fault because I had grabbed her horns while she was in a stanchion and I had twisted her head.

Lastly, there was the incident on the railway trestle. I and my pals had a place on the river where we could go to skate and play hockey and not be molested by those whom we did not want. The place was a mill pond some two miles from town and up hill all the way. We frequently were able to hop a freight train as it slowly puffed its way up to our pond, but homeward bound the trains went so fast that we could not hop on.

After one of our more strenuous hockey matches when I was nearly exhausted, I set out for home along the track, which went over a long trestle or bridge. We knew the times for the trains, so thought nothing of crossing the river by this route, although sometimes we would take the extra precaution of putting our ears down on the rail to listen for any train that might be coming. On this particular occasion, I did not take the extra precaution but struck bravely out along the track. My pals were all ahead of me: I was bringing up the rear at a very plodding gait. When I was about halfway across the bridge, I heard screams from my friends and shrieks from the whistle of the engine which was coming around the bend behind and aiming straight at me.

For a moment I thought I was a goner. The engineer threw on his brakes and I ran a bit and then as the cow-catcher was at the very seat of my pants, I jumped. Fortunately I was near enough to the enbankment so that instead of landing in the river bed some sixty feet below, I landed on a steep bank. The slope was so precipitous that it broke my fall, much as the steep incline of a ski jump landing breaks the impact of the jumper. So I was not hit by the engine nor injured in my jump. But the engineer gave me a tongue lashing which lasted me a long time and I never again crossed a long trestle without knowing the exact schedules of trains, and even then I did not relish being on a bridge from which I could not get off safely in a very great hurry.

Subsequently I did not have so many narrow escapes (except once in an automobile accident), for experience had made me cautious. Yet, I had plenty of problems. Those connected with the state of puberty were, I think, the worst of my entire life. Just as I was moving from grammar school to high school, I entered that period when the sexual urge becomes an obsession, and the evidence of sexual potency is abundant. In these matters I had no instruction and was really bewildered and frightened at what was happening.

Reluctantly and shame-facedly I went to my mother for help, and apparently she turned the problem over to my father. He, too, could not get up courage to speak frankly with me, but bought me a book, *What Every Young Boy Ought to Know*, which was a scary treatise on the subject—just the wrong type of book for a sensitive youth. I am sure that this work did me much harm, for it threatened nervous disorders and even insanity if great moderation were not practiced. It also gave the impression that there was something evil about sex, and it made no effort to explain why the appetite for sex was so keen at this age and why society provided no way to satisfy one's appetite. It only advocated the suppression of what one wanted so much. If it had only given some rationale for the taboo which had grown up around sex, I would have obtained some comfort from it. But it did not. From my experience I can only urge parents to take a frank and understanding attitude toward this problem when they endeavor to inform their children about it. I believe that they are alone the ones who have the love and the interest properly to perform the task. They should not leave it, as they are wont to leave so many things, to the school.

Chapter II

Prep School And College

In what has preceded, I have attempted to follow the precepts of those psychologists who are specialists in the field of personality formation. They teach, essentially, that an individual comes into the world with a given physical potential, that he develops this potential in reaction to his "environment," and that he forms fundamental personality traits in his very earliest years. Thus, I have tried to make clear that I inherited a rather frail constitution, that I came from stock interested in intellectual activities, and that I was reared in an environment which was a mixture of sickness, reading, roughness, sports, and work. In the next two chapters I aim at describing how I built on the foundation laid in my earliest years.

In 1915, at the tender age of twelve, I moved from grammar school to the local high school—enrollment seventy-five. The new environment was not particulary edifying. Teachers in such small secondary schools as mine were usually not very competent. They were mostly just out of college and had little experience in communicating their material to teen-agers. When complaints about them were made to school boards, the standard reply was: "They are the best the town can afford."

The first two years of the period of my secondary education were very difficult ones for me. I found little in my studies that was challenging, I was not big enough or strong enough to make any of the school teams, and the problem of sex was driving me mad. I was fresh to my teachers and morose to my family.

The headmaster of the school thought that I needed to be given responsibilities to bring me into line. He had seen that I discharged certain tasks well, such as those connected with being president of my class, to which I had been elected. So he gave me the task of answering the phone in his office and of receiving his vistors during my study periods. And he encouraged my father to give me more responsible jobs in the "yard."

Undoubtedly the remedies which he proposed did some good, but my behavior left much to desired. My parents realized that something was amiss and decided that a change in environment for my last two years of secondary education was in order. Consequently they arranged for me to go to Colby Academy, New London, New Hampshire, the school to which they had gone. This move proved to be one of those important turning points in life.

When I arrived at Colby, now Colby-Sawyer, I found a new set of friends who operated from a different order of values than I had experienced in Lebanon. In fact, the year before I arrived the school had had a kind of religious awakening and the aura of this revival still hung over the school. To be sure, students had for a long time been required to attend chapel services on week days and church services on Sunday, but now I found boys meeting voluntarily in their rooms to engage on their knees in prayer. This religiosity was not exactly new to me, for the family often had prayers, but to witness such things by boys was a revelation.

I was soon caught up in this wave which had broken over the school, and almost at once realized that I had found a mooring for my thoughts and passions. I became a leader in a continuing revival,was elected president of the local Y.M.C.A., led prayers in my room in Heidelberg Hall (I first learned about the University of Heidelberg from this connection), was chosen as a delegate from the Academy to various religious conventions for youth throughout the state, and became active in the Church. I even was so devoted to the cause that I considered going into the ministry for my life's work.

The intellectual and theological sides of this religious period were rather simplistic. I thought that some omnipotent force must have accounted for the creation of the universe and of man and thus I could postulate God as that force.The rest of it was visceral. I felt a need for someone to whom I could take my troubles. Who could have been better than an all-loving Heavenly Father, or his Son. The theological paraphernalia which surrounded these beliefs was also simple. By baptism, total immersion, my sins were washed away and I could keep them that way by true repentance. What my reward would be eventually concerned me only slightly (that comes later in life). I was getting my reward then and there by feeling at peace with myself and the world.

My religious experience in these years helped me enormously to cope with problem of sex, which was partially, at least,sublimated into religion. I remained faithful to Louise in my home town and only had short-lived affairs with girls at school. During vacations I would have dates with Louise almost nightly, but during the term I had virtually no female encounters. I did go to the weekly "promenades" (we were not allowed to dance for fear of arousing our passions) at which we literally walked around a hall, sashayed, and did the grand right and left. Only when there was some affair which was planned for couples, like a class picnic, did I manage to find a temporary partner.

These years at Colby coincided with those in which the United States was a participant in World War I, and this had a profound effect upon me. Like most other boys of my age, I wanted to volunteer, but perhaps my ardor was augmented by the fact that I knew that I was under weight and that I was under age, and that I probably would not get in. Some of my elder comrades did go to war and some of them never came back, but none who was lost was really close to me. In one sense, then, the war remained at a distance, yet we were all very anxious about it and made minor sacrifices because of it. I think that the ones which struck me the hardest were eating uncolored margarine instead of butter, and potato flour bread instead of wheat flour bread.

We also had a semblance of military training. A member of the Board of Trustees found a broken down marine of questionable ability and morals who came to school from Boston to instruct us in the eighteenth century manner of drill. The whole thing was a farce. In the first place, we had no respect for the captain, and we were so mean to him that shortly he had no respect for us. Marching drills made very little sense to anybody, for all that business belonged to another type of warfare—one that had proved futile even in our Revolutionary War. Before long the powers that were (including my father who had become president of the Board of Trustees) fired the captain and no replacement for him was found. The following fall the war soon came to an end. On the day of the "false armistice," classes were called off and we organized an impromtu victory parade. My grandfather Shepard was the moving spirit in the celebration, providing each of us with small flags (God knows where he got them) and buying buckets of hard candy (from the local general store) which he placed at intervals along the main street, our line of march, and into which we could dip at will. The free candy is still a subject of conversation when Armistice Day comes around.

Another great event of my Colby days was the epidemic of influenza in the fall and winter of 1917. I belive that we had no deaths in the school, but most of the students were very sick. My roommate, who came from the Boston area, was one of the sickest, but he pulled through. I was his nurse, but somehow I did not come down with the dread disease.

One of my relatives, only a little older than myself, who was in training at Dartmouth, died and his was the first funeral I ever attended, but it was soon followed by others. One of the saddest cases was that of a young friend who went canoeing one night with the captain of the basketball team , a lad who was a strong swimmer. The canoe tipped over and the strong swimmer could never find his partner in the dark. I remember so vividly that the victim's brother, who made great sacrifices to send his brother to Colby (they were orphans), came for the funeral. I was a pallbearer for the first time and suffered the agonies of the mournful as the brother sobbed his way through the service.

In spite of tragedies like this, fortunately few in number, my students days at Colby were the happiest school days that I ever had. The physical setting of the school was unique. It was on New London Hill with a beautiful view of Kearsarge Mountain. Our main building and the town were charming, and though most of the other structures were wooden and not distinguished in architecture, they were comfortable and livable.

A large amount of the enjoyment which I had at Colby undoubtedly came from the fact that I was successful in nearly everything I tried. I did well in my studies and was the valedictorian of my class. This gave me a chance to read an address that was very condescending to my elders. I organized a debating society that did not distinguish itself with glory but gave us good training and a lot of fun. I remember so distinctly the ignominious defeat—and in the presence of my Father—which we suffered from the hands of a team of a rival school, Kimball Union Academy.

I participated in sports, but I was too light for football, too small for baseball, and too short for basketball. I did play hockey, however, and was captain of the team my senior year, but our record was not very brilliant. I remember a disastrous encounter with St. Paul's School of Concord, New Hampshire, when we had not been able to practice on ice, and a shellacking we got from a Manchester High School team that arrived in New London a day when the thermometer was twenty below zero. We learned how to lose and maintain our dignity.

I took part in most of the school activities, including waiting on table. I was reputed to be very adroit, but one fine day I lost my reputation completely. I was chosen to serve the table of the headmistress, the imposing Miss Julia Gay whom we all loved and admired, when she had distinguished guests for dinner. On the occasion in question she had a tableful. We served "family style," that is, the food was placed in serving dishes, the dishes on trays, and we took the trays to tray stands and then placed the serving dishes before the head of the table. One who is uninitiated in the profession may think that unloading a tray is a simple, foolproof thing, but let me assure all such persons that it is not. In this particular instance, we had platters of meat in the center of the tray and then two serving dishes at each end—at one end potatoes and at the other coleslaw. Miserable that I was, I unloaded the meat and potatoes together (they seemed to go together naturally and were always closely associated in my mind), which left the coleslaw at one end with nothing to counter-balance it. The laws of gravity being what they are worked with inexorable regularity and with no respect of persons. The coleslaw fell with a resounding crash to the floor. This was ignominy compounded, and I hastened to get a dustpan and brush with which to clean up the mess as rapidly as possible. I probably overdid the speed somewhat, for in my anxiety to make amends, I fell down in the mess, and every time I tried to get up I slipped again. How I ever managed to extricate myself from my predicament is not, nor has it ever been, clear. At all events, the moral of the story is: keep things in balance at all times, whether dishes on a tray or yourself on your own legs.

There were many other episodes of this period of my life which are worth recounting, but which I must pass over very lightly. There was the time when someone dared me to go swimming in Little Lake Sunapee before the ice had gone out. I took the dare, caught pneumonia, and was very sick. There was the time when some of us went out to steal apples, I think, and returned after the doors of the dormitory had been locked and we were trapped by the master of the hall while we were half way up the pillars to the safety of the porch roof, and were campused for a month. There were trips to the apple orchard of one of my roommates, Percy T..., who later made a very good life for himself as a local printer. He and I produced the *Colby Voice*, the school newspaper, a not very distinguished sheet, but one that gave us some experience in journalism. And there were the victory celebrations of our very successful athletic teams, composed in part by "scholarship athletes" from the Boston area.

The instruction which we received varied widely according to the talents, leadership, and inspiration imparted by the teacher. Perhaps the part of my education which was the poorest was English. Our female teacher of the subject was pitiful. So far as literature was concerned, she could not do much damage, for the masterpiece being read could stand on its own legs. When it came to written English or to speaking, she was lamentable.[1] An English teacher must correct errors in composition. in grammar, and in spelling. The task is a hard one, especially if you don't know how to construct a paragraph, form a sentence, or spell. The beginner should be taught not to split infinitives, or to mix tenses. or to play hop-scotch with ideas within a paragraph. He must connect ideas as he moves from thought to thought or paragraph to paragraph, and to keep sentences and paragraphs short. Something like Fowlers' *The King's English* ought to be mandatory in every serious student's education, or library, and referred to constantly. Fortunately, in the last semester of my senior year this lady was replaced by a young ensign who had just been demobilized from the Navy. He was excellent and later became a professor at New York University.

Instruction in most other subjects was mediocre to excellent. Chemistry and physics were taught by competent persons, but not distingusihed ones. Latin was the province of the headmistress, who was inspiring but not a good Latinist. French was mostly a disaster, largely because of the translation method and lack of ability on the part of the teacher. History and political science were taught by the headmaster, Justin Wellman, who later went to the University of New Hampshire as a teacher, and he was excellent. He was a practitioner in politics. and although unreasonably Republican, he knew a lot about government. He did such things as to take us to the state legislature in Concord and on to the floor where we could speak with representatives. I had been there before with my father, but Mr. Wellman gave me insights that added much to my interest in the place. Moreover, I knew some of the representatives of the day (the membership totalled about four hundred in a state with a

---

1 One of the worst things she ever did was to have me recite when my mother was visiting the class and criticize everything I said in a disdainfully irritable way. In brief, she tried to make a monkey out of me. Both my classmates and my mother (after the class) thought that she had put on a shameful performance. My mother confided in me that she thought that my comments on *Julius Caesar,* which we were reading, were correct and that the teacher's were wrong.

population of less than 400,000, so knowing someone who had been unable to "avoid the draft," as the saying went, was easy). Mr. Wellman's classes in history were great and I am certain that he did much to turn my mind toward a serious study of the subject. He also directed the debating team and, in fact, took on almost any task that came along, for which he had any competence. He even refereed our hockey games, but we had to teach him much about the rules before he could do an adequate job.

I was very pleased with Colby—and so were my parents. In fact they were so pleased that later they sent my younger brother there, although it benefited him less than it did me, and also my younger sister. Unfortunately, the school, like so many co-educational academies fell on hard times in the depression of the 1930's. To save it my father, still president of the board, was responsible for converting it to a junior college for women and was able to get as president Leslie Sawyer who had been headmaster of the high school in Lebanon and who turned out to be a most remarkable and successful school administrator. By dint of hard work and careful financial management, the school prospered beyond the dreams of the most hopeful—and has continued to prosper to the present day.

My family is still interested in the institution and my sister, Barbara Clough, is a member of the Board of Trustees. We take much pride in the place, and one building is named Shepard Hall, for my Mother's family. I must confess, however, that we have a little resentment that no adequate physical recognition has been given my father for all he did to make the school a viable institution.

In the spring of my senior year at Colby, I had the task of choosing the college to which I would go. My father promised each of his children that he would put them through college but warned that they would be on their own after graduation.

The factors which influenced me in my selection were numerous. I was not sure that my preparation was such that I would be admitted to any of the "big three." College Board examinations were new and had not been given at Colby, so I had little objective evidence on how I would fare in stiff competition. Consequently, I sought institutions where Colby graduates had done well. I felt, that I should go where my religious experience would be continued. I felt, too, that I should go far enough away so that I would experience another enivronment—a consideration which ruled out Dartmouth. My attention began to focus on Colgate University at Hamilton, New York, and finally, I decided to seek admission there. The final factors for making this choice were rather trivial. One was that photographs of Colgate on the walls of Colby gave the impression that the place was very beautiful. The second was that the president of the University was Elmer Burritt Bryan, who, as I have said, was a close friend of my father at the University of Indiana.

I was in due course admitted to Colgate. When news of my choice was known, three of my classmates decided to accompany me to the Chenango Valley, which eased the transition from prep school to college.

From almost the first, I had certain misgivings about my selection. In those days, the train trip from Lebanon to Hamilton was a long, overnight one. Connections were poor and service, especially the last lap on the "Cannonball" of Ontario and Western was unbelievable. Then, to top off the trip one of the boys from Colby, who accompanied me, was robbed on the train.

Hamilon did not come up to my expectations for beauty and my first taste of college life consisted of being briefed by members of the junior class regarding a college rush. Students were divided into two groups—seniors and sophomores and freshmen and juniors. One or the other of these combinations held the remnants of the statue of "Mercury" and that group was required to carry on foot the trophy across the football field during one of the home games. The other group was supposed to capture the statue when this exposure of "Mercury" took place.

This event had attained such proportions that "Mercury" was kept in a bank vault and when the "rush" took place "blood flowed." We were told all this on the train even before we got to Hamilton!

My arrival in Hamilton was not any more reassuring than the train trip had been. After Hanover, New Hampshire,

Hamilton looked pretty drab. The architecture of the college was a hodgepodge of styles, much worse than the Dartmouth of the time. I went to the dormitory to which I had been assigned and had the letdown that most freshmen experience when they are among the earliest arrivals in a half-empty residential hall. I was visited by a sharpie who tried to sell me the furniture in the room, but I was just wary enough to escape this trap. No sooner, however, had I done so than it was eating time and I descended into a smelly underground commons room, where I got my first bit of collegiate indigestion.

Soon enough to save me from irretrievable despondency, I was enrolled in classes and my collegiate education began. Or so I hoped. Almost immediately I became aware of the shortcomings of my preparation. In a Latin translation, I split an infinitive. The Assistant Dean who conducted the class made me very cognizant of the fact that I came from Colby Academy and that Julia Gay, my Latin teacher there, had not done a good job on me. What a horrible awakening!

I was still staggering from this blow when fraternity rushing began. I was almost completely ignorant of fraternities and what they stood for or what they meant to one in a college like mine. At all events, I was entertained by several of the houses. At the end of the rushing season I had seven bids, that is, invitations to join one of the seven which wanted me. I was in a quandary. One of the houses was oriented toward religion and was composed of fine young men. I was inclined toward it. Yet, another invitation was from a house with a great reputation on campus—with several football heroes, editor of the college paper, and so on. Not knowing what to do I went to call on the President of the University. He listened to my tale and advised me to accept the invitation of the house with the great reputation. This I did, and thus I made my bow to worldly values.

I was not really happy with fraternity life. To be sure there were some good people in my house, but there were some with whom I could easily have dispensed. One of the troubles with fraternities is that one is forced to be associated with people who are "brothers," whether or not one likes them, and one is thereby partially cut off from others with whom one would like to be friendly.

After being pledged, I moved into the fraternity house and soon discovered the usual bullies who tried to make me wait on them and even run downtown of an evening to get ice cream. Fortunately, one of my friends was a football hero and a graduate of Colby Academy, and he saved me from much of the importuning of very second-rate characters.

In the fall of my freshman year my father came to visit me. He was a guest of the President, which gave both him and me status in the eyes of my peers. He surveyed my living arrangements and was not entirely satisfied with them. I think that he felt the fraternity detracted considerably from my studies and that I was with people, some of whom were not exactly of the type of which he would approve. This was also my view. He went with me to the Syracuse football game, our big game of the year, and marched with me in the parade there. I thought that he was a very good sport about the whole thing, for he was not a sports' fan. We were defeated, which matters very little from my present perspective, but which seemed important at the time. After our return to Hamilton from Syracuse, he pointed out how much more important in life my studies were than winning a sports event. He stressed the point that my future would be determined, in part, by the record which I made.

My mother also visited me that year. I was much pleased by the fact that some of my fraternity mates thought that she was very well-dressed. She did have a fur coat — mink I suppose — that had come down in the family but which had been remade by a local tailor-furrier so that it was, indeed, smart. She also was a guest at President Bryan's house, which once again made an impression upon the brothers.

Many other events of my freshman year are still vividly in my mind and some had a lasting effect upon me. As a part of my initiation into the fraternity to which I had been pledged, I had to find and bring in two animals within a half hour. One of my friends captured a couple of flies, but they were ruled insects and not animals. I returned with two hens that I had taken off the roost of the Director of Athletics. When I reported the source of my trophy, I was hustled back with the game in double time. We never did have any repercussions of this matter, but I heard that "Doc" Huntington's hens did not lay well that winter and that they molted very early.

Another aspect of the same initiation was that we freshmen were told that we had to cut ice in the local pond and store it in the fraternity's ice house. We were completely taken in by this tale — and we were so gullible that we did not take the pains to see if the fraternity had an ice house. I was sent to the Deke house to get the ice saw from one of the halfbacks on the football team. I was given a real run-round, much to the amusement of his brothers, and this was increased when I got angry because he would not give me the saw. In disgust I left and only on the homeward trek did I awaken to the fact that I had been taken in. It was such a good job that I had to laugh in spite of myself. I certainly was being cured of gullibility.

One of the most traumatic experiences of this period occurred at about mid-years. I came down with influenza and this brought on a severe case of jaundice. I tried to take care of myself in my room and failed — and the failure led to despondency. Finally I was carted off to the infirmary and did not recover until after midyear examinations had been held. This meant that I had to take make-ups, which professors do not like to give. I did fairly well in all my work except Latin. My professor in this subject gave me an examination at his house, part of which was oral. I was very weak and had a slight fever. He gave me a "C," the first one I had ever received. I made it a point after that not to get sick at examination time. In fact, students who work themselves to exhaustion before tests usually do poorly.

Shortly after mid-years we had our winter "house party." A house party consisted of inviting girls to come to the campus for a weekend of dancing. Usually those who lived in the fraternity house moved out and gave their rooms to the girls. I lived in what was known as the "sky parlor," a room and bath at the top of the house with one flight of stairs by which to get in or out. During the house party, when the girls and their escorts were having lunch, my roommate, who had brilliant red hair, thought that he had time enough to take a bath. He undressed downstairs and with one towel went aloft. He prolonged his ablutions a little longer than he had planned and when he got out of the bath, he heard the girls coming up the stairs. What to do? One bath towel between him and decency and identity. He decided to hide his identity, so he put the towel over his head and fled past the startled girls. All seemed to have gone well — he had escaped being recognized, or so he thought. However, at the hour of the girls' departure, and when the residents of the house had begun to trickle back to their quarters, he came into a group of departing girls without a hat and his red hair aflame. Whereupon one of the girls blurted out, "Oh, so you are the boy with the red hair!" Her curiosity was apparently satisfied.

By this time in my career, I was less inclined toward the ministry than I had been, but I still wanted to be of service to mankind, so I thought of becoming a physician. This idea was, however, shortlived. I was enrolled in a chemistry course known as qualitative analysis, in which, among other miserable things we had to do, was to try to find all of the chemicals mixed up and put in bottles. One day I was testing for a nitrate, which involved heating the mixture in a test tube with concentrated sulphuric acid and to watch to see if it would give off a brown gas. I heated the tube all right, but without shaking it, as I should have done. When the tube, unknown powder, and acid were very hot I turned the tube toward me and looked down it to see if the brown gas would appear. When the liquid hit the hot glass, it was blown into my face and eyes. Fortunately, a laboratory assistant grabbed me and put me under a faucet and washed the stuff off my face and out of my eyes, but for twenty-four hours I had my eyes bandaged and I was not sure that I would ever see again. When it was apparent that I would see, I went to visit my professor of chemistry. (He was Cookie Cutter Smith, so called because he had one leg shorter than the other and had an iron frame that "cut cookies" in the snow as he walked along). Cookie informed me that good physicians were usually good chemists and that if I were so unfit for chemistry as the late event seemed to indicate, I would be well advised to turn my thoughts to other callings. Thus ended my dream of a career in medicine.

In the spring of that first year of college, I was elected manager of the freshman baseball team. As fraternity members, we

youngsters of our house were encouraged "to scrub" for positions on the campus that would bring glory to our chapter. Scrubbing meant that one did a lot of dirty work for free in the hope that one would be elected to the sought-after job. I was chosen manager of the team all right, but the "honor" brought only headaches to me and very little glory to my fraternity.

In the summer after my freshman year I went back to my paternal home and worked in my father's business. My father tried to make things more interesting for me than they had been in the past, but that was difficult to do. I began to feel that, as the eldest son of the family, he wanted me eventually to take over. For my part, I was getting a taste for other things and for other places. A life in the coal, lumbering, wood, and ice business did not look very attractive to me.

My sophomore year was not much unlike the first year. I did become a member of the editorial board of the college paper and also became a correspondent for papers in Utica, Syracuse, and even New York — to report athletic news primarily and other things very secondarily. At least I made a little pin money. My studies went better than they had the first year. I knew enough and had leeway enough so that I could pick good professors rather than subjects. We had an excellent professor of literature, William Crawshaw, whose classes were a sheer delight. We also had a fine professor of speech and economics, Lionel Edie, who subsequently went on to Indiana and Chicago and finally had a very successful career as financial advisor, investor, and broker in New York. He taught me a great deal, but in a rather unsystematic way. Also I studied history and political science, both of which were of great interest, although my professors were not particularly distinguished. At all events, my sophomore year was more rewarding than my freshman year had been.

My junior year was a climax to my college career. I had made some close friends, particularly Paul S... from Utica and Dana S... from Rochester. I spent many a pleasant weekend at the home of the former and at the grandparents of the latter. Another close friend was Ted Pratt who became famous as the author of the *Barefoot*

Mailman, a story about the early days of Florida. He had me at his house on my first trip to New York (via the Hudson Night Boat from Albany). Then I had very good friends among the faculty, especially Lionel Edie, already mentioned, and Freddie Jones, a French professor.

I also became a campus leader in the sense that I was elected to several offices. I was chosen as editor-in-chief of the college paper for my senior year and this distinction led to my election to an honorary society, Gorgon's Head. At the Junior Prom, when I was to be officially "pinned" to the senior society, I invited a date from Syracuse. There was a dance Friday night, but after it she had to go to Syracuse for a Saturday morning class. Somehow she made the trip and returned, but the events of Friday night were too much for me and when she got back, I was sound asleep. No one woke me. And when I did come to, she was in tears and preparing to go home, for which I did not blame her. Somehow my plight appeared to be so desperate that she consented to stay for the big dance, but things were somewhat cool between us from that time onward.

The following summer I got the wanderlust. My father was a prominent Baptist and was a member of the governing board of the Northern Baptist Convention. That year it was to meet in June in Des Moines and he made arrangements whereby I was to accompany him there and afterward go on to Minneapolis. There I had a great uncle who was an important person in the Soo Line. He agreed to get me a job, which he did, as a sweeper in a machine shop of his line. Sweeping is one of the lowest jobs imaginable. I had not only to sweep the floor, but empty metallic shavings from the bins under machines, all the while being ready to duck locomotives that might be swinging in their entirety over my head. And then I had to clean the toilets! Once in a while I would be called into the office of the manager of the shop to do some typing, much to the astonishment of the workers.

Most of the machinists were Swedes or Norwegians and they invariably chewed snuff, which meant that they held a large pinch of the dry-as-dust tobacco under their lips. This made the saliva flow in abundance and the abundance could be used to get a sweeper out of the way or to move in any direction they thought desirable. In self defense I took up chewing tobacco, for the dust was so great that one's air passages would become completely stopped if the sediment were not periodically removed. I chewed scraps—tobacco leaf soaked in molasses. It was bearable stuff—much better than the bitter snuff. I got along with it fairly well until toward the end of my sweeping career when in the handful of scraps I was about to put into my mouth I observed a piece of finger cut off at the first knuckle. I was cured from chewing tobacco for some time to come.

My experience in Minneapolis was a great one. I saw new country, met different people from those I had known, and had my first living in a city. One thing that astonished me was that Americans of English stock looked down on the Scandinavians, while to me the light haired, blue eyed, and large framed people were very attractive. They were not at all like the minority which I had despised at a child. The country was very different from the hills of New England! One day my Uncle took me to North Dakota and I saw wheat fields, giant size. Here was farming the like of which made a New Englander's eyes pop. Then I associated for the first time with workers who were imbued with Marxism and some with anarchism. I remember so well a union rally (I could not belong to the union because my job was too low) at which the organizer said no man would ever profit from the work he did—he'd break the lathe first. He pictured the capitalist system as rotten, American society as vile, and advocated the destruction of existing institutions. Whatever appeared in their place could not be worse than what we had. This was strong doctrine, and I learned that subsequently he was fired from his job in the brotherhood, for it stood essentially for a full dinner pail policy and not the overthrow of society as it was.

I was impressed by city living, too. Here there were people with whom one could associate—all kinds of people. The buildings were impressive even as to size and the services which were rendered varied.The University of Minnesota looked enormous after little Colgate or even Dartmouth. The high schools were fantastic (in size) and I thought to myself maybe I could qualify someday for a job in them. Then the great range of opportunities of the city appealed to me. I took a girl, who lived next door, out to dinner one night and she allowed as how she would like to go to a Chinese restaurant. I took her there and was enthralled by the food. In later years I came to believe that the Chinese cuisine is the best in the world.

Time went by and inexorably the day for my departure arrived. I made it back to Hamilton via Montreal to begin my senior year. This should have been the height of my college career, but it was not for a number of reasons. One was that I was chairman of the honor system committee, a committee that was supposed to enforce a system of honor in examinations and classroom conduct. The system was in crisis. One of my close friends and a leader in the class was found guilty of having some stooge answer present for him when the roll was called. The captain of the . . . team was convicted of cheating and dismissed from the University. And my own roommate was indicted, which put me in a terrible position from which I could not extricate myself with glory (I abstained from voting). I did take pride in the editorship of the Colgate paper, the *Maroon*, but many of my efforts to improve the college and the behavior of students encountered tough sledding. As for the question of bettering the college, I was asked, "What do you want to make of the place, a key factory?" (The reference is to Phi Beta Kappa keys). The second was a campaign against professionalism, which was making some athletic stars ineligible for varsity competition. The culprits took the position that they needed the money and that the University gave them little or nothing for their efforts. Subsequently I realized that they had a point, but at the time I had a hard fight on what I thought was a clear-cut issue.

Probably my greatest source of dismay was that I became conscious of the fact that I was not getting a good education. I had learned no language well enough to use it; I was trained for no profession; indeed, I had no training that would allow me to earn a living; and the general education which I did have did not seem to me to make me a competitor for anything against graduates from large universities. About the only thing that I had accomplished in selecting a life's work was to have eliminated the possibility of being a minister or a physician.

My disquiet increased as the fall semester progressed. As I gave expression to it, I discovered that others felt much as I did. I began to wonder, if maybe, I should not spend the last semester of that senior year in another place.

Where? Just at this time the question of the Ruhr occupation was getting all the headlines—and so, too, reparations. My generation had become very interested in Europe because of the war and the tales which were brought back about France. Somehow it occurred to me that maybe I should take the Grand Tour in the second half of the year. First, I consulted the Dean of the college and discovered that I would have enough credits to graduate with my class in June, for I was given bonus credits for high grades and extra credits for work that I had done.

Then I consulted my parents. They did not seem to be opposed to the idea. My father did point out to me that it was going to cost money and that I had no job to which I might return. As regards the costs of the trip, I thought I could get by on what I would normally be spending in the last semester at college and by the use of some of the savings which I had built up since I was knee-high to a grasshopper. As regards the future, I thought that I would go into journalism and he suggested that I consult the editor of the local paper to see if he would employ me upon my return. I did, but the interview ended my thoughts of working in journalism at home, for the proposed salary would not have kept a mosquito alive.

I had also been considering teaching in the field of history. My professor, Dr. Lowe, informed me that he had heard of a possible readership at Cornell and arranged that I go there to see about it. I did and met several of the people at Ithaca, among whom was Thomas Peardon, who later came to Columbia, was appointed Dean of Barnard College, and became my very good friend. There was also Alfred Zimmern, an ancient historian from England, whose wife would interrupt him in a lecture to say, "Now, Alfred, it was not like that at all." But I did not meet professor Wallace Notestein for whom I would be working if I got the job. He was in London and inasmuch as I was probably going there, I could see him and he could make his own decision about me. On this visit to Ithaca, I had the privilege of talking with Professor George Lincoln Burr, who was a real personality, although he published very little. When I told him of my plans, he approved them most heartily and encouraged me to take full advantage of the cultural opportunities which would be mine. He counseled me to spend as much time as possible seeing plays and the opera, hearing music, visiting museums and architectural monuments, and not to concentrate solely on booklearning. That could come later. This was good advice from which I profited mightily. I have passed it on many times to my own students.

By this time, my mind was set to go to Europe and much to my surprise three of my friends and fraternity brothers at that—one senior and two juniors—convinced their parents and the college authorities that they should go with me. They were all to get academic credit for the work which they would do—or for the experience which was to come from travel. We were to leave college after mid-year examinations.

We purchased our steamship tickets from a member of the faculty who was an agent for steamship lines and made arrangements to sail on the S.S. Celtic of the White Star Line. We were to go third class, which was the lowest that one could get. We had hoped to receive some cut off the price of our tickets, but the "member of the faculty" who was wealthy, told us in no uncertain terms that rebates of any kind were forbidden by the North Atlantic Shipping Conference and that, if he made a concession, he would run the risk of losing his agency. So we paid full fare.

The departure from Colgate was not heart rending. I had an election for a successor as editor-in-chief of the college paper and I paid my respects to some of my close friends in the town. The most memorable was to Freddie Jones, professor of French. I found a bridge game going on at his house when I arrived and was invited to participate in it—auction bridge it was. Although I was not an addict, I did take a hand as a farewell gesture. I bid and made six spades doubled and redoubled. It was a good moment to go away.

Chapter III

"Le Grand Tour" and the Turn to History

Le *Grand Tour* was envisaged as a great adventure and as a supplement to my college education. I did not think of it as a means of deciding upon a career, but it turned out to be exactly that.

When I conceived the idea of going abroad, I knew where I wanted to go even though I did not know why I was going, except to satisfy some vague curiosity. One place to which I felt drawn was France because of the accounts of that country told by veterans of the war. The second was England, for the study of English literature and history made me curious to see the places where events with which I was familiar had taken place.

With these vague ideas regarding our trip in mind, we thought that preparations for our *tour* would be simple. Some were, however, more complicated than I had imagined. To get a passport, for instance, turned out to be a real hassle. I discovered that to get this necessary document one had to have a birth certificate or other evidence of having been born in the U.S.A. When I wrote to Bloomington, Indiana, for one, I was informed that such records were not kept in 1901. So I had to get affidavits from people who had known me for a long time and to swear that I was an American!

In order to attend to other matters, I left New Hampshire for New York several days before our scheduled departure. One of my tasks there was to get a visa stamp on my passport in order to enter France. For this purpose, I had to go to the docks on the West Side, which was, it seemed to me, a very rough section of the city. The person who gave this indispensable stamp had been badly wounded in the face during the war, a real *Gueule Cassée*, and won anew my sympathy for the entire French nation for what it had suffered.

For information about educational institutions in France, I and my companions had recourse to Columbia University and in turn, to its Maison Française, the University's Center for French affairs. There we were very cordially received, given much good advice, and instructed immediately upon arriving in Paris to go to the American University Union, directed by a former Columbia professor of French, Dr. Horatio Krans. We were assured that he would be of immeasurable assistance to us, and this tip proved to be accurate.

After attending to other matters of this kind, we finally boarded ship on a very cold day in February for our first transatlantic voyage. The vessel on which we embarked was the S. S. Celtic of the White Star Line, destination Liverpool. This craft was not of recent vintage. In fact, it had been torpedoed by a U-Boat and beached during the war and thereby had acquired an odor of bilge that smelled like a combination of urine, rotten cabbage, and carrion. Each cabin in steerage, where we were, had a tank a fresh water, but ours was frozen solid and did not thaw until we had been in the Gulf Stream two days. In the meantime we washed and shaved in salt water in a common men's room. A very common room, indeed.

Crossing the North Atlantic in February is not exactly what one would choose for a maiden voyage. We had some very rough weather and the effect of it on most passengers was obvious. Somehow I did not succumb. On the contrary, I developed a ravenous appetite, and I could not satisfy it with the regular slop which was served at mess. It got so bad that I would steal hard-tack from a barrel in the galley to allay my pangs.

We four college boys were soon very bored. We lacked

exercise. In desperation we tried throwing a baseball back and forth on deck, but after one of the lads, a pitcher, had thrown a couple of balls over the side, because he threw just as the ship rolled down from where he stood, we had to give that up. It was too expensive. We were not brazen enough to venture into second or first class, which was forbidden, but which I subsequently learned was not difficult to do. We had no movies, no books, no dances, no bar.

All things come to an end even as you and I, in one way or another, and our boredom finally was broken when we came in sight of Ireland. If anyone ever thought that it is not green, then he should approach it from sea in February after having left a frozen, dirty, snow covered New York. It was beautiful. But our stop at Cobh was short and soon we were on our way to Liverpool. We arrived there of an evening, with the tide so low that we could not get into the harbor until high tide the next morning. When we landed and had our first contact with the English, it was not at all happy. The customs officials, much to our horror, wanted to charge us duties on our cameras, baseball gloves, and baseball balls. What, free trade England? We had a big argument about this and decided that if these characters persisted in their demands that we would throw everything they wanted to tax over the side. When they heard of this, they relented. But they had spoiled our entry into Britain.

Our arrival in Liverpool coincided with a dock strike (February, 1923) and the city was very grim. We had not expected to stop there, and were glad that we had not. We went immediately to the nearby town of Chester—our first walled city. It was very picturesque. Indeed, everything seemed to be, including the waitresses in the restaurant to which we repaired to get our first land-based meal. The pink of their cheeks, kept so, I suppose, by the lack of sun and the great amount of rain and fog, the quaint dresses, and the "if you pleases," as service was rendered, were all delightful.

We had no very fixed itinerary, although we wanted to get to London for a stay before pushing on to Paris where the two junior classmen were to study French at the Alliance Française beginning about the first of April. By combining hiking and train rides we made it to Warwick Castle, Kenilworth, and to Stratford-on-Avon, where we saw a play or two. Then we went to Oxford, where we discovered some American friends. Then on to London, which was very impressive. I'd had so little contact with really large cities that everything seemed novel. We also found some friends there—wealthy ones—who wined us and dined us most regally. We visited all the sights from St. Paul's, to the Palaces, to Hyde Park, which intrigued me, to the London School, to the British Museum. Like tenderfeet, we tried to see everything—the Cheshire Cheese, which I can still recommend, Simpsons, the Tower, Pall Mall, and Petticoat Lane.

In London I had an appointment to see Professor Wallace Notestein of Cornell, for I was still interested in the readership for the following year. I went of an evening to see him in his quarters. He was a curious person, I thought, especially since he began to examine me about my knowledge of English history. While I was fumbling to answer his questions, he smoked cigarette after cigarette, always holding them between his teeth, and every now and again jumped up to go to the bathroom. I could hear the water running, but I couldn't understand the repeated visits. When my curiosity became too obvious to ignore, he confided to me that he was putting sixpences in a gas meter to warm the water. What queer plumbing the British have. And I did not get the job at Ithaca.

I did fall in love with London, however, and I have been devoted to it ever since. Our time there was, unfortunately, limited and before we knew it we were on our way to Canterbury. The Cathedral of Canterbury was my first sight of a real Gothic structure, and I was much impressed by it. From Canterbury we went to Dover, with its white cliffs, and thence to Calais. The crossing was not severe.

And so we were in France. Ah, France. I was prepared to love it. Everything seemed to me to be made to order for sight-seers. I still remember a street sweeping machine, a runt of a thing, driven by a man twice its size, who had a flowing conversation with it and anyone who impeded his progress. Everything was perfect—except the language. I realized, what I had already feared, that my secondary school French gave me an understanding of the language which approximated zero.

After paying our respects to Calais and Rodin's *Six Bourgeois*, we took a day train to Paris, arriving in the early evening. For Paris we were not prepared. We had no hotel in mind, not even a section of the city in which we wanted to stay. Thus we fell prey to some hangers-on, who are always to be found around railway stations, especially around those to which foreign visitors are expected to come. We made it clear that we wanted to go to the Y.M.C.A., thinking that that would be within our means. The "Y" turned out to be a flossy place on the boulevards, but by the time we arrived there we were too exhausted to complain, or to go farther.

A flossy hotel and no soap in the room. We complained, and learned the hard way that guests were to furnish their own. Oh the ways of foreigners! The beds were good and we had a wonderful night's rest. I was awakened in the morning by the music of a band marching down the street. I thought that it must be a victory-day parade. I bounced out of bed and rushed to the window and stretched out to the limit of my size. There was no band. There was no parade. French automobilists were honking their rubber horns at one another. That was the music. Moreover, most of the cars were surely taxicabs that had carried reinforcements to Joffre at the Battle of the Marne.

The first order of business that day was to find a place to live. Somehow we found our way to the American University Union on the Left Bank, Rue Fleurus, and were received by Dr. Krans. He was to prove very helpful. From his organization we received a list of cheap pensions and started ringing doorbells. I settled for one, along with my senior pal, nearby in Rue d'Assas. It was not much, but it provided three meals a day and had running water in the room. Still no soap. The Juniors wanted to live in a family in order to learn French and they settled in Rue du Suffren near the Champs de Mars.

We all enrolled in the Alliance Française in order to learn enough of the language to get by. As in America, we began the dull task of learning verb forms, phonetics, and translating at sight. It seemed strange to me that I, almost a college graduate, could not learn the language when so many obviously not too bright persons spoke it excellently and even babes in the nearby Jardins de Luxembourg could from infancy make themselves understood. I decided that what was wrong was the teaching method. What I needed was to learn the way babies did. I needed the direct aproach. It worked—to a point—but it had its own risks.

Let me explain. Every evening after dinner I retired with *les Grandes Dames de la Pension* to the *salon* to take *tilleul*—Linden tea to you. This gave me a chance to exercise my French and to extend my vocabulary, even though the method was not very direct. One night one of the ladies of the *salon* asked me how it was that my trousers were always well pressed. She and the others had noticed this fact, whereas they knew that the French boys let their trousers go baggy, trapped as they continually were by the rains of Paris. When I did not know a word in French, I would use an English word, give it a French pronunciation, say a prayer, and hope for the best. On this occasion I could not for the life of me think of the word for "mattress," under which I put my trousers every night. What I said in reply to my questioner was: "Eh bien, Madame. C'est tres simple. Chaque soir je mets mes pantalons sous ma maitresse." What joy. What a man.

Every mistake in learning a language is a boost. One must persevere. I did, but this was not the last of *mes gaffes.*

One of the first sights of Paris on my list was the Bastille. On my map of the city I ascertained where it was and struck out for it afoot from Le Louvre on a very hot day. I had the idea that to see a city one must go on foot and take one's time. The route I chose seemed endless. It must have been a good four miles. And when I reached where the Bastille had been, guess what, there was no Bastille. I had overlooked, what I must have learned at Colgate, that the Bastille had been destroyed stone by stone during the Revolution and never rebuilt. I was truly a Yankee at the court of Louis XVI.

I went from episode to episode, some good, some not so good, but I did see a lot of Paris and loved it. Yet time was marching on and money was running out. There was more to France than Paris. I must see the rest. So the senior pal and I decided to strike out. We further decided that we would get bicycles, go to Versailles, Chartres, the Chateaux country, the Rhone Valley to Marseilles, Monte Carlo, the Route Napoleon through the Alps to Grenoble, Geneva, and thence back to Paris—and presumably home. We both bought our bicycles—he a very good one; I a very poor second-hand one. First off I got a ticket from a policeman for not having a bicycle tag—my first run-in with the French law. These foreign ways again—a tag on a bike!

One misty, musty morning we started out . . . for Versailles. I think that the chateau, the *parc*, the Trianons, and all were every bit up to our expectations. We were learning history by the minute. We took the route that the women who marched on Versailles in 1789 had taken; we saw where Marie Antoinette had played at farming; and we saw the impressive Hall of Mirrors where the Treaty of Versailles had been signed.

Eventually we took off for Chartres. The Plaine de la Beauce is very rich and very flat. We had a contrary wind all the way. I had thought that pumping up the hills of New Hampshire was hard work, but it was nothing like pumping against the wind. We got a glimpse of the towers of the Cathedral at a great distance and like a siren they called us on, and on, and on.

We finally made the town, or I would not be spinning this yarn. The cathedral was as wonderful as we had expected it would be. I have been back to it maybe fifty times and it never ceases to reveal some loveliness which I had previously overlooked. I suppose that the main facade gives me the greatest lift: the donkeys, the woman with the broken nose, and the tympanum with its line of those rising from the dead and awaiting to be judged by being weighed to determine if they be found wanting. They seem much like those characters who wait in lines at supermarkets to be checked out, especially in southern Florida where everyone, it seems, is old and just waiting for the grim reaper.

Then the chateaux! I fell in love with them all, especially Chenonceaux. I had a bad bicycle accident, however, at Amboise. Fortunately, this event took place right in front of a country inn to which I was taken. Gravel was washed out of my hands and knees. My wounds were bandaged and my sprains rubbed down. My bike, which looked like a plate of spaghetti, was taken to a shop for its last rites. My tour de France had come, I thought, to an inglorious end.

But not so. By some miracle of workmanship the bike was put together. Gradually my cuts and bruises healed.

At the wayside inn, I had little to do but to rest and lick my wounds. As I felt my strength return, there was one thing at the inn that I could do, which was to dance. One evening at the weekly *bal*, I got into the hands of a buxom wench to dance *le Boston*. This dance is a waltz in which one turns and turns and turns. After we had been at it awhile, I was dizzy and my knees told me that I should rest. I wanted to suggest to my partner that we sit down, but I was having a lot of trouble with reflexive verbs and was not just sure of my grounds, that is, of my grammar. I made the effort anyway. What came out was not "Voulez-vous vous asseoir?" as it should have been, but "Voulez-vous s'asseoir?", which the girl understood to be "Voulez-vous ce soir?" This meant to her only one thing. This was my second big *gaffe* in French.

Gradually I recovered enough so that I could take short trips in the neighborhood. I became very well acquainted with the Chateau at Amboise and learned to my astonishment that Leonardo da Vinci had been brought to France by François I in an effort to bring cultural glory to his nation and that he, Leonardo, was buried on the grounds of the chateau.

I was particularly fond of nearby Blois, but by the time I had explored it, I was ready to continue my trek to Monte Carlo.

The route from Touraine to the Rhone Valley was a long one—through Bourges to Lyons, but I conquered it. Then I went down the Rhone to Arles, where the most beautiful women of France are reputed to live. From there I pushed on to Nimes, with its Roman remains (La Maison Carrée, which was the inspiration for the capitol building at Richmond, Virginia), the Arena, and not far away the Pont du Gard, a Roman aqueduct of astounding proportions. Then there was Avignon, with the palace which the popes had built when they established themselves in France. And the bridge where one dances!

Finally, I reached Marseilles, but did not like it, and took off, almost at once, on my two-wheeler along the Route de la Corniche. It was beautiful, but hilly, very hilly. At one place I could not pedal at all and was painfully pushing my means of transportation in front of me, when, all of a sudden, a blare of horns and a platoon of bicyclists on a local bicycle race rushed by me as though they were shot from a gun. What a difference between a real professional and a poor, ill-equipped amateur!

I made it to Toulon, where I spent a pleasant evening playing cards with a group of naval officers; then on to Nice, where I expected to have a swim (I had read literature about Nice as a winter resort) but experienced a snowstorm. Then on to Monte Carlo. I had attained my goal and was ready to return to Paris. From the Riveria I took a train, with no food or toilet on the train. This was something for an all-day trip, but I shall leave the details of it to the reader's imagination. The back platform came in for heavy use.

We arrived at Digne in the evening of a market day and I got the last room at the inn. After settling myself in my room, I went out to get something to eat. When I came back and barged into my room, I found a man and a woman in my bed. No arguing with them or the proprietor. He would not get them out, but the *patron* did fix up a bed in a bathtub, which I indignantly turned down. I left the hotel and tried a park bench, but the Alpine breezes were too cold, so I went to the local railway station and crawled into a coach. There I slept until daybreak when I was awakened by the train's taking off. I jumped off just before it entered a tunnel. (Fortunately I had locked my bike at the station to a post).

At the first opportunity the next morning, I took a train for Grenoble (I was following the *Route Napoléon*, more or less, that is, the route that Napoleon took when he escaped from his prison Isle of Elbe and made his way back to Paris). From Grenoble I went to Geneva and attended a meeting of the assembly of the League of Nations and was duly impressed by seeing in the flesh some of the big political personalities of the time. I was also greatly amused at stories told by a guide (stories that may have been partly apocryphal), especially the one about the architects of the League building who in planning the seats forgot to allow space for the delegates' legs and did not realize their oversight until the time came for the actual furnishing of the room.

Ultimately I had "seen" Geneva, I was longing to get back to Paris. So I took a night train which was completely empty, and arrived in Paris in the early morning with the coach jammed packed and my head in the lap of an enormous *paysanne*.

Paris certainly looked good to me. After the provinces, it was like sunshine in the rain. It was May and all the colors of the impressionist painters were at their best. I was delighted to see my friends from Colgate (the juniors) and we did a little celebrating, among other things by going to the Moulin Rouge where I tried to turn a handspring on a slippery dance floor and fell heavily on my backsides.

I had, however, personal problems which were too pressing to allow for much frivolity. The most urgent ones were to learn French well and to determine what I was going to do with my life. I went back to the Alliance Française with my Colgate pals and gradually made some real progress in the language. Incidentally, we tried to get some exercise by throwing a baseball around the cramped yard of the school, but after we had broken a couple of windows with wild pitches, the authorities put a stop to that.

By early June, I had come to the conclusion that I should remain in France the following year, if I were really to know the country and the language, and so I began to see if I could get a job. I tried the American Express, but they were not interested in a college boy on the *Grand Tour*—they had seen too many of them before. Then through pull I got a tryout with the *Chicago Tribune* (was I not a hot-shot journalist in college). I was placed at the end of a telegraph line from the States and was supposed to put the jibberish (abbreviated stories) which came over it into intelligible articles. I lasted two nights. I was simply not a fast enough typist to keep up with the messages. By the process of elimination I had been steered away from yet another vocation.

Not having a job and having no prospect of getting

one, I decided to cut my living expenses to the bone. I got my room by reading Dickens aloud to a hack writer who had some ambition to go to America. The room had bedbugs (they were new to me), but I stuck it out. At least, I could do some cooking there, which helped with my finances.

By reducing my budget, I had enough money to sign up for the Cours de Civilisation Française at the Sorbonne. The course was cheap and it was good. I was fortunate in hearing lectures from some of the country's most distinguished historians—Charles Seignobos, Charles Guignebert, Pierre Renouvin, Albert Mathiez, and many more. This was high level instruction and I took to it like a duck to water.

Moreover, I had a chance to visit Paris, and especially its historical monuments, more thoroughly than I had earlier. I went to those places about which the professors lectured and thus made what they said more vivid. On one such excursion I was at the Conciergerie where Marie Antoinette and Louis XVI had been incarcerated. By chance, I encountered there Professor Charles Downer Hazen of Columbia University, who had been a professor of my mother's at Smith College and who had been born at Barnet, Vermont, up the Connecticut River from Lebanon. We entered into conversation and he seemed interested in what I was doing and what I was going to do. He was very wealthy and invited me to an apartment which he had on the Quais. He was very gracious and considerate. His advice to me was to stay another year in France and to go to Germany some time along to learn the language. He thought that if I did as he suggested that I would be a strong candidate for a fellowship in history at Columbia the following year. He advised me also to run the financial risk. His clinching argument was that the most important investment which I would ever make in life would be an investment in myself, at that time. This advice I have frequently given my own students. I did as he thought wise and a small inheritance from my Grandmother Clough made the stay through the next winter and summer feasible.

At about this juncture I received word from Colgate that I had been graduated with my class and that I had been awarded a Phi Beta Kappa key. This honor encouraged me in the direction toward which I was tending. I have seen many times in my years how important it is to know where you want to go, if you are ever going to arrive at that destination!

By the summer of 1923, I was close enough to a decision about my future to apply myself with great diligence to my studies. In the fall, I enrolled at the Sorbonne. I went to history lectures with great regularity and read voluminously to make up for lost time.

In writing these words, a thousand memories come back to me. One of the most vivid pertains to French libraries. The French are allergic to drafts and to fresh air, with the result that the libraries, it seems to me, have never had any new air introduced into them since they were constructed. To make the situation worse, in some libraries, notably the Bibliothèque Nationale, a man would come around from time to time to spray a vile smelling substance into the air. By the end of the day the whole atmosphere was so vile that it would have been possible to cut it up into hunks. Moreover, the libraries were very crowded. At the Sorbonne library, one had to arrive when the place opened (ten A.M. and two P.M.) or one had no seat. To get a book one had to hand a bulletin through a peep hole and wait. When one left the reading room, one was frisked to be sure that one had taken nothing. All this was novel to me, for I had been used to libraries where few came to befoul the air and librarians tried to force books on their readers. Yet, with all the difficulties I encountered in France, I did get books to read, and I read them.

The toilet facilities of the libraries were, one might say, quaint. There were the ubiquitous *pissoirs* (the protective shield on the one I used was only shoulder high and it was peculiar to see a distinguished professor doff his hat to a passing lady with one hand when the other hand was obviously occupied). Then there were the *cabinets turques* (holes in the ground with footrests), which had a niagara type flush that would wash one out the door, if one did not jump in time, and there were the card catalogues, which were usually cards locked into books and arranged by years. If one wanted a certain book, one had usually to know the approximate year the book was published to have any chance of finding it.

My living arrangements in these days were extremely spartan. I continued to live with my hack-writer, receiving a room (unheated) in exchange for English lessons. I walked from his place, Rue Falguière, to the Sorbonne along Rue de Vaugirard each morning and back each night— a distance of some (I should say) six miles a day. For the most part this was my exercise. I ate in very cheap restaurants at noon, but I had a reasonably good meal in a pension, rue d'Assas, in the evening.

The pension was in the Montparnasse Quarter and this was the center of many of the important literary and artistic figures of the age. There I met James Joyce and Fujita (at La Rotunde, a cafe of some repute); Marcel Proust, who was becoming famous; Ernest Hemingway, to whom I sold my bike; and Gertrude Stein. These people were not, however, for me. I was in another section of a "lost generation" that was specializing in the social sciences, and we had little in common with *littérateurs*.

My social life was limited because of a shortage of funds and dedication to work. Yet I did have a girl friend, Dorothy Y . . . who went to dances with me at Reid Hall. Most of my male friends were at first Swiss and then Americans. I knew a few French girls, but I did not hit it off very well with them, and I had at that time absolutely no male French friends of my age. I was invited to the homes of some wealthy French, especially Deutsch de la Meurthe, who were members of Franco-American welcome groups, but I made no lasting friendships with people whom I met at such places.

The hack-writer who gave me my room was the only French person with whom I had much contact. We would go on walks together in Paris and on excursions to the countryside. Often we went to museums, especially the Louvre, and I came to know it so well that if all the pictures had been taken down and scrambled, I could have put them back in place from memory, or almost all. He was knowledgeable about many things. He introduced me to Karl Marx, whom I read at length, and to eighteenth century philosophers. By reading them my religious beliefs came in for some severe testing. I had already given up a literal interpretation of the

Bible, but now began to doubt the existence of an all-powerful and omniscient heavenly father. I wrestled with the thought that there must have been some force that created the world, but then ran smack into the propostion—what or who created that "force." After reading Voltaire's *Candide*, I doubted that our "maker," if he existed, were as all-loving as I had for a long time believed. In short, I had my religion undermined, took a skeptical position, and began to think of the world as a great mechanism, in a Newtonian sense.

Among my American friends who were studying at the Sorbonne was a fraternity mate from Pennsylvania, with whom I associated a great deal. One day he asked me if I did not feel the need of exercise and when I confessed that I did, he asked me what my sports were. In most of them we could not indulge because of the lack of snow or ice or tennis rackets or money. When it seemed that there was little or nothing that we could do together, he asked me if I had ever boxed. I confessed that I had been a sparring mate for the Colgate boxing team in my weight and that I could hold my own. Apparently that was what he was waiting for, so we found a gymnasium run by Methodist missionaries and prepared for a work out. Almost at once my nose was broken, and still remains crooked, and then he loosened a couple of teeth. His punches came from nowhere and mine went nowhere, or if they did, had no power. After a little of this one-sided combat, I yelled *camarade* and asked him who he was in the boxing world. The reply I received was, " I am the Eastern intercollegiate champion of my weight"—a weight above mine. The moral of this story is: do not put on boxing gloves with somebody you do not know.

Through that winter of 1923-1924 I followed the advice of Professor George Lincoln Burr. I was an avid opera goer, concert buff, and theater fan. Fortunately, by going to a high enough balcony and being uncomfortable enough, one could get a considerable amount of "culture" for little money. At least once a week and sometimes more often, I attended one of the state opera houses or theaters and by judicious selection found concerts to which I could go for next to nothing.

Along in March of 1924, I received word from

Columbia that I had been awarded a University scholarship, which would pay for my tuition. With it came a catalogue and a letter of admonition about a knowledge of foreign languages, if one were to do graduate work in European history. The award made me more certain than ever that I should go into the historical profession and the suggestion about languages made me decide that I should leave France and go to Germany. I had by then a good command of French and I was anxious to learn German as my second foreign language. My boxing friend also wanted to learn German. Both of us were getting very uneasy.

We decided that, if we left shortly, we could learn enough German to allow us to enroll in a university for the summer semester, which began in May. So we started out, going through eastern France at a slow pace. We went to Rheims and the battlefields (Verdun made a big impression on us, as did also Chemin des Dames) and on to Sarrebrucken, Mannheim, and thence to Heidelberg. We were impressed with the Neckar Valley and fell in love with Heidelberg. We arrived just at the end of the hyper-inflation and although we had to carry billions of marks around with us, the currency was manageable. So, too, were the prices, for they remained very cheap in terms of a high-value currency like the dollar. We found a very satisfactory pension in which room and three meals a day cost us just $1.00. Because the franc had also slipped, living had been cheap in Paris, but nothing like this. When the role is called up yonder, I shall have to confess that I got a good bit of my graduate education thanks to inflation.

My friend and I were both ambitious and hard working men, and soon were making ourselves understood in German and understanding even more. We were fortunate in making friends with one of the members of the pension, who was semi-retired, and who liked nothing better than walking with us. Herr Büdinger was a typical bourgeois. He took pride in his city, guided us everywhere, and introduced us to everybody.

Within a month we were at a point where we could profit from lectures at the University. For very modest fees we registered for a number of courses and were fortunate to hear such men as the philosopher Karl Jaspers and the Goethe specialist Friedrich Gundolf. We found the Germans of Heidelberg much more inclined toward establishing friendly relations with us than the French of Paris had been and this made the learning of the language easier for us. They invited us to go to meetings of local choral societies, which are ubiquitous in Germany, and even to participate in the festivities of drinking and singing. With them we took in concerts, the theater, and the most dramatic event in the town, the lighting with red fire of the Old Castle ruins on the hillside—an event which is supposed to recall the burning of the Castle by French troops in 1689.

Thus our days went by and our German improved. After about two months my companion thought that it was time that he seek a more urban setting for his sojourn and so took off for Berlin. I remained in Heidelberg for another month and then, reluctantly, left in order to visit more of Germany before I set sail for America. I went first to Stuttgart and on the train was, much to my satisfaction, mistaken for a German. From there I pushed on to Augsburg to see the Cathedral and the housing projects for the poor started by the Függer Family, who were Augsburg bankers. Then on to Münich, which I admired very much, particularly the Alte Pinakothek, which has an amazing collection. Gradually I wended my way to Bamberg, Nüremburg, Dresden, Leipsic, and finally to Berlin. There I met my companion from Heidelberg, took a course in German civilization at the University of Berlin, and got acquainted with the city. It did not have for me the charm of Paris or Münich, but it had much of interest for a budding historian. Incidentally, I lived in a pension in the Franzōsischestrasse where I was well situated. After World War II I went back to this part of town, but the devastation was so complete that I could not even find the street!

At last, the time arrived (late August) when my footsteps had to turn homeward, for my study at Columbia was to begin in the latter part of September. I left Germany via Hamburg in third class, so I was treated as an emigrant. I was put up in a dormitory-kind of quarters of the Hamburg-American Line, was given a perfunctory physical examination, and was fed at their expense. The ship, when we finally got on it, the *Deutschland*, was brand new and hence clean and free from ship's odors. The crossing was uneventful, except I was seasick the first day, a rare thing for me, and I attributed it largely to overeating. My parents met me in New York and we headed for Lebanon.

When we arrived in the home town, everything seemed exceedingly small. I was glad that I had taken off to see the world. Even Louise B . . . seemed more provincial than I remembered her to be. She wanted to pick up our friendship where we had left it, but I did not look favorably on that idea, largely perhaps because of jealousy. The "green-eyed monster" had been at work, quite noticeably, for absence makes the heart grow fonder for the other fellow. And another person there was, a person she eventually married.

My parents were concerned about my health, for I had not eaten well for some time. Furthermore, I had made the mistake of trying to live on potatoes, noodles, beans, and the like, for they were cheap and they were filling. My father insisted that I get medical assistance, but the physician whom I consulted at the Mary Hitchcock Memorial Hospital in Hanover did nothing for my trouble. Unfortunately I suffered from my malady for several years, largely because I had no real directions as to a proper diet. Then, too, nervous tensions aggravated the problem and unfortunately the life of a graduate student and then of a young instructor is certainly full of them. In fact, in Germany this malady is called *Privat-dozents Krankheit*, for those trying to get their professorships are usually afflicted.

Chapter IV

Graduate School And My First Jobs

In late September I left Lebanon for New York and Columbia to undertake my graduate training in European History. In passing through New York on my way home from Europe, I had reserved a room at the unfinished International House on Riverside Drive, so I had a place to which to go. To live in the International House was very important to me, for it threw me into contact with students with whom I could keep up my languages, who were at a high level of training and intelligence, and with whom I could exchange ideas on European affairs.

Columbia's history department was no disappointment. In fact, it was at that time one of the best in the country and perhaps in the world. To be sure, James Harvey Robinson and Charles A. Beard had left because of a row with President Butler, but there were still in European history James T. Shotwell, who was then preparing his great *Economic and Social History of the War;* Parker T. Moon, who had been at the Peace Conference with Shotwell; Carlton J. H. Hayes, who was just beginning his work on nationalism; Lynn Thorndike; William R. Shepherd; Charles D. Hazen; Robert Livingston Schuyler; and William Westermann. Three of these men became presidents of the American Historical Association. When I presented myself to the department, Professor Hayes, as the advisor, received me, and I worked out a schedule with him. I joined his seminar in nationalism and Professor Hazen's in French history. To do the work demanded by these men turned out to be a tall order.

My student associates were a mixed lot. There were some local persons, mostly from the city colleges, but there was a majority from far places, who had come to Columbia because they had fellowships or scholarships or because of the sheer excellence of the institution. My closest friends were those from a distance, several of whom subsequently had very distinguished careers. Because Professor Hayes would take into his seminar on nationalism students who were interested not only in Europe, but also in China, the Near East, Latin America, and Central Europe, we had people with a great many different area specialities. I liked the diversity.

The manner in which the seminars were conducted was as follows: at the beginning of the semester the professor would read off a list of subjects in which *he* was interested and the students were to choose or be assigned a topic on which *they* were to prepare a research paper. Professor Hayes was interested in theories of nationalism, so his topics were chiefly on individuals. Professor Hazen also took the biographical approach, but no central theme held his papers together to give the seminar some semblance of unity. During that first semester I wrote a paper on the nationalist thought of Jean Jacques Rousseau for Professor Hayes and a lengthy paper on Napoleon III, to whom I took a strong dislike, for Professor Hazen. Inasmuch as the two papers were due at about the same time my head swam with Jean Jacques and Louis Napoleon. Out of such papers one was supposed to arrive at a subject that could be developed into a doctoral dissertation. In those days dissertations at Columbia were published and so the thesis had to be about something that would make a book.

In the second semester of my first year, Professor Hayes put me to work on a Belgian scholar who had written on language as a factor in the formation of nationalities. In his works, which dealt particularly with the Balkans, he discussed the linguistic situation in Belgium and the results of the fact that the country was divided almost equally between Flemish (or Dutch) and French speaking people. This intrigued me and I began to read more widely in the field of Belgian history, the linguistic problems there, and the divisive effect of the dual linguistic situation. Gradually a doctoral dissertation seemed to me to be emerging—a history of the Flemish movement in Belgium—of which more later. I was greatly relieved when Professor Hayes gave this idea his blessing.

Incidentally, Professor Hayes and his wife were exceedingly kind to me. They entertained me and others of the seminar at their home. Mrs. Hayes even took an interest in my personal life and saw to it that I met many eligible young ladies—all Catholic, because Mrs. Hayes was very partisan. Indeed, Professor Hayes had been converted to Catholicism and his adopted religion had much to do with his interests and his actions. Unfortunately the young ladies Mrs. Hayes considered attractive were not attractive to me.

I thought that I did well in my first year at Columbia and I was encouraged to apply for a fellowship for the second year. I did so, but did not win one of the big plums, but a plum large enough to make possible my return for a second year. The juicy fruit went to others, none of whom was ever successful in the profession.

The big professional task before me at this time was to pass the oral examinations in subject matter. My major field was to be Modern History and my minor European Government. The latter was with Lindsay Rogers, a rough hombre. To prepare for this ordeal I invited with my parents' permission, one of my seminar mates to come to New Hampshire for the summer to study with me. We made a long list of monographs which we thought that we should read and we mastered a textbook (Hayes', of course) until we could recite it verbatim, or almost. Inasmuch as my parents' home was close to Dartmouth, we could get the books which we needed from the library there. We borrowed heavily, took the books to the "lake," and poured it on. Once a day we asked each other questions of the nature which we had heard were asked on the orals; and every day we put at least one book under our belts, or under our bonnets. I think we ate my mother out of house and home; we won the admiration of my father for our persistence; and we drove the rest of the family into some kind of shock. But we did prepare.

The next year at Columbia I did not join a seminar, but I kept reading in the lore of the Flemish movement. I was abetted in this endeavor by a young Flemish Belgian, Frans Olbrechts, who subsequently became a distinguished anthropologist and was director of the great museum near Brussels, le Musée de Cinquentenaire. He and I became close friends. For exercise we used to wrestle in his room, until one day I ripped his pants off and he was too poor to sustain such losses. After that we hiked, which gave him a chance to tell me about his work in anthropology with Professor Franz Boas, to whose lectures he would sometimes entice me, and about the Flemish movement. I became knowledgeable enough so that I wrote to Henri Pirenne at Ghent University about my plan; I started to learn Flemish (Dutch); and I applied to the Belgian-American Foundation for a fellowship to go to Belgium. This was turned down eventually, because, as I subsquently learned, Professor Pirenne thought I had a Flemish bias.

I worked very hard that winter. I went to a few lectures to catch up on details and to see how the minds of my potential examiners in my orals were working. Especially, I attended classes by Lindsay Rogers, but they were so uninteresting that I thought that I could get by on what I had learned in France and Germany and what I was learning from my reading. I took little time for socializing, but on New Year's eve I did go to a costume ball at the International House (I was still living there). This was a fateful event, for I met a young lady, I should say girl, who spoke French very well. I was impressed, and we saw a lot of one another. We went on picnics and walks in the country around Scarsdale and became fond of each other, so fond that we were practically engaged.

When my father heard that I was this serious about an Italian girl from the Bronx, for that is what she was, he found an excuse to come to New York to check upon the situation. He brought with him Leslie Sawyer, the President of Colby Junior College for Women. I am not sure that they were overly impressed with my choice, but they were considerate. I remember my father's telling me that a parent could do little about choosing a mate, but that I should remember that the girl who turns up when the male is of marrying age and in circumstances to permit marriage is the girl whom one must be sure measures up to all the requisites of a good wife. The ability to speak French was only one of those requisites. But more of this later.

Finally the time came for my subjects examinations—that tremendous obstacle which one must overcome, if one is to go on in the academic profession. The time set for this ordeal was May (this was in 1926). First came a written "qualifying" examination in Ancient, Medieval, Modern and American History, with some attention to the history of history. This was a three-hour stint, and I wrote an enormous amount and very illegibly. If it had been readable, I might have been stopped right there, but I was told that I had done well and had qualified for the orals. This was another three-hour trial and all oral. It was scheduled for nine A.M. of May 3, 1926, the day that the general strike was called in England. The first question was from Charles Downer Hazen: "Mr. Clough, would you name all the territorial changes in Europe during the eighteenth century?" Now Professor Hazen had asked this question many times before and any candidate who was not prepared for it simply did not get around or was too stupid to be in graduate school. I had the answer down so pat that I could have begun in the middle of the century and gone both ways at once. I rattled off the changes so mechanically that before I knew it the entire panel of questioners broke out into loud guffaws.

My next exanimer was William R. Shepherd who asked me to discuss the commercial revolution in the sixteenth century. In his lectures he had spent an inordinate amount of time to explain that there was no commercial revolution in the sixteenth century, but that there was a revolution in money and prices. Consequently, I began my reply by saying that he had argued that there was no such thing as a commercial revolution and therefore I could not discuss what had not existed. More laughter. He saved himself by then asking what was generally known as the commercial revolution. Professor Hayes, the chairman of the committee, examined me about French socialism, and out of the blue wanted me to talk about Jules Guesde. For the moment I could not bring to mind Jules Guesde, but Hayes very adroitly had me talk about French socialism and before I knew it I was discussing the contributions of Jules Guesde to this movement, much to the amusement of the panel.

Last but not least was Lindsay Rogers to examine me on my minor. As I have said, I had never had any serious course work with him or members of his department and he wanted to know why, which was embarrassing. Then he asked if I were familiar with Sir John Simon's brief about the legality of the general strike in England. I said that I was not. He then informed me that it had appeared in the *New York Times* that morning (remember that the examination had begun at nine A.M.) and wanted to know if I did not read the news. I allowed that I did, but that on this particular day I had put off the reading until later in the day because of a pressing engagement. He then suggested that I present a brief on the legality of the strike. I argued that the strike was illegal and on this premise developed my brief. When I had finished, he declared that Sir John had held exactly contrary to me. I thought that I was sunk, but replied, "I think Sir John is wrong." Lindsay, then, bless his heart, concluded by saying that he agreed with me. I was relieved, but after three hours of grueling strain I was exhausted. I remember that Professor Hayes said that would be all and that I would be notified of the outcome by mail. This was done to relieve everyone of the agony of being told on the spot as to the decision of the five wise men.

I do not recall anything about the next twenty-five minutes, but I imagine that I had something to drink and something to eat. I was naturally on pins and needles to know the outcome of my test. The department had in those days a secretary who was very considerate of the students, Miss Reilly, or "Ma" Reilly, and about 12:50 I phoned her office in the hope that I could reach her and learn my fate. Much to my consternation I got Professor Hayes, but I was too scared to ask him the question which concerned me. I asked for Miss Reilly only to learn that she had not returned from lunch. About 1:10 I phoned and this time Miss Reilly answered. She informed me that I had done excellently and that Professor Hayes wanted to see me as soon as possible.

About 1:30 I appeared at the master's office. He informed me that I had done much better than any of the faculty had thought I would. Futhermore, he congratulated me on my sense of humor and straightened me out on a couple of details. Then he asked me if I would be interested in working for him in Paris during the calendar year of 1927 on a book regarding French nationalism. The salary was to be $3,000. He explained that he had a grant from the Laura Spellman Rockefeller Foundation for studies of France in the period since the war. He thought that I would be useful to him and the team because of my knowledge of French and my recent period of living in the country. I accepted with alacrity. We discussed the project a bit and my own future. This conversation resulted in a decision that I should go to Belgium at once to work on my dissertation and then join him in Paris at the beginning of the year (1927).

When I left his office I was walking on cloud nine (I think that is the highest of the clouds) and went to a telephone to give my lady-love the news. We must have had a prearrangement for the call, because she was of a poor Italian family and had no phone. I explained what had happened and then said that inasmuch as I was to be away for nearly two years we should be married or absence would not make the heart grow fonder. She agreed with the proviso that she could get her father's approval (her mother had died when she was very young). He ultimately gave it, but, Italian that he was, feared that this was a shot-gun affair. Anyhow, my fiancee, a senior at Hunter, slaved for the next few weeks to complete her courses. I attended to a thousand things like tickets, passports, and visas and a place to live in Brussels, our first port of call and study.

We were married in the county court house in the Bronx and then in the rectory of a Catholic church, also in the Bronx, to please her father. My family came down from New Hampshire for the latter event. One of my college mates was my best man, Paul S. . . . When the ceremony was over he kissed the bride before I did! Then I handed the priest $10.00, which in Lebanon, New Hampshire was a munificent sum. The priest turned up his nose at the amount, however , and said that the fee for the job was $20.00. I was embarrassed, for I did not like to be made to feel cheap and I did not have another $10.00. I had to borrow it from Paul S. . . , a wonderful fellow.

The family, after a brief reception at the International House, which I put on, drove us to Lebanon via Albany. This was the first time my bride had been away from New York City. We had our honeymoon at the family cottage at Mascoma Lake, but soon returned to New York to sail on the S.S. Veendam of the Holland American Line, June 12. The ship was an old one and we were given a very poor stateroom in the very bowels of the ship. Thanks to the intervention of my father the room was changed and we improved our lot somewhat, but our accommodations remained very poor.

My brother Nathaniel sailed with us. He had gone to Colgate and had not done very well nor had he been very happy. The family felt that I had profited from study in Europe and that he might too. The voyage was not a very pleasant one. The ship was old and decrepit, and the service was akin to that in old-fashioned steerage. Moreover, my wife and I were having difficulty in adjusting to each other. And my brother was a care.

After twelve days upon the ocean, we eventually landed at Boulogne in France and took a train to Brussels. My friend Frans Olbrechts was at the station to meet us. He had taken a room for us in a very modest hotel where only Flemish was spoken. I had asked him to do this, for I wanted to learn the language and he wanted me to be with Flemish sympathizers who would give me the *truth* about the Flemish Movement. We stayed there about a week and then moved into a middle class pension in the Avenue Louise section—a French section where my wife would be more at home.

I plunged into my work.I began to interview leaders of the Flemish Movement like mad, to devour whatever literature I could buy on the subject, and to get oriented in the archival and library materials of the Belgian capital. I soon found out that my subject was a hotter political potato than I had realized from what I had learned in New York. I knew, of course, that Belgium was divided nearly equally between those who spoke Flemish and those who spoke French, that the economic, political, and social life of the country was dominated by French speaking people and that the Flemings wanted their language to be equal in law to French as regards its use in all public matters—from its use in parliament to its use in naming streets.

What I did not know was how bitter the struggle for linguistic equality had become. Perhaps I should been aware of how high feelings ran, for the issue had assumed major proportions under the German occupation during World War I. Indeed, the occupying power had given the Flemings some of the things they had been demanding. These included the use of Flemish in instruction at the University of Ghent, the use of the Flemish language in all public and governmental acts in Flemish speaking areas, and the creation of a Flemish Council, presumably for consultation on the matters affecting Flanders and the use of the Flemish language.

After the war some of them, "collaborators," so-called, had been tried for treason. Many of them feared for their lives and fled to the Netherlands for asylum. One of them, however, Dr. August Borms, remained in Belgium and was condemned to life imprisonment. Naturally feelings rose to fever pitch. Flemish students were active in demonstrations for the equality of Flemish with French and for demands that public officials be bilingual. Political Flemish groups were formed to push the Flemish cause in every possible way. All the major national parties had their Flemish speaking, as well as French speaking, wings.

In my efforts to know more about these matters I interviewed leaders of all the various political tendencies, including the most extreme. Consequently I came in contact with persons who were suspect of being anti-Belgian. Some were Senators, some members of the Chamber of Deputies, some mayors, others journalists, physicians, professors, and businessmen. I had no difficulties with the authorities until I went one weekend to Rosendael in the Netherlands to attend a congress of Flemish political exiles. A Belgian nationalist newspaper, *La Nation Belge,* got word that I was there and ran an article on the front page about me, casting doubts upon my seriousness and calling for my being thrown out of the country *sans au revoir et sans merci.*

Immediately I saw the article, I wrote the paper to explain what I was doing and protesting their allegations. I envisaged that all my investment in money and time in the Flemish Movement as a subject for a doctoral dissertation would be thrown out the window and was sick about it. Much to my surprise the paper published my reply in the same position as the original article. (I learned later that Belgian law required such treatment). Also to my surprise plainclothesmen appeared at our rooms at the pension the next day well before breakfast. My wife and I were told to get dressed and to follow the police. I protested that I wanted to know what I was being arrested for and demanded that I be allowed to call the embassy or the consulate. Neither request was granted.

We were taken to Le Palais de Justice, an enormous and unattractive building not far away. En route we were allowed to buy a newspaper and discovered my reply in *La Nation Belge,* which was very fortunate. We were put in a locked room (not a cell) and left there. Later in the day, we were taken to an official who handled foreigners who got into trouble. I learned subsequently that under Belgian law a foreigner cannot be thrown out of the country for political reasons without an express order by the cabinet. Obviously the cabinet needed someone to guide their actions and we were taken to this person. He gave big cigars to the plainclothesmen (French speaking) and told them that he would handle the case from then on. He was well informed about me and believed that I was in truth a scholar (I was in my early twenties). Moreover, he was a Flemish sympathizer and spent most of the time during our interview in giving me tips on whom to see and what to do for my study. He warned me that in the future wherever we went the police would call on us every week. And, indeed, they did. He then sent us on our way with the advice to give police visitors a bottle of beer.

Our reception at the pension was not very friendly. In fact, I was challenged to a duel by a relative of one of the pensionnaires, a challenge which I laughingly declined. The *Nation Belge* continued its campaign against me, but the Flemish press, on the other side, took up my defense. One of the best issues of a Flemish humorist magazine, *Pallieter,* was devoted to me. The cover had a portrait of me in which the artist made me look like Abraham Lincoln and the lead article was a satirical attack on the French speaking Belgians who could not take graciously the writing of a history of the Flemish question.

Perhaps the best article in that issue had nothing to do with me. It was a story in the style of *Thyl Eulenspieghel.* A lady, very obviously large with child, was on the platform of a tram just as the workers were pouring out of a factory in Antwerp. They kept crowding on until they forced her into a corner and were creating a considerable pressure upon her. Finally, she blurted out, "Look out for the child!" Whereupon a big, fat Breughelian character looked around and replied, "I don't see no child." To which the lady answered pointing to her midrift, "And what the hell do you think this is, a mosquito bite?"

Shortly after our arrest, we left Brussels and moved to Ghent, where we took quarters in the basement of a dwelling near the station of the main line. It was a miserable place, and the landlady was one of the meanest persons I have ever encountered. Our impression of Ghent was not improved by the fact that Professor Pirenne refused to see me on the ground that I was sympathetic to the Flemish cause. After some insistence on my part he did receive me, but he was very unpleasent and not at all helpful. On the other hand, I met many interesting people there, notably Dr. F. Daels, a surgeon, who was not only a great medical man but also a staunch Flemish leader. Then there was Professor Counson, in Romance languages at the University, who took a shine to us and had us frequently to dinner. On one occasion my wife drank so much of his excellent Pommard that I had to walk her for three hours in the countryside to sober her!

At Ghent I began to write my story. I discovered that I needed a quota of a given number of pages a day to get the job done, so I hit upon a chapter a month. I worked hard, but the basement apartment was terrible, and we left after a couple of months for Antwerp. There we lived with a physician who was sympathetic to the French speaking cause, but was not unfriendly to us. Fortunately

I met many interesting people, especially Frans Van Cauwelaert, who was the mayor of the city and subsequently president of the Senate. He was a leader in the Flemish wing of the Catholic Party and president of Gevaert photographic material company. Then there was Camille Huysmans, a socialist, who was frequently Minister of Education, and also Hermann Vos, once a member of the rather extreme Flemish Front Party,a Flemish party that had its origin among soldiers at the front. All of the men were very helpful to me. So, too, was the director of the extraordinarily excellent Flemish theater, whose name I have now forgotten. The plays which he put on were an excellent combination of classics, like Vondel's *Lucifer,* and the most recent experimental dramas. Then there were the police. As had been promised in Brussels, they came whenever we moved and when we remained in one place, the visits were weekly. We always had beer on tap and this seemed to have a mollifying effect.

Antwerp turned out to be a very interesting city. For one thing, it was a very active port, rivalling Rotterdam and Hamburg as the second largest in Europe (after London). Yet, it operated under certain physical handicaps, for it is located on the Scheldt River miles from the sea and its docks are located on waterways dug out of the plain. The Scheldt itself is narrow and has a fast flowing current that frequently alters course, which makes navigation difficult. Then, too, it is built up with dikes to such a height that in walking in the plains beside the river one has to look up to see the ships sailing by.

The city has many leftovers from the time of its greatest prosperity in the sixteenth century. There is the beautiful Gothic cathedral with its tower reaching toward the skies, the famous Plantyn Museum, one of the famous printing establishments of the Renaissance, and the paintings of masters native to the city, especially Breughels and Quentin Matsys. History exuded everywhere, even from the name of our street, Tollstraat, that recalled the differences with the Dutch over tolls collected on commerce passing to the sea via the Scheldt.

By dint of hard work, my manuscript began to take shape. By the middle of December of 1926 I had a rough draft completed. It was my policy then, and it is my policy now, to write a first draft of whatever I am doing in order to get proportions, pertinent information, and emphases and then to rewrite and to polish what I have. I was very pleased with the progress that I made, but I had worked very hard and my digestive disturbances showed no signs of abating.

We now set ourselves to planning our move to Paris in order to get settled and organized for the work which was to be undertaken for Professor Hayes. Just before Christmas we left on a through train to Paris, but had a very unpleasant trip because of the crowded train and the exigencies of the people in our compartment. (We were put in first class because the people in our reserved seats in second class would not budge).

To be in Paris was a great joy, but my wife was becoming difficult about living quarters. We tried a pension that I had thought was very good, but she thought was terrible. So finally we settled on a small apartment in a walk-up of seven flights on Boulevard St. Germain between Le Musée Cluny and the Place Maubert. It was a rather rough quarter but not inconvenient because the offices in which we were to work were at the Dotation Carnegie at 173 Boulevard St. Germain. I could thus take the tram in case of rain to get to and from work, or I could walk along a very interesting street.

Professor Hayes arrived with his family after the first semester's work at Columbia had been completed. I went to Le Havre to meet them and I helped them get settled in a new and comfortable hotel Boulevard St. Germain, close to the church of St. Germain des Prés, and much nearer our offices than my apartment. The two children of the family were under five and they put on quite a display all the way to Paris. We were then prepared to go to work.

One of my first tasks for the book which we were going to write—a book that eventually was published under the title of *France, A Nation of Patriots* and without my name on it—was to make a survey of the textbooks in history used in French schools. I bought some fifty of them and began my study of them. I knew which ones were most widely adopted by schools, for the ministry of education or its officials have a great deal of influence in determining choices and publishers are quick to advertise what their sales are—if those sales are large. Professor Hayes wanted,however, that I go through all the books with care and report upon them, which I did. Other assistants, especially William Buthman and Miss Vera Michels, made a similar survey of the press, and I had to arrange for the transportation of vast quantities of newspapers from the archives of the press at Vincennes to our offices.

Then I made a study of patriotic societies and of regionalist movements in Alsace-Lorraine, where I spent a month, Brittany, Flanders, and Provence. I wrote six chapters of the book in rough draft and submitted them to Professor Hayes. He would take my manuscripts and rework them for the finished volume. Other professors from Columbia were working on other aspects of post-war France. Professors Robert Haig and Carl Shoup produced a good work on French public finance, but I had little to do with that except to go with Professor Haig to the Ministry of Finance to try to track down a published error of some billions of francs. We were told immediately upon our arrival that the error in question was ours and not theirs, but our adding machine tape vs. their man with a pencil adding in his head won the day. The error was never, so far as I know, corrected.

William Ogburn produced a fine book on French social problems; and James Harvey Rogers of Yale had a good study of inflation. Parker T. Moon, Hayes' fair-haired boy, who was supposed to write on French foreign policy, never came through with a finished piece. Nor did Lindsay Rogers, who was to have written about French government and political parties. This entire experience aroused my suspicions of these great multi-faceted projects. Scholars do best when they are deeply committed to an undertaking: for some, it can only be one of their own devising.

I worked hard during the day and then usually spent some hours in the evening writing or rewriting my dissertation. Hayes kept begging to see my draft and although it was not ready for his scrutiny, I finally showed it to him. He told me that he thought it was great, that he would take it home with him and show it to the second reader who was to be Professor Hazen. I was flattered that he thought so well of it, but this haste cost me dearly.

During the year in Paris, my wife and I had made many good friends. There were Cyrus Peake, who was studying Chinese with Professor Pelliot at the Sorbonne; Ralph Barnes of the *Herald Tribune*; Harry Gideonse, later President of Brooklyn College, who was one of the worst spongers I have ever met; and Herbert Schneider, who had written a very excellent book called *Making the Fascist State*. As during my earlier stay in Paris, we had practically no French friends.

In the fall of 1927 Professor Hayes went home and I stayed on as per my contract to finish up a variety of things. Then in January of 1928 I returned to Belgium to polish my dissertation and to finish some research. As the spring wore on, I began to look hard at the future and wrote to several institutions for a job. New York University offered me a position , but before I accepted it I wrote to Professor Hayes for his advice. He cabled that I should wait one week. Before that week was up I had an offer from Columbia. That I accepted, and with alacrity. The salary was to be $2,400, but that seemed sufficient for the moment.

Hardly had this stroke of good fortune hit me than I had a letter from Herbert Schneider. Charles Merriam of the University of Chicago was editing a series in citizen training in several countries; his author for Italy was a professor from Heidelberg; this person had turned in a manuscript which was unacceptable; and a search was on for someone to write an adequate study of citizen training in Italy. Professor Schneider was asked if he would take on the task. He said he would, if I would go to Italy and collect material similar to what I had done for the French study. I agreed to do so and began an intensive study of Italian with my wife who was of Italian origin and knew the language well. I worked like a dog finishing the history of the Flemish movement and learning Italian. Within a month we left Belgium. By that time I could speak Italian well enough to be able to interview important Fascists when I arrived in the peninsula.

My first visit to Italy was a great thrill, as had been my

first to France. The climate was a relief after the rain of Belgium; the mountains were a delight after the polders; and the colors were eye-stopping. The trip was not all love at first sight, however. On the way down I stopped in South Tyrol to study the linguistic and loyalty problems there and ran into the same tensions as in Belgium. Besides I nearly got into a police trap.

An important personage was trying to organize German classes and groups of resistance to the Italianizing of the country which was going on. She called a meeting of her workers for two P. M. of a given day so that I could meet them, but her house was raided at noon. When I arrived for the confab with her cohorts, the house was locked, bolted, and shuttered. Nevertheless, my meeting with her workers was held with the understanding that, if the police returned, we would all hold still and make believe no one was there. In the midst of their explaining to me what they were doing, footsteps were heard outside. The steps finally reached the room in which we were. Then fingers appeared at the place where the shutters came together. They tried to find a crevice into which they could get hold to pull them apart. The fingers finally succeeded. They were followed by an arm in uniform. We all sat very still. Then the hand let drop a letter. The hand belonged to a friendly postman who was delivering mail on the inside of the house. Before this was clear, however, I nearly died of fright. I saw another investment in money and job go up in smoke. The experience gave me such nervous tension that I repaired to a sanitarium for the remainder of my stay at Bolzano.

From South Tyrol I made my way via Trent, Verona, and Venice to Trieste to investigate the problem of the Slavic minority in that city. Again I had a close call—I had an appointment with a leader of those opposed to the Italians and he was arrested two hours before I reached his house. I collected what material I could in a few days and took a ship to Ravenna, via Pola. The trip at night and in moonlight, across the Adriatic is a thing of beauty. So, too, is Ravenna with its Byzantine mosaics. Then on to Florence and hence to Rome. My wife had gone on ahead of me and had located a place to live, a pension in which the Schneiders had stayed. Both of us worked very diligently collecting materials on textbooks, youth organizations, schools, newspapers, and Fascism generally. In July we went to Frascati to study our materials and ran down to Rome from time to time to fill in gaps which we discovered.

At the end of July we left for New York from Naples on the S. S. Conte Biancamano; and from New York we went to Lebanon, New Hampshire, to my father's house, which was turned over to us. The Schneiders joined us there and we worked very hard to bang out a draft of our book before our teaching duties began in late September. I wrote rough drafts and Schneider rewrote them, an operation similar to the one I had been in with Professor Hayes in Paris. Somehow we got the job done, and the next year the book came out as *Making Fascists* (Chicago University Press). Everything considered, the book was not a bad one. It was reviewed very favorably and had a fair sale.

By the time we had most of the text completed, we had to move to New York. My wife went ahead, found a place to live, and bought some furniture. Our apartment was a walk-up of six flights, which was reminiscent of Paris. We were on Haven Avenue, where we were to witness the construction of the George Washington Bridge, or as my Italian brother-in-law used to say, "Giorgio Wash-a-da-bridge." Here I lived as I embarked upon my life as a young instructor in one of the great universities of the world.

For the person who enters the academic profession, the years as a young instructor are the most difficult of one's entire career. All the burdens of life fall upon one at once. One has to be a success as a teacher. One has to make a mark in scholarship and publishing. One earns very little, and yet one has to keep up a decent standard of living, build a library, and maintain a family (usually). Then as children come, one has added financial burdens, interests, and concerns. Lastly, one is uncertain about having or holding a job. All of these problems struck me in the next few years with varying degrees of severity.

Upon my arrival in New York to take up my first teaching assignment, I was dealt a severe blow. I was assigned to teach a section of Contemporary Civilization—a course required of all Freshmen—and for my "own" class, an elementary course in

American History. The first was great; the second was a blow. It was especially hard because I had not specialized in American history in graduate school and was not well versed in either the literature, the burning problems, or the source materials of the subject. I was informed that all the work in European history had already been taken care of and that it was American History or nothing for me. So like a good soldier, I marched in where any other fool would have feared to tread.

Contemporary Civilization was a wonderful experience. It was precisely the kind of teaching for which I had prepared myself. It was a broad survey of political, economic, social, and intellectual history from the Middle Ages to the present. It had been developed from a "war aims" course during World War I; it replaced elementary courses in European history, philosophy, political science, sociology, and economics. It was under the guidance of a philosopher, "Colonel" John Coss, and an American historian, Harry Carman. Among the staff were people who were later to make their marks in scholarship, education, and public life. Among them were Rexford Tugwell, later a brain-truster for President Roosevelt; Herbert Schneider, philosopher of political science and professor of religious history; Charles W. Cole, future president of Amherst College; Walter Langsam, future president of the University of Cincinnati; Joseph McGoldrick, comptroller of the City of New York; Jacques Barzun, author of *Teacher in America*; John H. Randall, Jr., author of *Making of the Modern Mind*; Irwin Edman, one of the best conversationalists I have ever known; Arthur MacMahon, future president of the American Political Science Association; J. Bartlet Brebner, English historian, and many more. Year after year the course in those years was voted the most popular one in Columbia College. It was a great way to introduce youth from a great variety of backgrounds to the past, and it was a magnificent device for making instructors learn about other disciplines than their own and to complete their educations.

When I began to teach the course, freshmen had to take the Thorndike intelligence test and then were grouped into classes of about twenty-five according to their scores. Sections of the course were given at all the morning hours, and five days a week. In my first year I was given those with the lowest scores at the most unpopular hour of all—nine A. M. I cannot say that either the students or I inspired each other. No one had ever given me instruction in pedagogy and if they had, it would, if I may judge from the products of teachers' colleges, have been wrong. Whatever teaching methods I adopted were derived from observing "good teachers" with whom I had been fortunate enough to have studied.

In that first year, I found myself imitating my graduate school professors. I was very demanding and serious—I acted as though all the young men who sat before me should be whipped into shape for becoming candidates for the Ph. D. in history. I drilled them in details which they could not remember and I assigned them extra reading for which they had no time. The only thing that seemed to improve whatever *rapport* there was between us was to invite them to my apartment for informal talks and refreshments. The latter, if one may judge from the rate of consumption, were very popular.

One of my particular problems that year was a young man who arrived very punctually but immediately went to sleep. I tried ignoring him; then I went out of my way to arouse him by asking him questions that I was sure he could answer; and finally I attempted to make him the butt of ridicule by his fellow students in order to shame him to stay awake. Everything I tried failed miserably. At last and in desperation, I asked him to see me after class, for I thought that I could reach him by a fatherly talk. When I asked him what was wrong, he replied, "I am an orphan. I have been in the building trades to earn money to go to college. I was not saving enough to permit me to do this, so I decided to work *while* going to college. I am now working on a building in midtown on the graveyard shift. When I arrive in class, I am so tired that I simply cannot keep awake. I know how hard you have tried to interest me and how patient you have been. But sleep is more powerful than my will."

How many times in the next forty years was I to hear similar stories. My reply was then and remained essentially unchanged: "Young man, the education that you are getting, or ever will get, with the handicaps under which you are living will amount to very little and will do you little good. Unless you can get a job that is less exhausting so that you can profit from your efforts, I advise you to go to an institution that is less expensive or drop the idea of going to college. There are many very respectable and honorable things that one can do in life without a college education."

Shortly after this interview, the lad did drop out, but some years later came back to see me. He thanked me for having been so frank with him and helpful to him. He was making a succss of what he was doing (he became a contractor) and he enjoyed it. I am of the opinion that higher education should not be rammed down the throat of every Tom, Dick, and Harry. For those who cannot or will not get anything from college, why spend four years at it? The waste of time and money is one thing, but college years are a period in life when young people are forming habits which will stay with them the rest of their lives. They will not be good habits if they emanate from an existence of laziness, wastefulness, and sloth.

In the conditions which prevail in our American society most young people have to look forward to a life in which they must earn their own living. I believe that there should be a closer relationship between the acquiring of culture, knowledge, and technological expertise and the acquiring of a capacity to earn one's way in this world. Furthermore, there should be a closer connection between college life and the forming of habits of self-discipline—the only discipline of value. Finally, college education would command more respect if it were not cursed with a quasi-professionalism in sports participated in by persons who show no evidence of being educated whatsoever—not even of being literate.

Now that I have delivered myself of this brief homily, I return to the course in general education at Columbia—a course that was widely copied throughout the world. In my second year I was given a group of students with the highest intelligence scores of the freshman class and at the ten o'clock hour, when most students had the course. This meant that I had, unlike my first year, *la créme de la créme*—no one had a score of less than 160. What a joy this class was. We immediately hit it off very well. Teaching them was no effort at all—I just had to be sure that I knew as much as they did. We went to foreign restaurants together; we went on trips to museums in the city; and we had social gatherings. In the spring we organized a baseball league among the "C. C." classes, and my boys, who now called themselves "Clough's Toughs," won the championship. The championship game was between my team and a team of athletes from a class taught by Robert Carey, which was known as "Carey's Fairies." My brainchildren, who were all small of build, slaughtered the goliaths.

Whenever objective-type examinations were given to all the classes in the course, my boys stood out like stars. Their grades went way off the charts. Of course, the "Toughs" attributed these accomplishments to my superior teaching, and I was not one to disillusion them. In fact, we were not allowed to mention that classes were formed on the basis of Thorndike scores. Almost over night my reputation as a teacher went from what it had been the first year to that of genius. This did not hurt me at all with the authorities or with the students.

Getting up the ladder in the academic profession requires, however, more than a reputation for "being a good teacher." This is a phrase which I abhor and which is used most promiscuously in the profession. Sometimes it means that the instructor is an entertainer; sometimes it connotes a person who has stimulating ideas and messages, like my colleague Mark Van Doren; and sometimes it stresses the ability of the instructor to train his students so effectively that they do well in the subject he is instructing. To get up the ladder, one had to publish. Publish or perish. How many times have I heard this admonition. One had to publish, but, if the book were a bad one, the slogan became "Publish and perish."

At all events, my dissertation was published in 1930 (all doctoral dissertations in those years at Columbia had to be published) and was very well received by critics. It had been held up for a long time because Professor Hazen, francophile that he was, thought that it was hostile to the French. I kept working it over and rewriting it and finally got it in shape for a defense. At a given moment, Professor Hayes called me to his office and told me that

Professor Hazen was going to be on a sabbatical leave and advised me to present the dissertation for examination during his absence. This I did. The examination went very smoothly and my examiners, including Professor Adrian Barnouw, Queen Wilhemina Professor of Netherlandish Literature and History, congratulated me on my impartiality, my knowledge of Flemish literature, and my handling of the Dutch language. The examination was marred only by repeated flights of aircraft over the campus in celebration of Air Force Day!

Financing the publication of the dissertation was another matter with which I had to cope. Once again I turned to my father for aid and again he came to my rescue—he lent me the money needed. He was always ready to help in a worthwhile project; but not in one where the principal would be whittled away to no constructive end. I decided to publish with Richard R. Smith, who had been for long with Macmillan's and handled their history list. He had broken away from this establishment house, had founded his own company, and had secured some authors, like Carlton Hayes, to publish with him. Hayes helped me in securing Smith to take my ms., but, of course, I had to subsidize the venture. I might have published in the Columbia University series in Political Science and History, but the costs were high, very largely because of an overhead charge that involved little more than mailing the ms. to the printer. If I remember correctly, the subsidy asked of me by Smith was $1,000, but my payments to him became mixed up because what I sent him was charged to his personal account, Richard R. Smith, rather than to Richard R. Smith, Inc. This matter was eventually cleared up, much to the embarrassment of Smith.

At all events, to have a book to one's name helps in getting up in the profession—and this was my second one. If one applies for a position, one is always asked what one has published. By publishing one becomes a specialist in a field, is called upon for lectures in that field, and is asked to review books published in it. I have always encouraged my students to publish, even if a subsidy is needed, and told them that they could expect to get their investment back in three years, mostly from promotions. Needless to say, this is only true of *good* books. In my case royalties in the first year were, however, enough to pay back my original investment, or rather my father's investment.

I received my degree in 1930, six years after I entered Columbia, which was about par for the course. The degree did not, however, perform the miracles which I had expected of it. With the onset of the depression of the thirties, jobs became fewer and farther between. In 1930 salaries at Columbia were frozen; mine was stabilized at $2,800. To have a job at all made one feel fortunate—and one I had for the time being. I knew, however, that to take another step up the ladder I would have to produce another good book. I had been turning to economic history and decided that my next endeavor should be a combination of my interest in nationalist economic policies in France from the Revolution to the present. To get on with the research I went to France in the summer of 1930—at my own expense. My wife would not accompany me. She insisted that she go to Italy. For a young couple in the early years of matrimony such separation is fraught with dangers. In such instances one or the other has to make sacrifices, if the marriage is not to be threatened.

I spent the summer of 1930 in Paris, with only a brief vacation in the Jura Mountains. I went there because I tried to get to know different regions of the country by sojourns in areas that I did not know. The summer was relatively uneventful except that I made good headway with my study. I sketched out a plan of what I intended to do and started writing the first chapters on French mercantilism. I was fortunate in being able to discuss my project with brilliant young scholars.

My wife and I joined forces in the fall and along in the middle of the scholastic year (1930-1931), she became pregnant. This news meant some drastic changes in our lives. She had to plan to give up the teaching which she had been doing at Hunter College; we had to move from our six floor walk-up to an elevator apartment at more rent; and I had to work harder to get up the ladder of academia. We moved to Riverside Drive, within walking distance of Columbia, to a section that was opposite the Claremont Restaurant (now demolished). It was not a great place, but it was better than what we had had and very convenient to Columbia. Then in order to get on with my next book, I began to lay plans to apply for a number of fellowships which would furnish me the wherewithal to spend a year in France.

In the summer of 1931 we repaired to my parents' places in New Hampshire and stayed alternately at their cottage or at their home. This was a very good arrangemnt, for I could use the library at Dartmouth; I could save money on rent (the place in New York was subleased); and the baby could be delivered at a supposedly good hospital (Mary Hitchcock) at Hanover.

Awaiting the arrival of the baby was a thrilling experience. So many plans were made and unmade about names; where he (or she) would be brought up; where he would go to school; and a thousand other things. I even painted a portrait of my wife at the height of her physical expansion, which is a vivid example (of very bad art) of the discomfort which women undergo. The trials of this period were greatly relieved by the fact that my very good friend and colleague, Bart Brebner, and his wife were also expecting and had come to Hanover to be with us. We shared each other's anxieties and expectations. (By a strange coincidence two other of the history instructors and their wives were also having children at about the same time).

Unfortunately, the Brebners' troubles were a little greater than ours, for the obstetrician at Hanover discovered that Mrs. B's baby was upside down and he expressed concern about it. So before the happy event, the Brebners took off for New York to see the M.D. whom we both had had there. He confirmed the facts discovered by the Hanover man, but he put Mrs. B. on a table, more or less with her on her head, told her to relax, and by a sudden turning of the table put the baby in the position that it was supposed to be in. When he explained what he had done, she said, "What will I tell Dr. X in Hanover?" He replied, "Say simply that the baby took a nose dive during the night." But Mrs. B. was nervous and decided to have her baby in New York. So we lost the comfort that we were getting from that source.

My wife's labor began one night at the cottage twelve miles from Hanover and as luck would have it my father had his car in town. I had to rouse a neighbor (per prior arrangement), drive my wife to my father's house, get his car, and then go to Hanover. Although the trip was rather long, we arrived at the hospital in plenty of time. In fact, the M.D. set up a schedule for developments and the next day went out to play golf. Action began earlier than he had planned and, as I learned afterwards, an intern held up the delivery (July 19, 1931) until Dr.X could be recalled from the golf course. If he himself did not deliver the baby, he could not charge his fee. That was a bad beginning.

After the then allotted time (about two weeks), I took my wife and baby and a very sexy nurse home. My wife was nervous; she did not like the nurse; and her milk did not agree with the infant. We called in a young doctor to see what could be done. He prescribed a formula in which the milk was treated with lactic acid. His instructions were so crude that the lactic acid formed great curds which the baby could not digest. Then the nurse thought that the child should be allowed to cry at night in order to get rid of the night feeding. What between indigestion and allowing crying to the point of exhaustion, the baby developed a hernia. An operation was advised, which was performed when he was only three weeks old. It came out all right, but nobody told me or the mother how things had gone until three hours after the event. The thoughtlessness of people in hospitals is beyond belief. And then when we got ready to go and the baby was on the point of being put in a car to be driven home, we were made to come back and pay cash for the whole affair, although my father was a trustee of the hospital and a well-known man in the region! But the baby was well and safe. We soon took him to New York and a good pediatrician there put him on a formula upon which he thrived.

As I have thought of those years in preparation for writing these pages, I realize once again, as I did at the time, that the greatest joy in my life has come from having children. There is the pride in creation, I suppose, a sacrifice to do things for the young, and the growing awareness of maturing, which are all beyond my powers of description.

Chapter V

On The Lower Rungs of the Academic Ladder

The next winter (1931-1932) was a momentous one. I realized more than ever how important it was to get up a rung or two on the academic ladder. To do so seemed as pressing as getting on the ladder in the first place. In fact, all through my life attaining the immediate goal that I had set for myself seemed just as urgent as reaching any that I had ever faced before.

That year I think that I worked harder than I ever had. I was allowed to have my own course in French history and I knew that I had to make it a success. The first semester only two students registered for it, but the second semester I had four—a very creditable increase of 100 per cent! Fortunately I was freed of my class in American history, so that I could devote all my energies to French history.

As I continued to do for the rest of my teaching career, I prepared my lectures with great care and I scheduled them in such a way that I covered the ground which the catalogue indicated I had contracted to cover. Furthermore, I kept my notes in folders to which I could add in future years. This I kept doing until toward the end of my career I had such bulky portfolios per lecture that when I came to class and spread my papers out on the desk I had quite a display. So great was my collection that I learned some students nicknamed me

"Recycling Clough."

Another procedure which I adopted that year was to have the preparation of my lectures dovetail with the writing of appropriate portions of my new book. To a degree, this practice gave me an opportunity to get my material organized, to try out my presentation in the "laboratory," and to learn if new ideas (if any) met the critical judgment of students. I was in a sense killing two birds with one stone. In this way, my new book took more and more the shape which I wanted and my ideas of what I wanted became more precise.

During that winter, I was relieved of some of the domestic work which I had been doing, for my wife had not returned to her teaching. This allowed me to concentrate more of my time on my own work. She had begun her graduate studies in Italian literature at the Sorbonne, when I was doing research in Paris for Carlton Hayes. She now picked up the quest of a Ph. D. degree at Columbia. Fortunately her studies were not so demanding on her as teaching was, for in those days one might progress toward the degree at one's own pace. Furthermore, Columbia had two excellent teachers in her field, Giuseppe Prezzolini and Dino Bigongiari. The latter became her sponsor and ultimately saw her to the degree with a dissertation published under the catchy title *Looking Back at Futurism.*

The center of our universe had, however, become our first born. Since we had returned to New York, he had enjoyed good health and become quite a charmer. My chief duty seemed to have been to take him to either Riverside Park or the International House Park for airings. These excursions were pleasurable, for the baby was always the object of obsequious admiration on the part of the ladies whom we encountered.

Although the baby was our pride and joy, I felt that I was impelled on his account more than ever to get on with my career. To do this, I was convinced that I would have to go to France to get the data which I needed for my book. I was far enough along with it so that I knew that I would soon exhaust the sources for it in America. Then, too, a year of work devoted exclusively to it would get the job along.

The person who works in a foreign field has one obvious handicap—he has from time to time to go to that area to do research and to catch up on what is going on in his field of specialization. He also needs to know what is happening in general, for he becomes automatically an "authority" on his area, at least among his colleagues. These necessary excursions to foreign fields require both free time and money, which academics always have in short supply. They do, however, have recourse to fellowships, which both their institutions, a few individuals, and foundations, recognizing the problem, provide to some degree.

It was with these various considerations in mind that I applied in January to the Social Science Research Council for a fellowship which would help me defray my expenses for a year in France. My office mate at the time, Charles Woolsey Cole, who was a very good friend, knew of my initiative and one day asked if I minded if he, too, apply for an S.S.R.C. grant. To this question only one answer was possible. He did apply and when the awards were announced, I learned that he received a grant and that I did not. Much later, when I was elected to the Council, I was apprised that an entire coterie of people in prominent positions had been turned down by the fellowship committee of this famous institution. We formed a small group which we named "Rejectees" and prided ourselves on our distinction, although we never wore an "R" embroidered on our vests, as Hester of the *Scarlet Letter* had had to do with her "A."

At all events, I did not take defeat without a struggle. Columbia at that time had a fellowship which was large enough to allow me to realize my plan. I applied for that and was awarded it. This meant that both Cole and I would be in Paris at the same time, which I thought would make our stay pleasant. I fear, however, that I never had quite the same feeling of friendship for Cole that I had had earlier.

My wife and I planned to go to Europe as soon as the spring semester was over, that is, early in June. By this time the depression was well upon us and my father's affairs were going badly.

He had bought, cut, and sawed over a million feet of pine for boxes. I thought that he was over-extending himself, but he argued that he had contracts for delivery of the lumber. The wooden box business was, however, in a slump, for cardboard boxes were taking their place. Moreover, buyers of lumber can refuse shipments on a variety of pretexts: for example, because they think that the lumber is not up to specifications (grade); they want delivery dates to be postponed; and they make payments so slowly that one's working capital is tied up. Moreover, they know that worms begin working in pine during hot weather and that the seller *must* move his inventory at any price. All possible misfortunes of the trade befell my father at once. Then one of his largest customers went bankrupt.

These were trying times. My father attempted to meet them by working harder—to seek out more lumber to cut. On one of his cruising expeditions, his car was stalled by another which had failed to make a snowy incline in the early but very cold fall. He had a chill and this brought on a stroke, which affected his speech. He was in no shape to carry on his business; and his business worries only aggravated his physical condition. Under these circimstances a decision was reached that the management of the business should be turned over to my brother-in-law, who was working for my father, and that my father and mother should go to Europe with me, my wife, and child. In this way father would have to make a clean break with his business. Thus it was that we all set sail for Bremen on the S.S. Deutschland of the Hamburg-American Line in early June, 1932.

The trip across the Atlantic was pleasant enough, except for the fact that in my efforts to have the baby get enough sun, I overexposed him and he developed an annoying rash. A stupid young German physician, or maybe a first year medical student, diagnosed the trouble as rickets, but the absurdity of that opinion was so palpable that we obtained permission to take our son to the doctor in first class. He was very competent. He diagnosed the trouble at once and simply told us to keep the baby out of the sun. The baby was over his rash at once.

This was a minor difficulty compared to the one we created for ourselves upon ariving at Bremerhaven, down the Weser

River some fifty miles from Bremen. There boat trains were lined up to go to Bremen, Berlin, Frankfort, and other places. Inasmuch as we had a considerable amount of baggage, I decided to put my father, my wife, and the baby on one of the trains destined for Bremen, where we were going to spend a couple of days, while my mother and I tended to getting the baggage through customs.

The process of clearing customs was slow, so my wife in her inimitable way left the baby and my father, who could not speak (in any language because of his stroke to say nothing of German), to see what was going on. Hardly had she left the train than it took off without any warning that we were aware of. My wife was fit to be tied; and I regretted that I had not tied her to the baby. But my mother, who had been through worse crises than this, remained cool as a cucumber. She went to the station master with me in tow; I explained the situation to him; he phoned to the station master at Bremen. When we arrived there an hour later the baby was cooing in the arms of a large German nurse, and my father, who had been attended by a physician, was happy as a clam. We were all full of admiration for German organizational ability.

Eventually we went on to Heidelberg, for we had decided that the best way for my wife to learn German for purposes of meeting the language requirement for the Ph. D. degree at Columbia would be to live in a German family. I was to go on to Rennes in France to study with the famous French economic historian, Henri Sée, and to get on with my work on French national economics. My parents were to remain in Heidelberg for awhile and then my younger sister was to join them and to take them on a tour through the Rhineland, Belgium, and France. Finally, we were all to meet in Paris in the fall. My parents were to remain there so that I could keep an eye on them and my sister was to take a course at Lausanne that would provide her with a training that would qualify her to teach French abroad.

I found a family in Heidelberg where my wife could stay and learn the language. The landlady was of some noble family that had fallen on hard times. Her aim was to expolit my wife to the fullest extent possible, and this, combined with an extremely parsimonious nature, resulted in very poor relations. In fact, the German landlady would not even let my wife heat the baby's milk!

I remained in Heidelberg long enough to celebrate my son's first birthday. We had a Chinese baby's suit, cap, and shoes, which had been given to us by Mr. and Mrs. Cyrus Peake, specialists in Chinese cluture, in which we decked out the child for the first anniversary. He was very cute and was greatly admired at his party by all those who saw him, especially his grandparents.

After this great event, I left for Rennes. This separated my wife and me for another spell, which turned out again to be a mistake. I had my career to develop and she had to learn German—neither of us would give in to the interests of the other. As I have said before, the separation of a young married couple is not to be recommended, if one wishes the marriage to succeed. I was very lonesome that summer. I missed my family more than I can say.

Once in Rennes, Professor Sée and his wife were extremely kind to me. They engaged a room for me at the Hotel des Trois Marches where the Dreyfusards had stayed during the Dreyfus trials at Rennes. The place had for a long time been boycotted by the conservative elements of Rennes, but it was making a comeback under the managements of an excellent chef, M. Gadby, and his son-in-law, M. Le Coq. They specialized in banquets, for which there was a great demand in Brittany. Every important event in life was not complete until it had been topped off with a feast consisting of excellent food and drink. This was the case with births, baptisms, confirmations, marriages, anniversaries of marriage, birthdays, and deaths. Inasmuch as I was the only *pensionnaire* in the place, they cooked no special dishes for me, but let me have the same menu as the celebrants. The fare was extremely good—the hotel now gets three stars in the *Guide Michelin*—and I learned a great deal about French food and wines. I had so much lobster (*langouste*) that I became surfeited with it, to say nothing of many other delicacies—*poulet en casserole, poulet Mornay*, tenderloin roasts, pigeon pie, etc., etc. I was served many dishes that were not part of the cuisine of Lebanon, New Hampshire—*tripe á la mode de Caën, timbales, quiches*, brains, sweetbreads, kidneys, and Breton pastries, made from buckwheat flour. In a similar way I was given a liberal education in French drinks, from aperitifs, through wines, to cognacs, armagnacs, and cordials. I never did, however, develop a taste for hard cider, which is as much a standard beverage in Brittany as it is in Normandy.

M. Gadby was very interested in me and gave me lessons in how to prepare those dishes for which I showed an especial fondness. He also introduced me to the hotelkeepers' wine cellar, the selection of wines, and the techniques of transferring these wines, from the casks in which they came, to bottles.

Both he and M. Le Coq sensed my loneliness and frequently invited me to go on automobile trips through the countryside, which sometimes took us as far as St. Malo and La Baule. I became familiar with Breton farming, was impressed by the relatively poor soil of the area, and the *bocages*, great mounds of stones cleared from the land and piled high along the edges of fields. On them bushes and trees were allowed to grow until they were so high that often in flying over them they made the land appear as totally wooded. These *bocages* or hedgerows proved to be formidable obstacles to the invading American and British troops in World War II.

My hosts were also aware of the paucity of my social life and made efforts to do something about it. They arranged with many of those who held feasts to invite me to be a member of the "party" and to join in the dancing which was usually, except for deaths, part of the schedule. Thus I learned a lot about French customs, provincial social life, and current styles of song and dance.

Professor Sée and his wife took me into their home as though I were one of the family. They had me frequently to dinner and family reunions. In fact, I struck up a friendship with their son which has lasted to the present day.

Professor Sée was a very interesting person. Unfortunately, he suffered from agoraphobia and had not been out of his house or garden since the outbreak of World War I. He was Jewish and had been appointed to a professorship in a traditionally anti-semetic region—the home of the Dreyfus case. Moreover, he was a Socialist and strongly opposed to the war.

This combination of factors had aggravated his malady and confined him to his house. There he remained and there he wrote excellent works on French economic history. They attracted many a scholar to his door: M.M. Knight, John U. Nef, Ernst Labrousse and many more. In fact, I read the galley proofs of Labrousse's *Esquisse des prix au 18e siècle* in Professor Sée's study. Together we appraised that work and recognized it for what it was—a prodigious investigation of prices and the ups and downs which they took in eighteenth century France.

Sée and I became, indeed, very close friends and so close that I made an effort to cure him of his fear of wide open spaces. To this end I rented a car and he agreed to go with me for a ride in the country which he had not seen for twenty years. This was for me a Rip Van Winkle experience. Sée remarked upon the great improvement in the living conditions of small farmers in Brittany, upon the progress made in rural housing, which appeared to me rather primitive, and upon the new asphalt roads. He seemed so much improved that he actually descended from the car to take a short walk, but this was not a success, for he suffered badly from asthma. I had hoped that this trip might rid him of his malady, but I fear that whatever help it gave him was very short-lived.

I learned a great deal from Professor Sée. He willingly read what I wrote, but complained at the length of the first chapter of my work on French national economic policies. I still remember his observations as though they had been made yesterday, "Cher Monsieur," he said, "il ne faut pas oublier que tous les chef-d'oeuvres sont courts." (one must not forget that all masterpieces are short). Whereupon we discussed that subject. I suggested that the Bible was the best seller of all time and yet it was long. He replied, not at all. The Bible is composed of many short pieces. The masterpiece is not the accumulation of them, but individual sections, for example the twenty-third Psalm, which he proceeded to read to me in French. To hear this familiar passage in a foreign tongue gave me a very strange sensation. Try it sometime.

On one occasion, he had a visit from a grand-niece who was an avid tennis player and had a national rating. In Rennes she had no one with whom to play and so the professor asked me if I played, and when I replied in the affirmative, asked me if I would play with her. I agreed to do so. The day of our match the weather was hot and muggy and after three rugged sets in which she humiliated me, we went to the professor's for a drink. I was heavily perspired and disheveled, and not very presentable. He took one look at me and said, "I cannot imagine a man of science spending his time and energy chasing little white balls around a vacant lot." He had a point. I could not resist at that point to ask him what he did for exercise. He replied, "J'ai fait la marche." (I went walking.) He had been brought up in Paris and to walk there is a pleasure, for the streets are interesting. In many other cities, walking can be drab.

Professor Sée died before World War II. Mrs. Sée was seized by the French Gestapo during the war and was taken to a concentration camp from which she never emerged. This was one of the great horrors of my life. One whom I knew and loved so well came to this barbaric end. Even today I can barely imagine that it was possible.

Sée guided me in my reading. Fortunately, I had access to the library of the University of Rennes, which I used freely and extensively, much to the annoyance, if not disgust, of the flunkies in the library. They were veterans of the war and had received their appointments, not on merit, but on the basis of wartime records. Library service in France after World War I was the worst I have ever experienced anywhere. In spite of everything, I read an enormous amount, especially in the afternoons. My mornings were concentrated on writing and I finished two of my chapters that summer. I stuck very much to my last, but I did receive a visit from my parents and took them down to La Baule for a stay at the shore. That they enjoyed very much.

In the fall our clan came together in Paris. I met my wife and baby and a German maid whom my wife had prevailed upon me to bring from Heidelberg to Paris in part to help her continue her German. The baby had developed rapidly. He had learned to walk in Germany and I witnessed his prowess for the first time as he strutted down a platform of the Gare de l'Est. Alas, however, I was a stranger to him, and had to get acquainted with him all over again.

I had rented a beautiful, modern apartment in the Avenue de Lowendahl, near La Place Cambronne—a square that always provided an interesting conversation piece. The apartment had central heating, running hot water, and a room for the maid, as was the custom in Paris, in the mansards under the roof along with other maids. My parents took a place nearby close to Le Village Suisse, and my friends the Coles and their baby were installed not far away just off Le Champs de Mars. My sister went to the University of Lausanne and did well.

I worked very hard, but did a lot of it at home. Cole spent his time at the Bibliothèque Nationale, copying reams of documents. Unfortunately, he did not realize that they were already in print in the works of Emile Levasseur. When ultimately his book on Colbert was published by Amherst College, American reviewers praised him for his industry and his finds, but French reviewers and especially Eli Heckscher, the Swedish economic historian, were very critical of his book. Subsequently, however, Cole had rapid promotions because of his work, but a very poor scholarly reputation abroad.

As for myself, my work went well. I bought what books I could for use at home, but went to libraries as necessity dictated. I made excellent progress with my writing and a manuscript was taking form.

Christmas was to be a big feast. My parents were to come to our apartment for the day and my sister was to come from Lausanne. We had the traditional menu planned and I was to do the carving. About ten A. M. I began to feel groggy and went to my study to lie down to see if I could not throw off whatever I had. The time for the dinner arrived, and I told my wife that I was not sure that I was up to it. She allowed as how I had just been feigning sickness to escape work and that I jolly well better get up and serve. I got up. I carved. And I collapsed.

I was put to bed. My temperature was taken and I had over 104 degrees of fever. A doctor in the house, Dr. Cahen, was called. He told me that I had a severe case of pneumonia. The cure was aspirin and bed rest, lots of *tisanes* (tea made from flowers, like cherry blossoms), injections of some eucalyptus concoction, and cupping. For the innocent who do not know about cupping, an import from North Africa, listen carefully: One obtains "cups," like cup custard glasses, but more rotund. One puts a bit of guncotton in the cup. One ignites the cotton, which flames up and creates a vacuum in the cup. Then one slaps the cup on the chest. The flesh is drawn into the cup. It is left thus for ten minutes. When the cup is removed, the flesh is black and blue (a counter-irritant par excellence).

I was very ill. After a couple of weeks I began to feel better, but I could not work. I took walks in the parks, ate well, and slept a lot. Dr. Cahen put me on a diet of raw horse meat to build up my hemoglobin—and I ate the stuff while my wife gagged. Finally, when progress seemed far too slow, we decided that I should go to Italy and look for a place where we could all get together and spend the summer. I left Paris in late April and visited several places on the Italian Riveria. I finally wound up at Forte dei Marmi, which I loved. There I rented a beautiful little house on the beach.

In the meantime I was out of touch with my family, and in this period my father had another stroke. He was at the American Hospital and was better before any news of his condition reached me. He had improved so much that I was told there was no reason why I should go back to Paris.

My wife and child joined me shortly after this event and we spent an enjoyable summer in Italy. We were fortunate in meeting many talented people while we were there. One of these was Ardengo Soffici, the painter, who was often at our house. He came by one day when I was painting a picture of our very picturesque place. He watched me in silence for a few minutes, then said, "Your drawing is not bad and the perspective is good, but how do you expect to paint a masterpiece by using only three colors. It is like writing a symphony with three notes." He was right, of course, and as I contemplate my picture today, as I do when I go to my attic where it is hung, I think how restrained Soffici's criticism was.

Another of our neighbors was Giovanni Gentile, who

had been a minister of education under Mussolini and had reformed the entire school system of the country. He was a philosopher by trade and a very entertaining man. He always had as house guests bright young men who were aspirants for a doctorate under his guidance. I was frequently at his place to discuss aspects of Fascism or to play a Sicilian card game, *Scopa.* I nearly always had his daughter, Teresa, as a partner and most of the time we were victorious. This success astounded the "old man," for he thought of me as the *analfabeto* (the illiterate one) because of the mistakes I made in speaking Italian and he equated my Italian with my brain capacity.

We had several acquaintances who visited us that summer. Among them were Professor and Mrs. Horace Friess (Mrs. Friess was the daughter of Felix Adler, the founder of the Ethical Culture Society), John Herman Randall, Jr., from Columbia, and Dino Bigongiari, who lived in the nearby village of Seravezza.

With the warm climate at Forte dei Marmi, I soon recovered my strength. I swam regularly, visited the marble quarries of the region, and took long walks on the beach with my son, who invariably ran out of energy at the extreme distance we had gone from home and would return only via piggy-back rides. Sometimes, too, we would accompany fishermen on excursions to nearby fishing grounds and watch them by the hour pull their nets into shore.

My father and mother came to visit us, for my father's health had improved and my mother, with her usual resourcefulness, arranged an Italian tour. They went to Florence, Rome, Naples, and Amalfi and then started home via Venice, Milan, and Paris. My sister also visited us, but did not remain long, for she was bent on getting her diploma to certify that she was qualified to teach French *à l'étranger.*

Along with all the visits and the diversions, I did work on my book. By the time we had to return to America in late August, I had a first draft completed. I was satisfied with the central theme, with the apportionment of space to most issues and periods, and with the length. I realized, however, that the manuscript required a great amount of rewriting and polishing before it was ready to be shown to publishers. Most of this could be done in my "free" time, if any, especially in the summers.

Eventually this was done, some of it even in an abandoned barn so that I could write undisturbed. When at last the manuscript was ready to be shown to others, I had the satisfaction of having the highest praise from Carlton Hayes. When, however, I began to show it to publishers, I became utterly discouraged. Eleven different houses turned it down, some without even reading it.

Later on, when I was on the Publication Committee of the Columbia University Press, I became more understanding of publishers' problems. The bare fact is that the American public reads such books very sparingly, especially outside colleges and universities, and readers there usually get the books from libraries. Then with television, reading became more and more a lost art.

Finally, my book was published, and very attractively, by Charles Scribner's Sons. Allan Nevins, my colleague and friend, recommended it to this house with great enthusiasm, and consideration of the manuscript fell to an editor who had known my father at the University of Indiana. Yet the judgment of the first eleven publishers was probably correct, for the book sold very poorly, although it was received very well in academic circles.[1]

From what has preceded, the reader may get the impression that I gave undue attention to my professional life, especially to getting a toe-hold on the ladder and not losing it, or perhaps to getting a foot lifted enough to place it eventually on the rung above. Great as these concerns were, I did have a social and a recreational life. My greatest joy, while in the city, was to meet with friends and to discuss the intellectual questions or issues of the day.

Fortunately, many of my friends were great conversationalists and one in particular, Irwin Edman, was extraordinary. He did, however, have the bad habit of appropriating to himself my stories. For example, I had a period of absent-

[1] Publishing is reputed to be as fickle as producing "leg shows." My experience seems to bear this out. When my book appeared (1938), a work on France that was mostly one of political gossip was brought out by Denis Brogan of Cambridge University. It was not a good book, yet it sold well.

mindedness when I frequently put a nickel in the subway turnstile on the way out. Thank God, that was a time when the subway fare was only five cents and not the astronomical sum that it has now become. Anyhow, I was at lunch at the Faculty Club one day and related to my companions, including Edman, that I had put money in the subway on the way out. By the time I had returned to my office the secretary elatedly said, "Professor Clough, have you heard the latest absent-minded escapade of Professor Edman? He put a nickel in the subway turnstile to get out. What a dope."

Well, Edman was a great person. One day he met a student on Broadway and the student asked him if he had had lunch, thinking that he might dine with the professor. Whereupon the Professor replied, "Let me see. When we met which way was I going?" The student replied, "North." Edman then said, "Let me see, what time is it?" The student replied, "One, ten." To which Edman then replied, "Well, in that case I have had my lunch."

Associating with people like this was a delight, but when summer time came around, the call of the country came to me clear and loud. In the first years of my married life, we went to my father's house in Lebanon, New Hampshire, or to the family cottage not far away. This worked out very well, and after our son Tony was born, we had especially great times with the members of the family who gathered at one place or another. My brother-in-law Willis Howard was very fond of Tony and was always thinking up things to do for his nephew. He was wonderful with children, but had none of his own. One summer he bought for us a fine dog, an English springer spaniel, but alas we had to leave him behind in the fall and the animal was run over before another summer rolled around. Another time, he bought Tony a lamb, called in our region a "corset lamb" because it was still nursing, and in this case from a bottle. Willis made a deal with a farmer to let us have the lamb for the summer with the understanding that it would be returned in the fall, fully grown at no expense to the farmer. This sounded like a fine arrangement for everyone.

For us it was great. The lamb was a pet for Tony and quite an extraordinary one. I made a harness for it, which allowed him to hitch it to a boy's cart. The lamb would pull my son around the fields with a patience that would have been the envy of Job. All went well, and the lamb was returned to the farmer in the fall. The next summer I met the farmer on the street and he reminded me of our deal. He said,"The lamb was returned grown up and I am not complaining, but I am curious about that animal. I have eaten a lot of mutton in my time, but I have never had any so tough as what I managed to scrape off the bones of that scrawny beast. What in hell did you do to make it so tough?" Then all was clear. Lambs are not good draught animals. I explained it all to him. His reaction was, "Well I never."

Sometimes our summers in New Hampshire were varied by excursions to other places. One year, for example, we visited friends on Martha's Vineyard. It was then a charming place and the part where we were quite wild. We did a lot of swimming to have the benefit of the salt water to which we were not accustomed. One day I had my son in my arms and was venturing into the water with him, when an enormous wave hit me and knocked me down. In the process I lost the child from my arms. The water was so roily from sand that I could not see him and had to search for him by swimming under water. Fortunately, I located him on the first try. He was choking badly, but I pumped the water out of him and he was no worse for the experience. I was scared to death, however, and was much more cautious in the future. I wondered if he were going to have as many narrow escapes as I had had as a child. Incidentally, on this visit, a cat crawled into my open suitcase and got sick. Moral: don't leave travel bags open when cats are around.

Our summers were very satisfactory. We did many interesting things, like collecting antiques, which at the time were reasonable. Inasmuch as we were near three families of Shakers and they were closing their houses for lack of recruits,[2] we were able to acquire many pieces of their work. Shaker furniture and rural primitives thus became the dominant style of our furnishings.

---

[2] They had served as kind of orphanages, but with the growth of state or county supported institutions to take care of orphans, the Shakers were unable to attract new members.

Chapter VI

Summers in Vermont and a Winter in Wall Street

Satisfactory as our arrangements were for the summers, my wife eventually thought that we should have a summer place of our own. I thought so, too, on the condition that we could find something that we could afford and that was not so run down that we'd have to put a fortune into it or devote our entire time during vacations to rebuilding it. We looked in the Hanover, New Hampshire, area, but found nothing that we could agree upon. My wife had a penchant for the run-down, picturesque; I, for the structurally sound (a house with good sills, good roof, and not out of line in price).

Our good friends the Herbert Schneiders had purchased a place in Peacham, Vermont. I had written the book *Making Fascists* with Mr. Schneider, as the reader may remember, and he had fallen in love with the region of the Upper Connecticut River. We had visited him for short stays at his place from 1929 onward and found the area he had chosen beautiful. We also thought that to be neighbors of the Schneiders would be very pleasant, but I knew that it was rather far from the library which was adequate for my work, that is, the library at Dartmouth.

In the summer of 1936, we went to Europe, I to France and my wife and son to Italy. I had a few bits of data to gather or check for my book and I was anxious to have the manuscript read by a French historian to catch any boo-boo that I might have introduced into the text. In fact, I had asked Georges Lefebvre to do this job for me and he had very willingly consented to do so. Fortunately, he found no *gaffes* and was very complimentary about my work.

At all events, in the summer of 1937 we decided to rent a house in Peacham and to scour that region for a farm. To cut our expenses we divided the rental time of our house with Moses Hadas, a classical scholar from Columbia and a good friend.

Once in Peacham, we spent a lot of time and energy looking for a place. Finally one of our friends, Sterling Lamprecht, a philosopher from Amherst College, took us to a house that had thus far escaped our attention, for it was up over a high bank from the road and on a curve where one could not scour the landscape for houses. It had once been a prosperous farm, but like so many hill-top farms in Vermont with thin soil it had gradually run down and was in the hands, following the foreclosure on a mortgage, of the Passumpsic Savings Bank of St. Johnsbury.

I went to see the officials of the Bank and they allowed as how, indeed, the place was for sale, that I could visit it, and that the people who were living there were simply the caretakers. So we went to visit the house. It was run-down. It needed a coat of paint and a new roof, but I could see that it was not twisted out of shape, that the sills were more or less sound, and that it had conveniences (running water, an inside toilet, and central heating in the form of a wood furnace). It was such, however, that we could live in it while we did the necessary repairs. There were nine finished rooms and an opportunity to finish more in the ell. It had a long red barn to tie up twenty-five head of cattle, an excellent spring, and a sugarbush, recently partly cut for lumber. There were 150 acres, more or less. The price was $2,300. That was a lot of money to me on my meager salary and just as meager prospects. So I hesitated.

In my period of hesitation, the Bank showed us another place—red brick with four fireplaces. It was, however, more isolated than the first one, had less of a view, and was in a somewhat worse state of repair. But it was beautiful; the acreage was about the same; and so, too, was the price. Both places were about equi-distant from the lake where we expected to go swimming. So here was another reason for hesitating. My wife rather preferred the red-brick place, but I, the former one, which by then we had discovered had once belonged to Thaddeus Stevens, and was known locally as the Stevens' Homestead.[1]

Still I hesitated, talked about it with anyone who would listen, figured, hemmed, and hawed. Finally, I asked the Bank if it would knock off something on the Stevens' place if I took the land only on one side of the road and thus cut down the size of the place by some thirty acres. Reluctantly they agreed to this suggestion and to a lowering of the price by $500. Still I hesitated. I think that my inability to reach a decision got on everyone's nerves and certainly on that of Mrs. James Gutmann, who was visiting us at the time. She got me to say that I would buy the place and to be sure that I would not change my mind went to St. Johnsbury with me to close the deal. I put $1,300 down, which was all I could raise, and put a mortgage of $500 at 4 per cent on the place for the rest. I thereby became a landowner!

It was so late in the summer by this time that we could do little more than take possession and start some of the renovation which we knew was imperative. One of the first tasks was to take down a lot of wallpaper that was loose. In performing this task we discovered that bedbugs in millions had squatter's rights. We were not versed in the eradication of these pests and sought help. The local health officer suggested burning sulphur candles in the house. An old settler proposed that we paint the infested places with turpentine and

---

[1] Thaddeus Stevens was born in the neighboring town of Danville, but his family moved to Peacham when he was old enough to go to the "Academy." When this area was organized, Danville had received a courthouse, and Peacham, a school. Inasmuch as Stevens was a cripple, he had to be near a school if he were to get there on foot. In a history of Peacham, written by the economic historian Ernest Bogart of the University of Illinois, the house which I purchased was not where Stevens lived at that time, but was a house which he bought for his mother when he was a member of Congress. Stevens made a reputation for himself as one who wanted a hard peace for the South after the Civil War. He was active in the effort to impeach Andrew Johnson.

iodine (later he said that if we really wanted to be rid of them, we should use corrosive sublimate in place of iodine); and the Department of the Interior, to whom I wrote, said to leave the house vacant for three months and the bugs would die. Bedbugs, it seems, need a shot of human blood every so often to survive. We tried all three remedies and the next summer we were rid of the pests. I think that the absence of a diet of human blood did the trick.

That first summer we also got a new roof on the ell with cedar shingles bought from my father's building material and lumber business in Lebanon. In our haste to get on with that job, I hired some inexperienced roofers (at least they were not experienced with very wide red-cedar shingles) and the job turned out to be a poor one, for the wide shingles split. The roof did, however, keep rain out of the house for fifteen years. I also managed to get some repairs made to the plumbing and I picked enough of the apple crop to show upon my return to New York that I was a landed proprietor. But pride goeth before a fall. At one of the early dinner parties of the fall, these apples were served. I had to boast about their excellent flavor, their glossy skins, and their white flesh. I put considerable emphasis on the fact that they were *my* apples from *my* place. Whereupon my young son Tony piped up to tell the company that they were only partly mine. "Don't forget the mortgage, Dad."

The purchase of the farm was one of the turning points of my life. I now had property in which I took great pride; which I came to love above all other wordly possessions; from which I received much peace and comfort; and which gave me physical exercise in doses that I could absorb. In the future, I repaired to the farm whenever I could. In the next three years, we went there for vacations, but then the War came. That also altered my life very drastically.

My life at the farm was full of interesting episodes, some funny, some tragic. In the next summer I had an exceptional amount of trouble with the spring. My neighbor up the hill from me had plowed a field above my source of water and had manured it very heavily. Every time it rained hard the water would flow into my water supply, bringing with it a distinctive amount of topsoil. I elicited a promise from the neighbor that he would not again plow and fertilize the land above the spring, but in the meantime I was faced with a problem of digging out the spring after every rain. To help me in the task of cleaning the spring, I hired a newcomer to East Peacham, one Ben Berwick. He was about my age, trying to get going in life, and was having a hard time of it. Together we went to work on the spring and got down as far as our long handled shovels would reach, but clearly not very near the bottom. At that point I said, "What do we do now?" He replied, "Go home." I answered not by a dam site. So I took off my clothes, took a pail, descended into the frigid water (it was actually about 40 degrees), and began to bail out the remaining mess. Now Berwick is one of the world's most vivid story tellers. By nightfall the story was all over town that the crazy professor had taken off his clothes, descended into the drinking water of his family, and bailed out the soil washed in from the neighbor's field. Summer people are something.

Our efforts were not very successful in fixing the spring, for with the next heavy rain, the soil flushed back in. By then I had had enough of wallowing around in cold water, so I hired a mason, carpenter, and friend to solve my problem. We built a concrete fortress around the spring that kept out the neighbor's soil and a spring house over all. That kept the spring clear of wash from the field above and from pollution from wild animals and birds.

Incidentally, I asked Berwick after the day's work what I'd be owing him. "Well," he said, "I planned to ask what the road-workers are getting, two dollars a day." Oh, for those halcyon days again. Those were the best two dollars I ever invested. Ben became my lifelong friend and bosom pal. He read and wrote with difficulty, for he had had to leave school as a child to support his brother, but he was smarter than a whip. I have traded cows, horses, dogs, guns, hay, and maple syrup with him, but I have yet to get the better of him on any deal. I truly believe that he is the only man in the world who would literally give a leg for me, and except for members of my family, he is the ony one for whom I would do likewise.

In that same summer, I rented my fields and pasture to a neighbor (not the one who owned the field above the spring). He put in a large piece of potatoes and cut the hay, but in the fall his barn burned. I let him put his cows in my barn for awhile, but they fell off in their milk and he decided to give up farming. The cows were sold and the man I was relying on to keep up my place and to prevent it from going to bushes moved away.

In my extremity I turned to Ben. After some dickering we agreed that for the use of the pasture and the fields he would keep up the fences, keep up the fields (he would plow seven acres a year and furnish the fertilizer and seed), provide me with firewood from my woods, watch over the place, and give me $25 a year. Such was the deal then, and it has continued the same up to the present time. Unlike the farms of most of the summer folks, my place has not gone to bushes. It is still a farm—and it looks like one.

In that same summer we painted the outside of the buildings and had many of the rooms inside papered and painted. In fact, we seemed to be on our way. But in the fall of 1938 an act of God took place—the hurricane. I was in New York at the time, and it was very severe there. Much to everyone's suprise the storm turned inland in Massachusetts and headed for Peacham. When it hit, it unleashed all its fury on my place, or so it seemed. It took the roof off the barn clean as a whistle from the plate up and pieces of the roofing were found two miles away. It took down two giant silver maples in front of the house, and only the Lord knows how much of my woods. Fortunately, my friends the Schneiders were there and they hired the reliable Pat McGill to put the pieces back together. In those days of little work, he was happy to have a job and the entire labor cost of restoration was just $500. My friends chipped in and bought some trees, which they set out in place of the silver maples that had gone with the wind.

One of the biggest jobs was to clean up the silver maples that had blown down. They were so large that we could not move them; we could not split them; and we could not saw them up into small pieces (this was before the days of chain saws). So Berwick, who claimed to be an expert at blasting with black powder or dynamite, conned me into blowing the things to bits. I still don't know how much powder or dynamite we used, but I do know that we blew a window or two out of the house and we blew pieces of hardwood over the road just as the town clerk was passing by. Berwick loved every minute of it, and I can't say that I didn't have some fun, too.

By this time my son was getting to the point where he could do considerable work. I had the theory, and it was a good one, that he should traipse after me and learn by seeing and doing. Furthermore, I thought that he should have all the experiences of a farm that I had had as a boy. I think that we started out by having hens and/or chickens. I lent him the capital for the investment, bought his eggs, and taught him how to keep books. At the end of the summer he sold his hens and/or chickens and with what he received was able to pay off his debt to me and hopefully show a profit.

In most years, this system worked very well. He learned how to keep accounts, pay his bills, take care of livestock, and become an entrepreneur. Oh, that those early lessons had stuck!

One year, however, many of the chickens died with the pip and he had to be a veterinarian, which he did not like. Then another time, he became ambitious and had two hundred and fifty chicks. When the time came to return to the city, he could not find a buyer for his fryers, so the family had to eat them. We had chickens for breakfast, chickens for lunch, and chickens for dinner. It got so that chickens were literally running out of my ears.

If we had had freezers in those days, everything would have been all right, but we did not. We did not have even an icebox. We kept our milk and other things that needed refrigeration in a milk cooler, cooled by spring water, and those things that needed very cold treatment were tied by strings and hung in the water. The system worked, but it was not very convenient. Later we did get an icebox, but then the cutting of ice in the pond in the winter, the storing of the stuff packed in sawdust, and the bringing of it to the farm were major problems. Later, we had electricity installed in the house and could have an electric refrigerator. That was a real joy. Also it made study and writing at night much easier than it had been when we had to rely on kerosene lamps. They were a nuisance to take care of and were a fire hazard.

As my son grew older, the sophistication of his farming was stepped up. First, there was a cow. It came in very handy during World War II, for it gave us all the milk we could use. We bought a wonderful separator (table model from Sears) and he used it to get the cream. We bought a churn, also a table model, in which he made butter. And then he turned the skim milk into cottage cheese. Our experiments at making other types of cheeses were not successful. The boy was wonderful with cows and became an excellent hand-milker, something that I was never good at. In fact, when farmers got behind in their chores, he was enlisted to help out. He kept close tabs on the milk and once had a bad time with stringy milk (something was wrong with the udder of his animal).

For the most part, the dairy part of his enterprises went smoothly. We had excellent Jerseys from a neighbor, who would buy them back if in good condition when he left in the fall. Only on one occasion did we have some trouble. That came about as follows: On our local "fair day" our family and the Berwicks went to see the sights and to meet our friends. Somehow Ben slipped away from us and was gone a long time, so long in fact, that my wife decided to go home with most of the children and Mrs. Berwick. I was left to locate Ben and two of his sons. When I finally found him, he was at least two sheets to the weather. I loaded him into his car with his boys and drove to my place. The closer we got to home, the less ability Ben seemed to have to control his faculties, including his tongue. By the time we arrived home, he was out. My job was clear—I had to sober him up so that he could get home to milk (cows have to be milked on time twice a day, or they will dry up). Inasmuch as the weather was good, I put him down on my lawn and began to pour hot coffee into him. It did not seem to be a very effective remedy and so I played the hose of cold spring water on his head. That waked him up, but it didn't get the poison out of his system. So I forced more coffee into him—coffee so hot that, as he claimed, it cooked his tripe.

Finally, milking time came, when my son had to attend to milking his own cow. Inasmuch as we had been away all day, we had not consumed very much milk and the refrigerator was almost full. So, after milking when my son had put his milk in bottles, he edged them in and held them in such a fashion that when he closed the door, the door would keep them from falling out. At this crucial moment, a neighbor and deacon in the church came to borrow some gas. Although the nearest gas pump was only a mile away and all down hill, he was not sure that he could make it with the gas he had. So I siphoned some gas out of my car for him. While I was away doing that Ben got into an argument with the deacon on the virtue of getting drunk once in a while, and the deacon countered with the virtues of going to church. The discussion became a little heated, but it did not make the gas explode, for which I was thankful.

I kept on administering my first aid to Ben, but the cure was not effective. I was about ready to admit defeat, when the deacon returned with the gas that he had borrowed. He was exceedingly warm from his exertions and asked for a drink of ice water. Hurriedly I rushed to the refrigrator to serve him as fast as possible before he and Ben got into another argument about sin and virtue. I flung open the refrigerator door to get ice and the milk bottles tumbled out. I was engulfed in a flood. To make the situation worse, the deacon thought that was funny. Ben lost his temper and upbraided the holy man. I began to mop. I never had known how hard it is to clean up spilled milk. I almost cried over it!

Finally, I had to give up on sobering Ben, so my son and I decided that we would go down to his place and milk for him. As we drove into his driveway, we were met by Mrs. B. who told us to get the hell back to her drunken spouse and that the damn cows would dry up and rot before anyone but her husband would do the milking. So back to the sobering up process, this time with my wife overseeing the therapy which we were using. By dint of patience, my son and I finally got Ben so that with a little propping up he could walk. We loaded him into his car and took him down to his place. It was then late, but we got him on his milking stool and by keeping time with the streams of milk which he shot into his pail and the words of a very bawdy song, he got his cows milked. But his wife wouldn't let him sleep in the house that night and, as we heard it, he finished the last cow just in time for the morning milking.

Trying to educate sons into the mysteries of farming is,

like learning history, an accumulative matter. One thing leads to another; each enterprise is built on to what one already has. So to dairying, we added a horse, borrowed from Ben, which could be used for haying and other chores around the place. The horse's name was Babe, an old skate, but a lot of fun and very gentle. A veritable ancient mariner.

My son was very good with this old nag and took much pride in keeping her well groomed and her stall immaculate. He almost wore her hide off with currying and brushing and he developed a system whereby he could do his chevaline chores with ease. He built a large scuttle behind the horse to facilitate his work. For those unfamiliar with Vermont barns, a scuttle is a hole in the floor, with a cover, through which manure is thrown or pushed below to be recovered and put on the fields when the snow was not deep and locomotion on the good earth was possible. This particular scuttle was, as I have said, large of size, and the cover which fitted into the hole was very heavy. To clean out the stable one had to remove the cover, and the job was easier if one also removed the horse, that is, put her in the feed floor. My son used this method, putting the horse outside the stall in the main part of the barn, while he pushed, hoed, and shoveled the manure down to the nether regions.

On one occasion the cover to the scuttle fell through the hole to the manure pile below with the horse in the feed floor and the door between it and the stall open. When my son went for the scuttle cover, the horse, left to its own devices, walked into its stall stepping over the hole. Once in the stall, however, dear old Babe got a bite on her fore-quarters and backed up. Her hind legs, alas, alack, went into the hole and as much of her body as would or could go went after them. When my son returned with the heavy scuttle cover, there she was hung by her belly between heaven and what ever might be below. Following his instincts and a well established practice, he rushed to the phone and called dear old Ben Berwick. He explained that Babe was hung by her belly in the scuttle and that so far as he could see we would have to draw and quarter her to get her out. Ben's usual advice followed this description of the horse's plight: "Don't let your water boil. I'll be up."

Tony aged a thousand years before he saw Ben's old "war" Dodge come steaming up the hill. Much to his relief, he saw that Ben had aboard pulley blocks and tackle and a number of short two by fours which he immediately guessed were to pry our loved one out of her predicament. Breathlessly he helped unload these things and rushed to the scene of the tragedy. As he went to the barn and Ben had a chance to survey the anatomy of the horse and the size of the hole, he allowed as how "this'll be an easy one." (By this time he was used to us and our misfortunes).

He held the horse's head and Tony went down under the barn to pick up the pieces. Well, Ben spoke loving words to that horse, she began to do a hula-hula dance, the like of which has never been duplicated by the equine species, and little by little, aided by a grease that Ben applied to her belly, Babe slithered through the hole, landed on the relatively high pile of her own manure, and rolled off to a semi-standing position. Tony took hold of her bridle, gave her gentle encouragement, and got her on to her feet. Gratefully she nuzzled him and walked as proud as pudding out from under the barn to the plaudits of the family. Between my son's tears of joy and Ben's "Gawd, what a hoss," we watched as Babe went once again for her stall, now with the cover to the scuttle in place, stepped warily over the scene of her disaster, and started munching her oats. Verily, verily, what a horse.

At this point the account of my life during our summers in Vermont has to be interrupted in order to explain other happenings which impinge on that story. Without knowledge of these happenings, certain parts of my autobiography would not be comprehensible. We shall return to life at the farm on a later page.

Although I had been promoted at Columbia to the Graduate Faculty, my salary had not gone up and with a son in a private school and with the expenses of the farm, I was perennially short of funds. My wife was teaching, but her salary was not great and, except for paying for a maid while we were in New York, resulted in very little surplus. She did not save for a rainy day or old age. This issue was a source of endless bickering within the family.

My financial straits were such that I considered

seriously moving to another univeristy. I did go out to the University of Nebraska and gave a lecture which was well received, but this took place in March when the ground was a quagmire of mud, the earth forlorn, and everyone's spririts at the low level attained in the last days of winter. Universities in the country who want to hire new talent would find their recruitees much more amenable to offers at any other time of year than March. When the offer came from Nebraska, the salary offered was not very high and my feeling about Lincoln was that it was a land of desolation. I turned the offer down.

Then came an invitation to go to Hamilton College. I and my wife went up for an interview and for the usual test lecture. The President of Hamilton was amiable and the reception I received was made particularly pleasant by the fact that the President had as another house guest that weekend, a trustee by the name of Alexander Wolcott, who was as good an entertainer in a small group as in a large. I was favorably inclined toward Hamilton. It was a place of quality education and the countryside was beautiful (it was late spring). Of course, I knew the area well, for it was close to Colgate; but my wife did not like it, and she formed an opinion of the place not unlike the one I had formed of Nebraska. So when an offer came from Hamilton and the salary was not munificient, I turned it down.

So I kept on at Columbia, but the wolves kept howling up the elevator shaft. Then one day I had a call from an insurance company wanting to know if I would come down and talk to a certain Mr. Donald Woodward. I smelled a rat. An insurance salesman was using a new tactic to free me from some money. I wanted to know what the purpose of the visit was, but the voice at the other end allowed as how no explanation could be made over the phone. It did say, however, that Professor Leo Wolman of Columbia, professor of labor economics and a trustee of the insurance company, had spoken very highly of me and that I was being phoned upon his recommendation. This intrigued me. So I agreed to go down to an address in Liberty Street, in the financial district, that was given me.

A few days later I went at an appointed hour, but with so little time to spare that I did not even take notice of the name of the company into whose office I was walking. I found Mr. Woodward to be a very affable young man. He took little time in explaining that he was in the research department of the insurance company, that Lewis W. Douglas was the president; that the company was going to have a hundredth anniversary in three years; and that the officers had been contemplating the possibility of having a history written of its first hundred years. Would I be interested in doing such a history? I did not jump at the chance. I wanted some time to consider the matter. If I were interested, would I prepare a prospectus of the book that I would write. If I were to write such a book, what kind of compensation might I expect to receive.

So I went home to brood over the matter. On the way out of the building, you may be sure, I read carefully the name of the company involved—the Mutual Life Insurance Company of New York. Once back home, I read up on the company. I phoned Professor Wolman in order to make an appointment to discuss the matter with him. I also phoned the chairman of my department to arrange a meeting to hear what his reactions would be. I took the matter very seriously. My university salary was low and promotions seemed to be way off in the future. My wife had consented finally to have another child (the elder one was then eleven) and I knew that family expenses would mount. Moreover, war was threatening and I realized that if we became involved, as we most certainly would, there would be a dearth of students.

I had taken some precautions about increasing my income so that I could have a better chance of balancing both sides of the family's ledger. Alan Nevins was then the editor of a series of historical textbooks for D.C. Heath & Company of Boston and he had persuaded my office mate, Charles W. Cole, to write an economic history of Europe for his series. Cole had trouble getting down to this task and, because of incessant pressure from Nevins and Heath, was nervous about it. Finally, he reached a point at which he confessed that he was stymied and suggested to me that I collaborate with him to do the text. He would do the earlier part, which had become his speciality with the writing of the book on French mercantilism, and I would do the latter part, which had become my period with my work on French national economic policies since the middle of the eighteenth century.

We went to work and had completed our task by the time the offer to do the book on the history of the Mutual Life Insurance Company of New York came. Although this work on European economic history had been finished, I knew that, even if the book sold well, some time would pass before it would help to relieve the financial pressure on me. Hence I took the proposition from the Mutual Life more seriously than might otherwise have been the case.

Leo Wolman was the first person with whom I discussed the writing of the history on insurance. I was curious to know why he had recommended me for the job. His reply was interesting. He said that he had observed me at oral examinations for the Ph. D. degree and thought that I asked important questions and treated the students with respect and compassion. He added, too, that he had read the economic history text that I had done with Cole and had thought my part excellent. Finally, he added that the Mutual Life Insurance Company of New York was an old and respected company and that I would find the writing of its history rewarding.

After this interview I went to see the chairman of the history department, Carlton Hayes, to get his counsel. He had his own view of the situation. He could not say that any promotion for me in the department was imminent and that even a future at Columbia was certain. In short, he felt that I would be well advised to accept the proposal made to me. Together we worked out an arrangement whereby I might write the history of insurance in America and at the same time might keep my foot in the door at Columbia. I was to retain my seminar in modern European history at the University, which meant that I would give face-to-face instruction only two hours a week, and that I would surrender my other duties, that is, my lecture course, my role as adviser to candidates for the Master of Arts degree, and my giving of oral examinations for the Ph. D. except in my very special field. For what work I was to continue, I was to receive one-third of my ordinary salary. This seemed to me to be a satisfactory solution to my immediate problem. Thus it was that I turned my mind to the drafting of an outline for the book that I *might* write for the Mutual Life.

I knew very little about life insurance, but I did know how to go about writing a book. I had been involved in the preparation of five different studies by that time and I knew quite a lot about business history. I was of the opinion that the history of the Mutual Life should be written within the framework of the entire life insurance industry and that the history of life insurance would only make sense if placed within the context of the whole economy. I thought, also, that the history of the company should be divided into time periods, which would be determined by major differences in the nature, size and problems of the business. Then, it seemed to me, that within each period sections should be devoted (1) to the products (services) which the company had to offer the public, (2) what the market was for these products, (3) how the products were sold to this market (marketing), (4) what the costs of the products were (actuarial questions), (5) what the financial aspects of the company involved (premiums and reserves), (6) the relationship between the company and the state (regulatory agencies), and (7) problems of organization and management.

On the basis of these ideas, I prepared almost overnight an outline for an entire book and presented it to Mr. Woodward. He was immediately, favorably impressed and presented my plan to Lew Douglas, who was also favorably inclined toward it.

At this stage, we were prepared to draw up details of an agreement for the job before us. It was determined that I should be paid a salary ($5,000 a year), and I estimated that I could prepare the manuscript in one year. I did not want to produce another "puff" history, but to turn out a serious, analytical study. I specified that I should have access to all the company records and that I should write the story as I saw it. When I had completed the manuscript, the work was to become the property of the company. If any changes were, however, to be made in it, I was to approve them or disassociate myself from the book, if it were, indeed, to be published.

Mr. Woodward agreed to all of this arrangement and, so, too, did Lew Douglas. Some of the trustees were a little reluctant to meet my terms, but finally they did. So I went to work in Wall Street.

I thoroughly enjoyed my work on this project. At first I had some misgivings because of the enormousness of the task. One of my first experiences was to be taken to the "archives" of the company, which filled a six story building, half a block square. When I entered the building, I saw at a glance that the building was chuck-a-block full of papers. I wondered how in the world I could ever wade through that mountain of material—how I could exhaust the archives, as the saying goes in the profession. Upon closer scrutiny I discovered that much of the paper consisted of cancelled policies that were being held pending the lapsing of the period provided by the statute of limitations. I realized that there was no sense in looking at every piece in this great depository, but that I could find here at least samples of the various types of policies which the company had issued over its hundred years of existence.

Another source of information I expected to be of great use were the minutes of the board of trustees and of committees of the trustees. Much to my surprise these documents contained very little except what was legally required. What was of especial value to me turned out to be the records kept in the normal course of business—types of policies, amounts of insurance by policy and by agency or agent, actuarial data of all kinds, investments by types of holdings and how they fared, and correspondence from one branch of the business with another. In addition, I found to be useful certain investigations by regulatory agencies and the defense which the company prepared in such cases.

My associations within the company were very pleasant and instructive. Some of the old timers considered me something of an upstart because I was so poorly informed about the business, but I was a willing learner and gradually I won the respect of all, with the possible exception of a crusty actuary. He was, indeed, more than even the management could abide and was retired soon after my arrival. My closest friends were those with whom I had daily contact in the research department, especially Donald Woodward and Eleanor Bagley, but I had friends in all the departments and learned much from them. I enjoyed, also, the associations which I had in other businesses in the financial district. One cannot work for long in this area without some of of the excitement and knowledge of the "Street" being rubbed into one's system. I have ever since having been there taken an avid interest in the stock market.

The most unpleasant part of my experience in Wall Street concerned getting there from the Upper West Side and traveling home again. I tried every possible (and reasonable) schedule to get to and from my job, but to little avail. Even very early in the morning, the subways were crowded, usually with scrub women and maintenance workers; and late in the evening the trains usually would have vacant seats but got me home at an hour when the family had had dinner. In fact, the problems of travel were so great that I vowed after a bit that I would not work in Lower Manhattan the rest of my life if it were all given to me. The next most unpleasant aspect of the work was that I was tied down in the summers and had to forego long stays in Vermont.

Inasmuch as I could not go to the farm because of my work, I decided to make arrangements for my elder son so that he could spend his summer in the country. My married sister and her husband solved his problem by inviting him to their place in Lebanon, New Hampshire. They got him a job on the farm of a well-known deacon of the First Congregational church, or the Congo Church, as they say up there. This meant a bicycle ride of some three miles morning and night, but he was game for that. In order to make the arrangements businesslike, or to seem businesslike, I gave the deacon money out of which he was to pay my son a wage. Hard as it is to believe, that man made these payments with great irregularity and reluctance (that was his habit with other obligations) and this made my son feel like a heel. Why people cannot be more considerate of others as they live life is one of the mysteries that has puzzled me as I have made my way through this vale of tears.

As the year wore on my history of the Mutual Life Insurance Company of New York began to take shape. In August of the first summer that I was on the job, I took my materials to

Peacham and wrote like mad. By the end of the first year I had a draft done. How I managed to get so much written in such a short time astounded many of my professional friends as well as my employers in the company. Not the least perplexed was Matthew Josephson, who was writing a history of Pan Am at the time. My secret was that as soon as I knew enough about my subject to allow me to do so, I made a detailed plan of the book and stuck to it closely enough so that I did not go down every side-track that I came to in order to satisfy my curiosity as to its destination. My research was always focussed on finding out something that I could put directly into the text and my writing turned up gaps which I could readily fill.

Also I worked very hard. Not that the hours per day which I put in were excessive, but I stuck everlastingly to my task. A writer needs to put himself into a chair, pen in hand, or typewriter before him, and *WRITE.* Distractions of a phone, secretary, or assistant are disastrous. One has to be alone, and "turn it out." I find that writing the kinds of books I write engenders thought. In order to have chapters, paragraphs, and sentences follow rules of grammar, one has to think.

By the time I had my manuscript in shape to be read within the company, World War II had broken out and the United States had become involved in it. I spent the summer of 1942 polishing my book, while the research department of the company checked a lot of my mathematical data (they only found one error in the entire manuscript and that was a case of transposed figures). It is extremely important to work with such care that errors do not creep into one's work. Once in, they are extrememly difficult to recognize or to eliminate.

Some of that second summer on the insurance job, I was able to be at the farm, but I was not there enough of the time to make it feasible for my family to be there. My wife was expecting and life on the farm would have been difficult for her. The result was that I found a place on a neighboring farm for my son. This did not work out much better than the first job had. Unknown to me, both his employers, husband and wife, whom I knew well, had a falling out and began to graze in other pastures than their own. They would literally wait until my son went to bed and then they would take off in opposite directions. On one of my visits to Peacham in this period my son complained that he did not think that he was welcome where he was and wanted to leave. I, still ignorant of the situation, urged him to stick it out. I tried to discover what was going on but failed to do so. It was a tough ordeal for my son, but he learned from it—and so did I.

As fall approached, I began to get inquiries from Washington asking if I would be interested in this or that war job. I was approached by the Office of Price Control, the Board of Economic Warfare, and the Department of State. I discussed these opportunities with Professor Charles Cheney Hyde, who had been in the class of '95 with my father at Yale and who had "adopted" me, along with the children of other of his classmates. He was always glad to lend a hand in any matter in which he could help. As an international lawyer he had had a distinguished and happy career in the Department of State before coming to Columbia, and he urged me strongly to accept the job at State. And that is what I decided to do.

I went to see Frank Fackenthal, acting president of the University, to see if I could get a leave of absence and to learn what would happen to the salary that I had already received (Columbia's fiscal year began on July first, and it was already September). Much to my surprise Mr. Fackenthal encouraged me to take the job. Furthermore, he told me that I could have a leave of absence and that I would not have to pay back any of the salary which I had received for the fiscal year. I thought that the univeristy was being very generous with me, which it was. I was surprised because I had not been certain that I was part of the vice-president's plan for the future. Subsequently we became close friends and he wound up being one of my staunch supporters.

Thus it came about that I became part of a group in the State Department whose mission it was to make plans for the peace conference that everyone believed would eventually be held. We had to think up all the possible questions which would arise and prepare alternate answers to all of them, with briefs regarding the pros and cons. In addition, we had to train negotiators for the conference.

My immediate superior was Julian Wadleigh, who came to the public's attention during the Hiss Case. He was lazy, unpleasant, and unreliable. Our more general boss was Leo Pasvolsky, who gave us little time while he cultivated his garden higher up. Above him was Adolph Berle, egotistical and distant, and Sumner Wells, still more distant and noncommunicative. The job was, however, very interesting.

Chapter VII

World War II In Washington

The war years constituted an important benchmark in the history of the entire world, of Western culture, of the United States, and, indeed, of myself. The war resulted in a change in the military and political power structure of the whole globe, both within and among the nation-states; and it taught violence and the use of violence for the settling of human differences. For Western culture, the war was in many senses a civil war, which resulted in a relatively weakened condition of the countries belonging to it. Although the struggle was in large part the consequence of an attempt to reduce the power of one segment of the culture which had forsaken its basic values, the sanctity of human life and the orderly conduct of relations were greatly impinged upon.

The United States was a victim of these changes, but in addition experienced changes which greatly weakened those institutions which regulated our behavior as social beings. The strength of the family was undermined, for people were torn from their physical and social moorings—8 percent of the population moved at least once. Members of families became employed in more diverse concerns than previously; individuals were able to get out from under restrictive forces because of easy transportation (all means of transportation provided 834,500,000,000 passenger miles in 1943 as compared with 16,000,000,000 miles in 1900); and the population tended to move away from personal rural areas to impersonal urban centers. The size of families declined and divorce rates went up.

As for myself, I, too, was torn from my moorings. I had, of course, to live in Washington, but my wife wanted to remain in New York to pursue her career and my son stayed with her to continue his schooling. She was then pregnant and wanted to remain in an area where she had friends, family, and doctor. On weekends I made the trip from Washington to New York and return, and this was a big burden on me, particulary in that many others were doing the same thing and all facilities were crowded.

The trip was bad enough without any untoward incidents, but with them it was horrendous. The worst occurred one Sunday night near Princeton Junction, when I was returning to Washington. A hot-box in the coach in which I was riding froze the axle and finally twisted it in two. Obviously that carriage was not going to move. Foreseeing what might happen, I left the car and went forward into one near the front of the train. As I had anticipated, the front end of the train was detached and went on to Washington with me. The rear end of the train was left behind, and held up a number of trains behind it. They did not get to the capital city until the next day! Those left in the rear coaches put in a bad night, according to a friend who was in one of them.

During the week I lived in rented rooms, which were no substitute for a home. I never did have a satisfactory living arrangement until I moved to the Cosmos Club, which was then located on Lafayette Square in the Dolly Madison House. The place was old and not very comfortable, but the food was good and the companionship excellent.

My work was interesting, but had its unfavorable aspects. In the first place, I realized at the outset that the reputation which I was building up in my profession stood me in little stead in my new position. I had to begin all over again to become established. Secondly, the work which I had to do was poorly planned, if planned at all. Those who should have been attending to this part of the effort were too busy with other things, usually participating in interminable conferences according to Parkinson's Law, or were too lazy, or were too devoid of qualities of leadership to make efficient use of the talent at hand.

As I have already said, our section was supposed to prepare documents on *all* the issues which we could imagine would come up for discussion at a peace conference and to train persons who would presumably be our negotiators. The first idea was to prepare handbooks on various countries in which we would include a kind of encyclopedic body of information, a list of issues of possible concern for international settlement for each country, and the probable positions which various nations would take on these issues. The handbooks were to be available to the president, his close advisors, and to possible negotiators to familiarize them with foriegn regions and to assist them in the formation of policy.

I was given the assignment to produce a manuscript for a handbook on France. After I had written nearly three hundred pages of text and had taken three months of valuable time, the activities of our section were completely altered. Instead of preparing country handbooks, we were instructed to identify all the questions which might come up at a peace conference, to write memoranda on each one, giving the pros and cons of them all, suggesting what our possible policies might be, and the probable consequences of them, and the positions which other countries would take regarding them. Some of the questions were of a regional character and were to be handled by experts on these regions and some were of a more general nature, largely economic, and would be dealt with by specialists in various fields, primarily economists. In fact, our entire division was soon divided into a Political Section and an Economic Section.[1] I was placed in the Economic Section, but I was called on at first to work on issues pertaining to problems of France, Italy, and Belgium—countries in which I had my chief regional competence.

The other part of our work was, as I have indicated, to

---

[1] Little has been written about this activity, but see Harley Notter, Chief of the Political Section, *Post War Foreign Policy Preparation, 1939-1945*. U. S. Department of State, 1975.

train negotiators for the peace conference. Everyone assumed then that such a general conference would, in fact, be held. Curiously enough the old adage about military planning, that each war is fought on the basis of the last war, applies also to planning in diplomacy. Because there had been a peace congress after the Napoleonic Wars and after World War I, not to mention other lesser conflicts, we went ahead as though the calling of a large peace conference were a foregone conclusion. We wanted to have this time, contrary to what we had at Versailles after World War I, a body of negotiators who would be well versed in the issues which would come up for discussion and settlement.

The persons within the department who we expected would be active participants were Adolf Berle, who seemed to have a personal mission to put the world on the right track; Sumner Wells, who was somewhat above the battle; Herbert Feis,who was sure to be prominent in economic discussions; and Leo Pasvolsky, who had written an excellent book with Harold Moulton on reparations and war debts after World War I. From outside the department, we had as trainees Myron Taylor of United States Steel and formerly our representative to the Vatican; James T. Shotwell, emeritus from Columbia University and a specialist on the peace settlement after World War I; Dorothy Thomas of the *New York Times*; and Isaiah Bowman, president of The Johns Hopkins University and an economic geographer by trade. These were all gracious people, except for Bowman, who was unpleasant to all of us "experts" and forever attempting to belittle us and extoll himself.[2]

Fortunately, most of my colleagues were agreeable and able. One of my closest co-workers was M. M. Knight of the University of California whom I had known at Columbia and then

---

2 During these months I had occasion to go to The John Hopkins University in Baltimore on a very cold winter's day. As I crossed the campus I encountered President Bowman. As we met, I drew off my glove to shake hands, but he shook without removing his. He remarked on our respective actions. Whereupon I said impulsively but with conviction, "Well, President Bowman, we say up in New England, once a gentleman always a gentleman." This seemed to get some respect from him.

later in Paris. He never wrote much, but he was well informed, very intelligent, very talkative, and very good company. Also close to me was an assistant, Ralph Bowen, who had done his degree with me at Columbia and who was exceedingly able. Then there was Eleanor Dulles, who was much smarter than her more illustrious brother John Foster, and more modest. There were also A. J. Brown, of Brown University, who was an expert on international exchange; Grayson Kirk, a future President of Columbia University; Phillip Mosely, an expert on Russia and a future colleague at Columbia and a very warm friend; Dorothy Fosdick, who was largely responsible for the first draft of the American plan for the United Nations; and many more.

The poorest of our group were from government service, and they were the ones who were put in positions of bureaucratic authority, at least so far as administrative duties were concerned. Inasmuch as this was my first experience in government, I was not prepared for some of the shockers that soon came to my attention. One was that these people were not well informed and were either very lazy or exceedingly zealous. For example, Leo Pasvolsky made an ass of himself one day over plans for the French railways, because he did not know that the railways had been nationalized. Julian Wadleigh usually came in very late and often missed occasional briefing sessions given by Berle. And Harley Notter, who became the head of the political division, was so tense that he acted like a master sergeant and had his group in a perpetual state of jitters.

My second shocker was that my superiors, incompetent as they were, had to make a periodic rating of my work for purposes of individual promotions or increases in salary. This practice was conducive to a high degree of boot-licking against which I reacted strongly, and probably to my own detriment. My third shock came from the fact that the career men thought that we should give the higher-ups what was believed to be their desires. Thus for Mr. Hull, we had to take a strong anti-tariff stand; for Mr. Berle, an anti-De Gaulle stance; and for Mr. Roosevelt, an anti-German position.

My biggest disillusionment in the first months of my

work was that we had no idea what happened to the material which we prepared. We never knew what position the government or the prospective negotiators would take on the issues which we raised and documented—what the ultimate position would be on our "position papers." Only gradually did we come to realize that Mr. Roosevelt was going to call the final shots and that he might or might not use our work, or even hear of it.

Let me illustrate the two cases. One of my special questions was reparations. As a student of this problem after World War I, I was strongly opposed to creating a network of reparations and war debts that would upset post-war international trade and payments. My position papers were against any reparations, but everyone realized that there would be a demand from some segments of the public to make the Germans and Japanese pay. To see what the reaction to my proposals would be, I was encouraged to appear before clubs of business men and on radio to present my case. I debated Norman Thomas on the subject, but this experience was not very revealing because he insisted on using the opportunity not to debate the pros and cons of reparations but to sell socialism to our listeners.

Subsequently, I spoke on the question to the Lions Club of New York. I argued that reparations would upset normal commercial transactions and, furthermore, that capitalist economies would be unwilling to receive reparations, for payments would have to be made in goods and services and that to receive such goods and services would mean injuring some national, vested interests that could provide these very goods and services. In view of the fact that Russia had come out for reparations, I explained that a communist economy, especially one in short supply of many things, could receive goods and services with no special interests being hurt. The response to this argument, at least by some people, was that they guessed a capitalist economy was as good as a communist one and that we could receive all that we could get.

In spite of such experiences, our government went on record early as being against reparations; we fought the Russian position tooth and nail right down to the end. We also opposed the building up of war debts and promoted our lend-lease policy to minimize them. Also, in our division, we worked on the creation of a bank of international settlement to ease imbalances in trade and payments after the conflict and an international monetary fund to maintain some stability in the exchange rates of currencies in the post-war era. We also planned for a continuation after the war of the United Nations Relief and Rehabilitation Administration, for it was clear that many countries were going to have trouble getting back into production. In fact, our work provided a base for the subsequent Marshall Plan.

Another thing that began to be apparent was that few decisions were being made on any questions. For one thing, the course of the war was such that conditions for firm decisions were in many cases in a state of flux. We did not know who the various participants in a peace conference would be or from what positions of power they would speak. Secondly, questions which would come up for discussion were so numerous that final determinations regarding them were difficult. Thirdly, our bureaucratic organization made impossible even keeping us abreast of what was going on. President Roosevelt was legally responsible for policy and he wanted to form it whether or not he had the benefit of our memoranda. In fact, decisions on international matters were so far behind the actual course of military events in the field that the military frequently had to make policy determinations, although they were not equipped by training or briefing to do so.

A case in point later on was the agreement as to where the forces of the Allied nations would meet the Russian troops and where the line of military occupation should be drawn. This was left to Eisenhower to decide. After the war, when he was President of Columbia, I asked him why he chose the line that he did. After explaining that the decision was made far in advance of the meeting of the armies and that it was not possible to estimate how fast each would advance, he added that in those days where the line should be was not considered very important. Any matter of this kind was considered to be only temporary and that "in the brave new world" after the war, any mistake of the nature in question could easily be rectified. How unprepared he was for such activity is accentuated by the fact that in the first draft arrangement on this issue no provision was made for access to Berlin by land! Fortunately this oversight was caught by John Winant, a member of the European Advisory Commission at Rheims.

One of the issues on which I worked illustrates another of the difficulties confronting experts. One morning Mr. Berle called me to his office and said that he wanted us to investigate the possiblity of bringing back to a Germany reduced to the area inside the boundaries of the Oder-Niesse Line, Upper Silesia, and the Sudentenland, ethnic Germans in Europe outside these lines. He wanted to know how many of these people, estimated to number three and a half million, could be absorbed into agriculture and how many into industry and commerce. He wanted to know what the costs would be to establish them in these areas of activity at viable standard of living levels and on what assumptions of German economic recovery. I decided to study the agricultural side of the problem, while a colleague was to do industry and commerce. We were given a week for the task.

Needless to say, I worked like a devil. Fortunately for me, the Nazis had had a "settlement program" on the land in certain areas and created a great amount of information about costs and opportunities for expansion. The opportunities were few and far between, for Germany had a very intensive use of its agricultural land. About the only areas not heavily cultivated were on the sandy soils of Mecklenburg or on marginal land in such places as the Sauerland. According to German agronomists it was possible to settle more people in agriculture, but only, if they were to become self-supporting, at an inordinately high cost. From experience based on their own efforts, they presented estimates of this cost. Thus for my report I multiplied this figure by half the people who would be brought into the smaller Germany. I no longer recall the precise amount that would be required, but it was enormous—many billions of dollars at 1938 prices.

Whatever the exact costs were estimated to have been, however, my report got into the hands of Henry Morgenthau and was used by him as the basis for his proposal to make Germany an agricultural nation in order to keep it from becoming again a threat to the peace of Western Europe. Here was a concrete case of the way our information was used to other purposes than those intended. When our reports were taken out of context and without our knowledge or without an opportunity to explain our findings, our morale was greatly weakened. In fact, this particular episode made me extremely unhappy with the position in which I found myself and led me to think about devoting my energies to other tasks.

Opportunities for employment were numerous in those days. I had friends in many other agencies and I met frequently with them to discuss their work and mine. There was Franz Neumann in the Board of Economic Warfare, a German refugee, who was well informed about the Western European scene. There were R. K. Gooch, of the University of Virginia, Geroid T. Robinson and John Wuorinnen of Columbia in the Office of Strategic Services, who frequently talked with me about joining them. There were George Woodbridge, a former colleague in history from Columbia, and John Orchard, who had been acting dean of the School of Business at Columbia, in the United Nations Relief and Rehabilitation Administration. And then there were many friends whom I saw from time to time: Bill Langer of Harvard in OSS, James Phinney Baxter III, President of Williams College, and many more. From them I learned of many chances to move to other pastures.

Moreover, I was used regularly as a representative of our section in State to other groups, both inside and outside the Department, which were studying economic matters of Europe or other problems of areas in which I had some competence. Thus I was, for example, in on planning for military government in Italy and France, on the blockading of North Africa from Italy, on the supplying of Italy by Germany, on the German labor force, and on inflation in France and Italy. Such contacts got me around Washington with the result that I heard even more about job-opportunities than I otherwise would have.

Sometimes my work had tragi-comic aspects. On one occasion Mr. Berle asked me for a report on Charles De Gaulle and, as usual, in a hurry. I gathered all the information which I could find in the Department and picked the brains of French friends who had recently come from France, both occupied and unoccupied. One of these persons I took to dinner in a French restaurant in order to talk at length about my assignment. To the dinner I brought along a brief case full of documents on my subject in order to study them at my leisure. The dinner was pleasant and instructive, but when I arrived home, which at the time was beyond Chevy Chase Circle, a long way from the Department, I discovered that I did not have my brief case with me. In great consternation I phoned the restaurant where we had been to see if I had left my papers there. I feared that I might be in real trouble because many of the documents were marked "secret" and even "top secret" and should not have been taken from the Department in the first place. Much to my relief the papers had been found and put aside for me. On this occasion I hired a taxi and hurried into town to retrieve my materials. Even as I write this, I shudder at the thought of what would have been the consequences, if these papers had fallen into unfriendly hands. They contained confirmation of the well-known fact that the President was very hostile to De Gaulle and that the Department was acquainted with some of the shenanigans that the Free French were indulging in at their London headquarters. Episodes like this relieved the tedium of regular work. I use the word tedium, because, as I have said above, we had no idea of the use to which our material was being put, also because, as professors, we were accustomed to telling people in a pontifical way how things were—we were not overjoyed at not being able to do the same thing in government!

I also met a number of distinguished people in those days. One was Archibald MacLeish, then director of the Library of Congress. We came together because of our mutual interests in preserving war records. He was an amusing conversationalist and was full of anecdotes of his travels. One, I remember distinctly. He was coming back from England and was grounded by fog at Foynes. The wait became wearisome and he and a friend amused themselves by betting on who could compose a Limerick on a given subject in the shortest time. The one which remains in my head was composed by

Archie on the subject of Foynes. It went something like this:

There was a young lady from Foynes
Who made her way with her loins.
From early to late
She was ready to date
For anything that could be changed into coins.

In the same group, there was Vice President Henry Wallace, who got away with a lot because of his political position. I recall that some of us had a plan for a coordinator of war records at a time when coördinators were being named to perform every conceivable task. In fact, Washington was stuffed with coordinators. I guess that Mr. Wallace thought that the world had had enough of them, for he killed our plan by asking us if we knew the definition of a coordinator. When we allowed as how we did not, he said, "Well, a Hoosier friend of mine told me that the best definition he had heard to date was that a coordinator is one who can keep all the balls in the air at once without losing his own."

At about the same time, I was appointed as an unpaid adviser to a small body known as the Historical Service Board. Our assignment was to have pamphlets prepared for our fighting men on a great variety of subjects ranging from what the war was all about, to the problems of various regions, to problems on the home front, and eventually to questions about demobilization and being reabsorbed into civilian life. I suppose that two or three hundred such documents were published and they proved to be both popular and useful. They were important enough so that President Roosevelt cited each member of the Board for his services.

Outside of such excursions into other matters, I kept very close to my last. In those years Washington had no theater worthy of the name. Its musical life was very limited, and tickets were hard to get for anything of any moment. The city did have the National Gallery, which was and is excellent, but the availability of the Gallery was limited because of working hours. We labored from nine to five and a half day on Saturdays, which cut us off from many things and which left us so fatigued that we had little energy left. Even social life was restricted largely to dinners arranged by colleagues or friends.

Only rarely was there some event like a meeting of the Columbia University Club of Washington. I remember that I attended one such function, which was graced by the presence of President Nicholas Murray Butler. Although I must admit that he had many good qualities, he was not a modest man. When he came to speak, he concentrated on his autobiography which was then coming out volume by volume. Among other things he said: "I regret that Dean Acheson is not here tonight, for if he were I would remind him of what I said to Lloyd George in 1918 that if we impose too hard a peace on Germany, we shall reap a holocaust, as you will see if you turn to volume I, page such and such of *Through the Busy Years*. I also am sorry that Adolph Berle is not in the audience, a member of the Faculty of our own Law School, for if he were, I would refer him to what I told Aristide Briand in 1933, that the coming to power of the Nazis may well mean war, as you will see if you turn to volume 2, page such and such of *Through the Busy Years*." When Butler sat down and the President of the Columbia Club of Washington rose to make a few remarks in appreciation of Butler's talk, he said, "Well, boys, it looks as though we would have to buy the whole set."[3]

Still another activity outside of other "diversions" from my regular task concerned the Industrial College of the Armed Services. In my efforts to promote "history while it was hot," as the history of the War was called, I met the Commandant of the College, General Donald Armstrong. He was a graduate of Columbia College and a Latinist, and these things drew us together. We became good friends, and he invited me to become a member of the Advisory Board of the College. This College was on a par with the War College, but it devoted its attention primarily to the economics of warfare, especially to the production of goods for war, the delivery of them, and the planning for all economic eventualities. Many of our leading military men had studied at the Industrial College, Dwight Eisenhower among others.

I was flattered at the invitation to be on its Board and

---

[3] I should add that I am writing these words from memory and I am sure that they are not exactly accurate, but in the main I report what was said.

accepted the invitation willingly enough, for I had an interest in these things and some competence. I found myself, however, in the company of men who seemed to have some special interest to promote—the chairman of the board of a leading airplane company, the president of an important steel company, the head of a prominent business school, and so on. I began to fear, as time went on, that I might be compromised by some of the recommendations of this board, for I could not devote the time to it to be sure that I was not party to something that I really opposed. When I returned to academe after the war, I resigned from the Board of Advisors, but before I did I participated in several interesting experiments. One of the most important was a program for shadow economic mobilizations to find out whatever bugs there might be in our plans in case of another conflict.

Relief from my regular work was also had by giving lectures at the Army's school of military government at the University of Virginia in Charlottesville. The trip down on the Southern Railway was pleasant in the early morning, which was enhanced by an excellent breakfast. The town of Charlottesville is very pretty and the older buildings at the University superb. The Colonnade Club, where I stayed, was designed by Thomas Jefferson and its architecture was beautiful. Unfortunately the more recent structures were very humdrum, which leads me to express my amazement that architects, once they have found a beautiful style, insist on leaving it. Why cannot they understand that variations on a style can be as original as departing completely into something new that clashes with what exists. Many of our colleges and universities began with buildings that were not bad, but all of them have been ruined by a hodge-podge of designs and materials that destroys all harmony. My activities were unfortunately concentrated in the Law Faculty, which was then housed in one of these new and very mediocre structures.

My lectures were focused primarily upon difficulties that might be encountered in a cross Channel invasion of Europe, whether the invasion were, let us say, along the Belgian coast near Ostend, the French coast near Boulogne, or the Normandy coast. I emphasized at great length the difficulties in the Flanders Plain at various seasons of the year. Inasmuch as I had lived there for a couple of years and had hiked over most of it, I assured my listeners that operations in that flat country with its innumerable canals would require more Bailey Bridges than anyone had ever seen at one time. Flooding some of the countryside would not be difficult as a means of defense. In fact, along the Scheldt River which flows through Antwerp, I have often looked up, as I have said earlier, from the roadways in the plain to see great ships floating by overhead, so high is the River from the land beneath. Moreover, the rains of winter and spring turn most of this area into very soft going when one leaves paved roads. I pointed out the logistic advantages which the Germans would have in operating there because of their proximity to German bases. I was of the opinion that the Belgian population would be sympathetic to the Allied cause and that there would be few Flemish activists who would favor the Germans, as had been the case at the end of World War I. Finally, I pointed out that landings at Boulogne would be very much like landings along the Belgian coast.

So far as landings in Normandy were concerned, the problems which would be encountered would be quite different. I thought that the distance from Germany and hence longer supply lines for our enemies would offset the longer cross Channel haul for our own forces. The terrain in Normandy and Brittany did, however, present problems of its own. Not only do high bluffs exist at many points along the coast, but the countryside has a major characteristic of high mounds of stones, soil, and trees between fields, the so-called *bocages*, which I have already mentioned. These hedgerows are much more formidable than most people realize, especially when one compares them with English hedgerows, the English word that is used as a synonym for them. Indeed, these mounds rise twenty-five to thirty feet in the air and can impede movements across the country. Moreover, neither roads or railroads were very good or highly developed in this relatively poor countryside. Therefore, transportation seemed to me to be one of the major obstacles to a war of movement in this area.

So far as Italy was concerned, my opinion was that an

attempt to move up the Peninsula should not be made, for the Apennine Mountains provide from Sicily northward a very strong barrier to invaders and one that is easy to defend. The numerous mountain rivers that are raging torrents in the rainy season and that are nearly bone-dry in dry seasons cut the Peninsula or at least its coastal plains all the way along. My opinion was that a *threat* of advancement would tie up a large German force with extensive supply lines and would leave to the Germans the task of feeding and administering the Italian people, a no mean task. I was greatly surprised when the Allies began to move northward and when they landed at Anzio.[4] Subsequently I learned that Winston Churchill had been the one who had insisted upon the Italian campaign. He had a *mystique*—a fixation— about taking Rome, no matter the cost in lives and destruction of the country.

Another issue to which I had to address myself was that of refugees from the fighting in Italy. One of my colleagues from Columbia, Joseph Chamberlain of the Law School, was in charge of work in this area and consulted me at length—and the results of the consultations were reported to my students in the School of Military Government. My opinion was that Italy would not have a great refugee problem like Eastern Europe and that for a variety of reasons. One was that Italians fleeing from the war would go to the mountains until the front had passed and then would return to their homes. There would be no great influx of people, for Italians who had gone abroad had migrated to areas whence they could not come back, or would not, at least until conditions were greatly improved. I also thought that the transportation of refugees would not present a major problem, because those who did flee to the mountains could return fairly easily and refugees from cities in the coastal plains could be repatriated by sea.

Undoubtedly the most burning issue with which I was confronted in these days was what the nature of military government should be. My view was that for the countries which I was

---

[4] One of the most remarkable books to come out of the war is *Vessel of Sadness* by William Woodruff. He was with the British forces and was one of the few to live through the horror of Anzio.

considering — Italy, France, and Belgium — every attempt should be made to return governmental functions to local citizens. These countries were certain to be friendly toward their liberators and did not have to be coerced into following the dictates of the conquerors. Secondly, the governmental administrations of these countries were highly intricate but well organized and that for foreigners to take over would lead to unnecessary clashes of authority. Thirdly, I felt that the centralized nature of administraion in these nations meant that there should be a recognized and well-accepted central authority to which local government agencies could look both to obtain obedience and guidance.

Thus I placed much importance on the selection of central authorities that the Allies would support. In the case of Italy, I was at a loss as to whom to recommend. The Fascists would be eliminated from consideration and the royal authority had lost favor because it had been so highly compromised. I thought that support should be given to some of the leaders in public life and that their counsels should be given great weight. I had in mind persons like Luigi Einaudi, who did become President, and Benedetto Croce, the historian and a famous critic of Fascism. In the case of France, I favored Charles De Gaulle in spite of the antagonism of several of the war-time American leaders to him, for he seemed to me the only one who had the charisma to hold the French together in the period of reconstruction. In the case of Belgium, I supported the cause of King Leopold III, for, in spite of his rather questionable war-time record, he seemed to be the one who could unite the people, both Flemings and Walloons, until some more suitable leaders could be found.

Lastly, I concerned myself with problems of immediate relief and the time that would be necessary to get the economies of these countries back into production and functioning more or less normally. I argued, largely by analogy from post World War I experience, that the recuperative powers of our highly technical economic systems were extraordinary and could work wonders. I thought that the key to the situation was the restoration of a high level of commercial exchanges among nations, and of confidence in the future. I estimated that there would be a terrific drain on the United States for raw materials and machinery and that we would have to do a lot to help finance these purchases. I believed also that post-war inflation would be a major problem. Hence I advocated policies of low tariffs and freedom of commercial exchanges without embargoes and the development of multinational exchanges. I was also of the opinion that we would have to furnish a considerable amount of aid to control inflation and to get the economic machine to function properly. In fact, the group in which I was worked out the basic ideas for the Marshall Plan, for the International Monetary Fund to help control inflation, and the International Bank for Reconstruction and Development. I made a guess that Western Europe would be back at its pre-war levels of production in both agriculture and industry within five years, if the United States followed in general the lines which I have outlined here. I was not far off the mark, but I did not anticipate in 1942 that some of the European nations would have the economic successes which they did have, successes which warranted the appellation of miracles.

Although the work that I did in the Department of State does not seem so futile in retrospect, it seemed very unrewarding at the time. I had no respect for my immediate superior, Julian Wadleigh, who subsequently admitted to illegal acts in giving information to the Russians.[5] Not only was I of the opinion that our section was very badly directed, but I was dismayed, to put it mildly, when my expertise was used for ends of which I disapproved. This was the case of my memorandum of German agriculture that was taken up by Henry Morgenthau, as I have reported above.

My discontent was not, however, limited to my job.

---

[5] This was brought out during the Hiss case. I knew Alger Hiss during my stay in Washington and then came to know him very much better at Peacham. A professor of Philosophy at Yale, Brand Blanshard, had a house at Peacham and he let Alger use it when he was not there. Alger's son was about the age of my younger son and they played together a great deal. In his feud with Whittaker Chambers, I was convinced all the way along that Hiss was innocent of any charge of being disloyal to the United States. Although I do not profess to be an expert on the Hiss case, I am a judge of persons. When I compared Hiss to the supporters of Chambers who had attended Columbia College, I had no doubt on which side the right lay.

The fact that my wife and son were in New York and that I saw them only briefly was a thorn in my flesh. And then a second son was to arrive. In fact, he did and right on time, May 9, 1943. On a Sunday morning I received a telegram that the son had been born. It was sent by my elder son, at the time aged 12. I caught the first train for New York and rushed to my apartment expecting to be received by an excited son. But no one was at home. I called the hospital and could get no satisfaction, not even concerning the sex of the child. I learned from a neighbor that my elder son had gone to a baseball game and that my wife's brother, who was frequently with us, had gone to his Italian club in the Bronx to play cards. So I rushed to the hospital, saw my wife and baby, and determined that all was well. We had already decided upon a boy's name — Peter to keep the Italian flavor alive and Nelson, my grandmother Shepard's maiden name, to maintain the Yankee tradition.

I remained in New York on leave for about a week and made arrangements for the return home from the hospital of my wife and child and for some one to help her. I still marvel at the fact that my elder son had not awaited my arrival from Washington, for he had been very much interested in the coming of a new child. In fact, he had saved money from his allowance and from odd jobs in order to buy a collapsible stroller that his mother had expressed a desire to have. Such savings on his part required some real sacrifices. When the baby came home, he was very solicitous for his welfare and for years after was a kind of deputy father to his brother. The relationship was wonderful to behold.

With the arrival of a second son, my absence from my family was more painful than ever. My wife still insisted on remaining in New York and wanted to get back to her teaching job as soon as possible. She had taught almost to the time of her delivery, which was against my better judgment, and now she wanted to cut the time of recovery as short as possible. She went back to work in the fall semester of 1943. She tried to pass the summer in New York, but that proved too hot for her and the baby and they eventually went to Peacham for a few weeks. Unfortunately she took along two of her colleagues (maiden ladies) and they were unsympathetic both to the baby and to rural life! That was a combination to try the souls of men.

Thus my family situation and my unhappiness with my work in the Department contributed to my desire to find some employment that would allow me to meet the bills which the new child entailed. I was getting from government the munificent sum of $5,000 a year! Finally the Social Science Research Council asked me to head a group that would promote studies of World War II—to catch history in the making. This offer would allow me to be in New York halftime and paid much better than the job in State. My superiors in government tried to persuade me to remain with them, but they could not give me what I wanted. So I accepted the proposition for war history.

I had been a member of the Council for some time and so knew what I was getting into. This organization was dedicated to the proposition that the proper study of man is the whole man, not just economic man, or social man, ot political man, but man in all his activities. Its members were chosen by the various national, professional organizations and were representative of all the social sciences. Accordingly, the Council wanted studies of the war in all of its ramifications. The Carnegie Endowment for International Peace had sponsored a history of World War I in some one hundred and fifty volumes and I thought of that as a model for my work.

Unfortunately, I expended a lot of effort and time in trying to get publishers to undertake the mammoth history which I had in mind. In fact, I had Macmillan deeply interested in being the publisher of a large history of World War II. At all events, I had an opportunity to get acquainted with several of the large publishers of the day and learned much about them. To my surprise I was received unsympathetically by Alfred Knopf. I liked the honesty of Cass Canfield of Harper Brothers; and was rather amused at the small boy interests (especially in sailing) of George Brett, Jr. of Macmillan's.

Finally, it was decided that my task was not to promote a multi-volume history of the war, but to encourage individuals and agencies to write monographs on those aspects of the war with which they were closely concerned. Already the army had a history of the military under way. It was under the able leadership of Kent Roberts Greenfield, with Robert Palmer his close assistant. There was also a history of the Navy and Naval Operations being prepared by Samuel E. Morrison, and several of the war-time agencies were laying plans for histories of their activities. I was instructed to familiarize myself with all such efforts and to further them in any way I could. In the course of time these governmental efforts came to have a central direction from the Bureau of the Budget and I came to have an appointment in that Bureau in order better to carry out my assignment.

In addition to such work in Washington, I was also to get in touch with individual scholars who had thoughts of working on the history of some phase of the war. Thus a great many studies came into being—on population and the war, social problems of war time, the use of manpower in war, the migrations of people in war time, and so on. These works were published in various places by various publishers and were so scattered that it was not easy for me to have a clear picture of what success I was having in my endeavors. I was, however, able to travel extensively in this country; I was instrumental in getting fellowships or other financial aid for scholars in this work; I did manage to get those interested in war-history together to exchange notes and to avoid duplication; and I was successful in lobbying for the cause in various governmental agencies.

My job allowed me to be in New York about half of the time, which was desirable from a family point of view. It also gave me experience at the offices of the Social Science Research Council. I became very friendly with the deputy chief Donald Young of the University of Pennsylvania, Pendleton Heering, an active head of the work in political science and a subsequent director of the Council, and with Paul Webbink, the head of the Washington office. The Director of the Council, Robert T. Crane, who had been on the job for a long time, won neither my admiration nor friendship. He was devoid of humor and was of an intellectual capacity of a very limited nature.

In those years, the Council had some very distinguished members, as it had previously and has had since, and I felt privileged to have an opportunity to be associated with them. I was logically drawn to economists and historians by my professional interests. Fred Dewhurst was on our staff and I found him to be full of ideas and fun. Happily I could be of use to him when he undertook the preparation of *Europe's Needs and Resources*, which I thought was an excellent and useful book. I was also very friendly with Edwin G. Nourse of the Brookings Institution, who was the first chairman of the President's Board of Economic Advisers, and I had a chance to become better acquainted with Wesley Mitchell than I had ever been able to at Columbia. He graciously agreed to write an introduction to my history of the Mutual Life Insurance Company of New York. And I developed a close friendship with Simon Kuznets, a future Nobel prize winner. He chaired a committee on economic growth, sponsored by the Council, and I served on it for several years as a specialist in economic history.

Among historians, I was particularly close to Roy F. Nichols, later dean of the Graduate Faculty of the University of Pennsylvania, and to Merle Curti, who had been at Teachers College at Columbia, but, for some reason I had never comprehended, was not appointed to the Graduate Faculty of Political Science and moved on to the University of Wisconsin. I was also very fond of Louis Gottschalk, a specialist in the history of the French Revolution and the biographer (in many volumes) of Lafayette, who preceded me on the Council. These three and I were dedicated to the proposition that general history should include all aspects of human activity—the political, economic, social, intellectual, and religious - and we endeavored to propagate this idea by lectures and books.[6] I presented a paper about it at a meeting of the American Historical Association, but my pleas for a "new" history were not accepted favorably, judged by that audience's reaction. Academic historians

---

[6] A little later this group was responsible for two studies: *Theory and Practice in Historical Study*, Bulletin 54 of the Social Science Research Council (1946) and Bulletin 64, *The Social Sciences in Historical Study* (1954).

are great traditionalists.

In these ways I passed the war years. The end of the conflict came somewhat more suddenly than I had anticipated. I was at Princeton University lecturing about the problems of making peace when news came of the Japanese surrender. Like so many others I was confronted with the task of beating my personal swords into plough shares.

Chapter VIII

Back To Academe

The surrender of the Japanese came very suddenly, as I have just said. The atomic bombs which were dropped on cities of that nation were so devastating that our enemies had little choice but to give up the fighting. Those bombs unleashed at once a debate regarding the wisdom of their use. I was inclined to believe that they should not have been dropped immediately on populated areas, but in some place where the toll of life would have been minimized. I realized, however, that there was another side to the story and this was brought home to me very forcefully by a veteran of the war who had been badly wounded, yes mutilated, by conventional weapons. He said with great feeling that if I had gone through what he had been through and if I had seen buddies fall by my side, as he had seen them, that I might have had quite another opinion.

In this connection, the opinion of Harry Truman on the subject impressed me greatly. Several years after the event, the ex-President spoke at Columbia. In a discussion period following his address, he was asked what the most difficult decision was that he had to make while in office. With no hesitation at all, he replied, "To decide that the atomic bomb should be dropped on Hiroshima." He added that subsequently he realized, horrible as the effects of the bomb were, that it had by shortening the conflict resulted in the saving of a great number of lives, particularly American lives. I believe that this was the case.

The surrender seemed to clear the way, or so we thought at the time, to hold the general peace conference for which the division that I had been with in the State Department had been preparing. A general peace conference was not to be, however, for the victors were deeply divided concerning a myriad of issues of the settlement—from boundary questions to the restoration of all parties to a functioning international community. Some peace treaties were actually negotiated, but in certain cases arrangements of non-belligerency were arrived at *de facto*. Perhaps this procedure was better than trying to arrive immediately at a general settlement, for the time which elapsed before any agreements were reached may have served as "cooling off" periods and thus the treaties may have been much less vindictive than they otherwise might have been.

The years involved in peace-making were marked by a falling out among the victors—a falling out that probably would have taken place even though peace negotiations on a grand scale had been attempted. The "cold war," as this falling out came to be called, was essentially a state of discord between the U.S.S.R. plus its satellites on one side and the United States and its allies on the other. The rift was already visible during the conflict, notably over the questions of opening a Western front, the matter of giving aid to Russia, and the issue of military government of conquered territories. Fear existed even over the possibility of fighting between the armies when they met in the conquest of Germany.

On this last issue, the danger seemed so great that arrangements for where the armies should stop moving forward were settled well in advance of the time at which they actually did meet. This agreement, which resulted in a division of Germany, was made by General Eisenhower and his staff, as has been said. How inept the military were in handling such matters is indicated by the fact, which has also been mentioned above, that in the original plan no provision was made for a corridor by which the Allies could reach Berlin. Fortunately John G. Winant and his staff at Rheims corrected this omission. This case was a sample of the failure of the Department of

State to be alert to the emergence of ever new problems. It shirked its duties either because it was uncertain as to what to do, or because President Roosevelt wanted to keep in his own hands the making of all international decisions, or because the President had so much to do that he could not keep on top of everything.

The end of the war meant that I would have to reconsider my own future, for promoting histories of the war would obviously soon come to a halt. I was reluctant to return to the History Department at Columbia because I had not been promoted to the rank of Associate Professor, which would have given me tenure, and because the pay was small in comparison with what I had been receiving. I had the feeling, also, that some of my colleagues, notably Jacques Barzun, were not anxious for my return. I was definitely in the market for other employment. I was considered for the directorship of the Social Science Reasearch Council, but I blew my chances, whatever they may have been, by some ill-considered, but accurate remarks about the administrative staff at the Council. Donald Young was chosen for the job and, I am pleased to report his qualifications for the job were greater than mine.

I was still debating what I should do when the Economics Department's chairman, Fred Mills, approached me with the propostion that I come back to Columbia and take over the work in European economic history. This subject had been handled for several years by Vladimir G. Simkhovitch, whose main explanation for the course of history was the exhaustion of the soil. His most famous work was an essay entitled "Hay in History," and his training of specialists in the field was almost nonexistent. He made his way largely on a policy of self-praise.

I was asked to take up this work because I had already made a reputation for developing studies in my fields of specialization, for giving attention to students and their needs, and for a success in business history. In the offer made to me, I was to be an assistant professor but I would be promoted very shortly, if everything went well. I decided to accept this proposition, inasmuch as nothing better was available, but as a bit of insurance for the future I asked that I be allowed to continue a seminar in the History

Department for candidates for the M.A. degree. Thus I went back to academe.

From the first my affiliation with the Department of Economics was not all roses. Before my formal appointment was made, I was asked to present a program of what I wanted to accomplish. The draft of what I aimed to do was not received favorably. In fact, I was asked to revise my plan very considerably, and even then at least one member of the department (Joseph Dorfman) voted against me on the ground that I had not had a formal economics training. Subsequently most members of the department were very friendly, including Dorfman, and some like Arthur F. Burns, Robert M. Haig, and Leo Wolman were very helpful. I had a large enrollment in my lecture course and it was larger the second semester than the first, which is a good sign of student acceptance. I had a small seminar in economic history from which I soon realized that graduate students in economics were primarily concerned with becoming professional economists and not in becoming professional economic historians. It was apparent also that most specialists in economic history would come to me via the History Department. Hence I worked out a major and minor system whereby students in history might take a major in European history and a minor in economic theory and statistics, and whereby a major in economics might have as one of his minor fields European history. My efforts were not without success, for I had three students, at least, from the lecture course who decided to do their dissertations in economic history, which was more than Simkhovitch had had in many years and which was more than my successors, Karl Polanyi and David Landis, had in the next ten years. I heard indirectly that Fred Mills was very happy with what I was accomplishing.

In spite of the success which I was having, I sensed that I was still on trial. I was given two different dissertations in economics to whip into shape after others in the department had thought them to be more or less hopeless. I accepted the challenge, although I was not qualified to do either one, for I wanted to be helpful and to show what I could do. This was a mistake on my part, for although I received the approval of "second readers" for both works, examining committees turned one of these theses down flatly and returned the second to the author for major revisions. These decisions reflected adversely on me. Moreover, I received little thanks for my attempted salvage operations. Then, too, I never felt entirely at home in the professional or social life of the department. I was made to feel that I did not really "belong."

Consequently, when in the spring of my first year in my new post I began to get "feelers" from other institutions, I took such approaches seriously. One of these was from Cornell, where I was invited to go to "take the place" left vacant by Carl Becker. This was very flattering and the chairman of the department there, Paul Gates, seemed very anxious to have me. I was inclined to accept that offer, unless the Economics Department at Columbia would give me some precise assurances about a promotion. The upshot of the matter was that the department thought that Arthur R. Burns should be promoted before me and that only one promotion was possible at that time. This about sealed the matter, but just before I was to inform Cornell of my acceptance, the head of the History Department (John A. Krout) came to me and asked if I would remain at Columbia if I were transferred back to the History Department and if I were promoted to the rank of associate professor, a rank which would give me tenure.

This offer was, indeed, tempting. It meant that, if I accepted it, I would have arrived at one more rung up the ladder. I wanted, I think, to remain at Columbia, even though I had backed into a permanent post. The cultural advantages of being in New York were obvious and the University had much to offer in research facilities.

My wife was even more set upon remaining in New York than I was. To have left would have meant either the giving up of her teaching or the making of difficult adjustments to get a position in the area of my new post. Thus we decided to accept the offer of the History Department at Columbia.

Upon my return to the Department of History, I buckled down to a tight schedule. My lecture courses consisted of a history of France and Italy from the end of the eighteenth century to the present. In addition, I alternated from time to time with a course in European economic history from the beginning of the eighteenth century. Then I was called upon to give a course in contemporary French affairs for the School of International Affairs. In those days a number of West Point officers were receiving instruction in areas where they might serve, which was in a sense a remnant of the Navy's School of Military Government which had been established during the war. This course was mostly of a service nature, but for it I received no extra compensation or recognition. Indeed, most of the research funds of the school, to say nothing of other funds, were going into regional institutes—Russia, the Far East, the Middle East, Latin America, Africa, and Central Europe. They reflected the greatly expanded interests and responsibilities of the United States commensurate with its power position in the world.

The regional institutes were conceived as covering a wide range of interests. Thus each institute had to have an historian of the region, an economist, a political scientist, a sociologist, a linguist, and a *littérateur*. The Institutes were expensive to operate, especially when considered on a student per capita basis, for enrollments were low. I warned of the danger of establishing such an elaborate array of regional institutes and of ignoring the old stand-bys of Western Europe, where most of the student interest resided and where professional jobs were the most numerous. My voice cried in a wilderness, for the new institutes had at their inception support from the foundations, especially the Ford Foundation, and the day when the costs of the Institutes would fall upon the University's budget seemed far away.

In addition to my lecture courses, I gave a seminar in the modern history of Western and Southern Europe and a colloquium in the same areas and time-spans. In the seminar I endeavored to launch students on research topics which would eventually be developed into doctoral dissertations. My procedure was to interview each student at length in order to discover what his or her interests really were and what his mastery of the necessary languages was. To attempt to do research in an area without knowing the language, as I had seen it tried in the Economics Department, seemed completely out of the question.

In the first semester, the student's assignment was to write an essay on the entire subject of the proposed dissertation, complete with bibliography and a report on the availability of the sources involved. This essay would tell me if the student understood the subject on which he was working, whether or not he knew how to write, and whether or not the material which he would need could be obtained by him, including the problem of getting to that material in Europe. The second semester was then devoted to working on one of the chapters of the proposed thesis, usually the first. This way of attacking a research project was supposed to get the student to the point where he could carry on after he had left his residence at the University.

If all went well, the student would normally go to Europe the year after his residence at Columbia had been completed and put in a year of research. In order to guarantee that the student would continue to get expert guidance in his work, I was always able to put him or her in touch with a foreign scholar who could help do the guiding. Usually these foreigners were friends who were glad to be of assistance to students of mine. Thanks to Fulbright fellowships, as well as their own resources, most of my students were able to manage at least one year abroad.[1] The writing of the dissertation was then carried on, usually when the student embarked upon his first teaching job. In most cases the thesis was completed by the end of the seventh year after the beginning of graduate work, if it were completed at all. Fortunately, I had a high proportion of completions, although there was some attrition along the way. Health problems, finances, and marriage accounted for the greatest incidence of noncompletion.

In my colloquium, the procedure was to read a book a week—all of us read the same book; then we would come together to discuss it. Thus the students were given an opportunity to increase

[1] Incidentally the Fulbright fellowships were financed from funds owed by foreign governments to the United States for supplies, mostly of a nonmilitary nature, which had been purchased from the United States upon the conclusion of hostilities. In this way some of what might have been considered "war debts" were settled. Of course, most of what our allies received from us was under "lend-lease" and these credits were canceled.

their knowledge of historical literature and to talk over all manner of problems regarding the field, from the philosophy of history to bibliography and to individual historians. This was a great course for students. For one thing they were given a chance to talk, which they loved and otherwise had few opportunities to do, and for another, they were given some idea about the nature of the oral examinations in history for the Ph. D. degree. This latter information frightened some, especially when I told them that the first question which had been asked me on my orals was to name all the territorial changes in Europe in the eighteenth century, but it provided a challenge to others, who strove mightily to meet the demands of the test.[2]

In the colloquium students were also made to think about their discipline. Students in economics or political science had some idea of what they were trying to understand of man's behavior, but all too frequently students of history were flabbergasted when asked what the discipline of history was aimed at accomplishing. I wanted them to think about what the historian could contribute to the understanding of man's behavior through (or over) time. I also wanted them to know more about the profession of the historian—what kind of life they were getting into as professional historians. I did not shrink from a description of the sordid aspects of university life—the low salaries, the difficulty in becoming established, the jealousies and animositites that one might find, and the drudgery of some of one's duties like correcting papers and tests, attending committee meetings where nothing was accomplished, and associating with people who did not always measure up to standards of conduct which are called civilized. On the other hand, I did not skimp the good sides to the profession—the opportunity to satisy one's curiosity about a myriad of things, to be creative through thought and writing, to train young persons who might achieve great heights, to travel, and to associate with people who were gentlemen

---

2 At Columbia these oral examinations in history were given by a panel of five members from the department or departments of the major and minor. The examination was entirely oral. The major subject was the object of about seventy minutes of the examination time and the minor about forty. Between the two parts the candidate was given a ten minute break.

and scholars.

In addition to these scheduled training periods, I encouraged students to form study groups at which they would try their hand at both examining and answering typical examination questions and through which they might exchange knowledge of bibliography and points of view. Sometimes professors, or other intellectuals, were invited to these groups to comment upon what was being done. I remember well when one of my former students, Christopher Herold, popped in unexpectedly one day, on his way to receiving a National Book Award for a work on Napoleon, and spoke to the group on "How to Write a Book and Get it Published." He was excellent and very helpful to his listeners.

I remember distinctly many of the things he said. He stressed the importance of knowing English very thoroughly. His was a special case in this regard, he said, for he was of Swiss origin and English was not his mother tongue. I was inclined to question this condition as a handicap, for I have seen individuals with such ingrained misuses of their language that I have often thought that they would have been better off if they were starting from scratch. Before I carry this argument very far,however, I am reminded of the difficulties in writing my one book in a foreign language—French. I find some comfort in the thought that the French are very intolerant of mistakes made in their tongue!

Then I should report that Herold stressed the importance of having a regular schedule for writing. He made his living by serving as an editor for the Columbia University Press and so had to work his writing into a very busy life—into evenings, weekends, and vacations. He also put emphasis on having a theme about which one has something to say, upon the importance of not being frightened by a "blank sheet of paper" in the typewriter, and upon the necessity of keeping eternally at it—to write and rewrite.

For the most part, the training which I gave my students fitted Herold's prescription very precisely. What I attempted to do was in the long run greatly appreciated by those who studied with me, although not always in the short run. In fact, one student confessed to me that he wanted to punch my nose when I told him that he would have to rewrite his dissertation (for the third time) before I would approve it for examination.

In the course of time, I trained many of the leading historians of Europe in the United States; and my students followed my general pattern of instruction in the various universities to which they went.

In addition, to producing an acceptable doctoral dissertation, aspirants for the Ph.D. degree had to submit to rather formidable oral examinations of the fields they had selected for specialization. These tests were real ordeals. When I first participated in them as an examiner, I used to come out of them completely done in. I suffered along with the student. When I returned home after one of them and related what had gone on, my elder son remarked, "There must be a better way of ascertaining whether or not a student is qualified to continue with his graduate work." Perhaps there is, but I do not know what it is. We did have an elaborate system of steps toward the orals and if the student stumbled on them either he or his sponsor should have seen the signs and acted on them. Most professors were unwilling to tell students the hard fact that they were not cut out for a scholarly life, and students had to make most of the decisions for themselves. I have, however, been thanked (long after the event) by all the students whom I have told they should not go on. My advice put them into fields where they could do well.

The examinations were, as I have said, very hard on students, but these tests made the students do a lot of work that they might otherwise have shirked. Yet they were sometimes very rough. Students took various measures to relieve the tension. One took phenobarbital to relax the night before so that she could get a good night's sleep, but she overdid the dosage and actually dozed off during the exam. Yet, she passed, barely. Another tried to get a lift from alcohol, but took too much and had to call off the exam. Still another fainted during the test (he was being pushed rather hard by his examiner). I rushed out to get a remedy, which was very good whiskey that I kept in my office for emergencies; the examiner, Jacques Barzun, came back with smelling salts. To no one's surprise the student chose the whiskey, which he drank from the only cup available, a paper cup, for I had failed to bring a glass. In time the whiskey ate away the wax coating on the cup and every time it was put down, it made a ring. For years afterwards the examination-room was known as the "whiskey ring."

The examination gave the staff an opportunity to determine whether or not the student had mastered a modicum of important facts rather than trivia, could show valid relationships among varied data, knew a considerable amount of bibliography, and lastly whether or not he would try to bluff when his information gave out. The last was the most heinous sin of all. It is not what you don't know that hurts you, it is what you do know that is not so.

The examinations were also times when the professors were on display. They were human enough to want to show off to each other, and frequently did. They also used these occasions to advance some pet theory—some even to give lectures to their fellows. Unfortunately, sometimes they could work off a grudge against a colleague. At the last defense of a dissertation by a student of mine, which I attended, one examiner practically accused the candidate of plagiarism. Yet these examinations served the purpose of maintaining some standards among diverse members of the faculty and different departments. I remember on one occasion Arthur F. Burns had a student who had written on the German labor movement and who did not know German well enough to read it. I thought that this was outrageous and voted against accepting the dissertation because the work was ill-conceived and did not represent a mastery of the German literature on the subject.

Incidentally, some professors were unorganized and were forever forgetting about their exams. Others repeated the same question over and over and the word to this effect got around. Others were conscientious and excellent in probing to find out what the mind of the student was, how it worked, and what it contained. Wesley C. Mitchel was one such; Carlton J. H. Hayes, another; and Garrett Mattingly, a third.

For the most part students performed according to their abilities and knowledge, but there were exceptions. Once in a while a really poor student got by, although not with a good rating (for internal use we rated the students, but for public information they were graded "pass, failure, but could try again, failure and could not try again"). In all of my experience with students who had trained under me, of some two hundred and fifty who reached the oral examinations, I had only three complete failures and one of these passed on the second try, and fewer than ten failed on the first attempt. Sometimes brilliant students failed. This was the case with David Saville Mussey and J. B. Brebner, both of whom had great careers as members of the department. For that matter, one might do well in the profession without the sanction of the Ph. D. This was the case with Alan Nevins, who received his basic training in journalism, plus a lot of study and writing.

In these first years after the war, students were numerous and were very highly motivated. Many of them were veterans and were anxious to make up for the time which they had lost professionally. Moreover, they received governmental aid, as veterans, and this allowed them to devote all of their time and efforts to their studies. They were a joy to teach and a great inspiration for a young professor. In two or three instances, however, there were individuals who still suffered from battle-fatigue and who simply could not make it.

As time went on, I felt that I was solidifying my position in the department and was becoming more necessary to the University. Professor Hayes returned for a time, after his ambassadorship at Madrid, but he concentrated his attention more on general lecture courses than on research. Charles W. Cole left Columbia for the presidency of Amherst College and was replaced by a much more distinguished scholar, Garrett Mattingly, who came to be a very close friend and colleague. And then we had John

---

[3] The history of Wuorinen's life was a real saga. He was a native Finn and was determined to flee from Russian domination. During World War I he escaped by skiing at night across the Straits of Bothnia. Several persons were lost in making similar attempts. Wuorinen made his way to the United States and to a Finnish group at Gardner, Massachusetts. Incidentally, immigrants into our country frequently clustered around fellow countrymen and only became dispersed geographically in subsequent generations.

Wuorinen in Scandinavian history, who for a long time assumed the duties of chairman of the department.[3]

By the end of the decade of the forties I thought that the time had come for me to take a trip to Europe, which was to be the first since 1936, for I needed to renew my contacts with European scholars and to catch up with what was going on in my fields. My younger son was then old enough to travel and conditions of life in Europe were reestablished to a point where we believed we could get adequate lodgings and food. So in the summer of 1949 the family took off by ship for Europe—the last time that I went to Europe by sea.

The voyage was not without its little experiences of interest and excitement—and annoyance. My elder son was the object of an extreme form of infatuation by the daughter of a very wealthy friend of mine, infatuation which unfortunately was not reciprocated. Then the steward on the last night out "offered" us an extremely expensive wine, which I thought meant that it would be complimentary, but which was charged to me, much to my chagrin. Then when we landed, my wife took our younger son to a cafe while my elder son and I saw our luggage through customs. It was a hot day and she ordered what she thought would be water for the two of them. She thought that she was getting Perrier, but she had apparently said Pernod, a very highly alcoholic anise drink, and to save face drank both her glass and also that of her son. So I had a mildly inebriated case on my hands all the way to Paris. Finally, at Paris, the usual bedlam existed in trying to get taxis, and I with my three and a mountain of luggage did not look like an attractive fare to the drivers. The result was that I was the last to leave the station and that very late in the day.

We put up at a pension where I had lived as a student and where I had made the terrible gaffe about putting my trousers every night under my "mistress," My wife complained about the place from the moment we arrived and fought with everyone, including all of the maids. Nothing was right—not the rooms nor the toilets, nor the food. Finally, things became so unpleasant that the sensible thing seemed to be to move, which we did. We went to a hotel, little better than the pension, and ate in restaurants, an arrangement that put some strain on a very limited budget.

The stay in Paris was, otherwise, very rewarding. I renewed my contacts with many of my French colleagues and met some of the newcomers to the field. Meetings of the Société d'Histoire Moderne, of which I had been a faithful member for many years, proved extremely valuable for such purposes. My elder son was at an age which he could enjoy and profit from many of the works of art which were made available to him. He spent day after day in the Louvre, the Museum of Modern Art, and the Rodin Museum, especially the last, and an equal amount of time visiting the architectural gems of the city from the Basilica of St. Denis, Notre Dame of Paris, and the Ste. Chapelle to the Musée de Cluny, the Tuilleries, and the Panthéon. He was and is an excellent photographer and took pictures of Paris at night that have even today a professional touch. His smaller brother often tagged along after him, but was particularly pleased when I hired a car to visit the chateaux of the Loire, the chateau of Versailles, and the town of Barbizon.

From Paris we went to Italy via Basel, to see the Holbein paintings and drawings. We were enchanted by the city, especially by its red stone town hall, which we admired over an excellent meal in a restaurant *en face*. Then on to Italy, where our main stop was in Florence. We put up in a *pensione* opposite the Boboli Gardens, in the Via Romana—an address that was in proximity to the Pitti Palace and not far from the Uffizi. Again our older son spent most of his time in these galleries and loved them all.

From Florence our road led to Rome via Perugia and Assisi. From our Roman *pensione* in the Via Vittorio Veneto we could see Saint Peters, the Pincio Gardens, and the Alban Hills. We explored them all and tried to instill in our childern our love for and admiration of the city. At that time, and for some time thereafter, Rome was my favorite city and I had dreams of returning to it in my retirement.

When our visit to Rome came to an end, our time in Europe was running out, but we meandered back to Paris via Genoa and the South of France. I showed the boys Avignon with its bridge, where according to the song which my younger son knew, *on y danse, on y danse, tout en rond*, its Palace of the Popes, which my elder son had learned about in his history courses, and the vineyards, where we went to help with the *vendange* in the vineyard of a friend.

This last episode was one of the high spots of our trip, for we could all enter into the spirit and work of the fields. There is much more to harvesting grapes than meets the stranger's eye. One uses a very sharp knife to sever the bunches from the vines and has to be extremely careful or one can get badly cut, as I was on this occasion. One does not go faster than the leader of the crew, for to do so would wear one out very early in the day and would result in very poor production. Withal, the harvesting in the field is real work and not a matter of singing songs and of dancing—an impression one gets from comic operas.

Many of the practices which have become sanctified by legends have been drastically changed in modern times. Grapes are not trampled by bare feet, but are loaded into a cart and then crushed down by a man wearing rubber boots and who treads them down in order to get on a larger load than he otherwise could. The grapes are actually crushed by a machine, like a grinder, and then put in open pits to ferment. In this process they give off carbon monoxide, which is strong enough to extinguish a match held over them. White wine is made from white grapes or from red grapes before fermentation begins. *Rosé* is produced by drawing off juice before pressing. Red wine comes from fermenting juices after pressing. The quality depends largely upon the kind or kinds of grape used; their sugar content in relation to their water; the care taken in the whole process; and the period of maturation once in the vats. The final product is delightful and a part of the diet of all Mediterranean people in Europe.

After the stop in the vineyards, we took a train to Paris, to which "all roads in France lead," and then went on to Rouen, en route to Le Havre and our ship. Our stay in the City of Jeanne d'Arc was brief, but we did see where Jeanne was burned at the stake, and the Cathedral, which had been much damaged during the War, and the famous marketplace. By this time my funds were running so low that I had to refuse my elder son's desire to have a lot of film developed and pictures printed, much to his annoyance, which bothers him even to the present day. When we arrived in New York, I had one $20 traveller's check left. This got us to our apartment, but just barely.

In what has preceded, I have referred several times to my sons, but I want to say something about them in this place because so much of my life revolved around them and was deeply influenced by them. In fact, one of the reasons for the trip we had just taken was to introduce them to Europe and one of the reasons for returning to academe was that in my professional calling I could have much more time with them than I could if I were in business or almost anything else. One of my notions about raising children was that the successful adjustment of youth to life was directly related to the interest which the *pater familias* had in his offspring. Not only was a good *camaraderie* important for them, but the parent also receives much from being with them. At least, I did.

One of the major decisions that I had to make regarding their growing up was the matter of selecting a school for them. Both boys went to the "Greenhouse House," a morning kindergarten that the University ran during morning hours for faculty children. The place derived its name from the fact that the building used by the group had been a hot-house belonging to the botany department. This structure had ceased to be used for plants—too drafty—but was considered good enough for teacher's kids. One of the school's redeeming features was that the children could indulge their interest in all manner of things, like carpentry, gardening, and simple electrical circuits of batteries and lights. The other great blessing was the character of the directress, who mothered several generations of faculty children while their own mothers were engaged in other things.

The big problem after the Greenhouse was to find a school for my boys. I considered this of extreme importance, for the years in elementary school, at least, are the very ones when the innocence of infancy is tempered by contacts with the large world. The older boy tried Barnard School, but it was far away; then he went briefly to Horace Mann, at Teachers College. This was purported to be an excellent place, but I became disillusioned with it when I made a visit to it and was spat upon by several of the children as I walked past them on the way to lunch.

At this point, I was about ready to consider a public school, but the one which served our district was located at 125th Street near Broadway. This was a rough neighborhood and futhermore, a priest in our district told me that the incidence of venereal disease in the school was high, and that I would be well-advised to look elsewhere. In addition, the children in this school came from families of such low income levels that my sons would have made very few friends with them. Snobbish as this may have been, it was realistic.

After much more searching, I finally chose Trinity School for the elder son, and the younger one later on went to the same place. This was a conservative, Episcopalian institution, where the children were taught manners and respect for others, where discipline was the order of the day and self-discipline encouraged, and where the object was to give the boys a good education. Both the boys did well there, finishing high in class academic ratings, and both were able to participate in extra-curricular activities. The elder one did well in football and glee club; the younger as a manager to some of the athletic teams. Finally, both made more life-long friends in this place than either did in college or in any other place in which they lived.

I knew that schools would not provide all the things which young people need. One cannot expect them to furnish parental love, all aspects of character building, or interest in many extra-curricular activities. I made a real effort to supplement the school's work with those things that I knew they were not receiving. We went frequently to museums, to concerts,to factories, to banks, and to farms.

Perhaps the most unique thing I did for them was to encourage hobbies which could lead to vocations from which, if necessary, they could make their livings. My elder son was much interested in radio building, and I found friends who would take the time to give him help in getting over the tough spots. My younger son learned from his brother and both became experts in the craft and ultimately went to the more exacting building of television sets.

Another thing which I did that was good for them and for me was to join them in games. We began by playing with building blocks.[4] Then we went on to such things as Flinch from which they learned to count,to add, and to subtract. Then we advanced to checkers and chess. What surprised me no end was the rapidity with which they arrived at a point at which they could beat me every time—or nearly. At the beginning I had managed to let them take a game from me from time to time in order to keep their interest up. If they suspected me of doing such a thing, their ire was aroused, and they never reciprocated in this kind of treatment.

Still another thing that I did with them was to engage in sports. Every weekend, weather permitting, we would go to a playing field in the outskirts of New York for baseball in the spring and football in the fall. Often we combined such junkets with a picnic with a fire over which we cooked meat. Sometimes their mother joined us, but she did not enjoy sports and little by little accompanied us less frequently and finally not at all. In the winter we would go sledding or skating. We knew of small ponds in Westchester County and would go to them as soon as the ice would hold us. As a former hockey player, I was bent on teaching them to handle a puck and to shoot hard enough to beat the best goalie. Unfortunately the opportunities for week-end hockey matches around New York were almost nonexistent and the boys never got beyond the stage of having exercise with me.

Later on we took up skiing. The elder son, Tony, and I were die-hards and would put on our skis whenever we found a patch of snow. When we had time, we would go to some nearby place in Jersey or Fahnstock Park, and once in a while we would make it to southern Vermont or the Hanover area of New Hampshire. I taught the younger son, Pete, to ski in the Alps during sojourns in Europe, a matter to which I shall return later. I fear that skiing around New

---

4 The blocks we used were ones that we made together by cutting up scraps of lumber.

York, as I had done with my first son, was tame stuff for him. At all events, much to my disappointment, he would not go skiing with me, as he grew older. I went by myself and was very lonesome without him.

In addition to the outings which I have described, we had other little minor diversions, which were lots of fun. In the fall, we would walk in the woods to "kick the leaves," which makes a rustling sound that only a country boy can enjoy. Or we would go to an orchard owned by a friend and pick apples. Then in the spring we would go to streams created by melting snow to build dams, direct the water to prevent erosion, or float "ships" down swollen brooks. When that pastime came to an end, we would gather wild flowers. I knew where trailing arbutus could be found, where hepaticas and anemones announced the change of season, where the first trilliums were available, and where blue violets were in abundance.

These various ways of getting exercise, of watching the boys grow up, and of maintaining some semblance of personal youth made life in the city just tolerable. From time to time I became so fed up with my urban existence and with the ivory-tower character of academic life that I was tempted to throw up the whole thing and move to the farm. I thought also that some measure should be taken to draw my wife back into the kind of family life I dreamed of as my ideal. I might have made some drastic move, but I knew that I would have a rough time making a living in the country and so I continued with the kind of existence which I have been describing. I have often wondered if I would have been happier in another kind of environment.

At all events, we returned from our European trip just in time to put my elder son on a bus for Ithaca to begin his first year at Cornell. He was a little late and missed "freshman orientation." He also was so late for freshman football practice that he was not encouraged to stick with it, for which I was very relieved. The younger son returned to Trinity School to continue his happy years of schooling. My wife went back to her language teaching at Hunter College, which she cherished so highly and at which she was so excellent that I have never found anyone her equal.

As for myself, I went back to Columbia to my previous routine, but I had a new enthusiam for it, a store of fresh ideas for my courses, and a new body of information to impart to my students.

Chapter IX

The Academic Boom Of The 1950's

My advancement up the academic ladder was greatly facilitated by the fact that there was a boom in higher education after World War II and then all through the 1950's. There were many students clamoring for admission to graduate faculties. The youth of the country were being bombarded with propaganda to the effect that those with at least a college education enjoyed higher incomes than those without it; that nations with the largest proportions of those with a high level of education enjoyed the longest expectations of life at birth and had the highest incomes per capita; and that job opportunities abounded for those who were well trained. Moreover, funds for fellowships were available in such abundance that universities began to bid for talent, just as football recruiting coaches did.

Money was being poured into buildings for libraries, laboratories, classrooms, offices, and dormitories. Curricula were being expanded even to fields where there was little student demand or social need. Indeed, many universities seemed to feel that they should extend their offerings into all the most esoteric fields instead of dividing among themselves training in these areas. Even academic salaries were increased to a point at which professors did not have to live as though they were poor country cousins. They could go to their own "clubs" for lunch, albeit often rundown faculty clubs, and they could do away with lunches carried in brown bags, at least some of the time. Partly because of better economic conditions for staff, more and more persons from less well-off circumstances were seeking training in institutions of higher learning. Lastly, graduate faculties were changing from places where the development of scholars was their main reason for being. There were many fewer gentleman scholars to accomodate than there had been a half-century earlier, but there were many more who aspired to be college teachers.

So far as I know, there has never been a study of the "business cycle" in the development of universities, but I am certain that such a study would be most enlightening,especially to university administrators and to boards of trustees. I have experienced two "cycles" in my career and can point out some noteworthy characteristics. In periods of "boom," teaching staffs are expanded at a rapid rate and soon those appointed are given "tenure," that is, they cannot be discharged except for excessive malfeasance, or morally offensive behavior, or some criminal act, which incidentally, almost never occurs. Inasmuch as teaching personnel is protected in office by tenure, in spite of a possible mediocre performance,[1] and inasmuch as the longevity of professors is well known, universities keep their teaching staffs unchanged for long periods of time. One has to wait for retirements, deaths, or appointments to other universities in order to change staffs. The system operates in a fashion to keep a university stuck with its weak-sisters and to make the demand for new personnel in periods of "doom" almost nonexistent.

If one comes into the university job market in a period of depression, he is likely to remain unemployed until he is unemployable because of age. If one is trained in a field in which job opportunities are very limited even in good times, the situation is tragic. In France, for example, sociologists were being turned out in

---

1 The story is told that a professor from a mid-western university who had been appointed to a great university of the East Coast remarked to a former colleague, "Thank God that I am at——, now I won't have to sweat out any more books. I don't have to work any more to get to the top. I am at it."

the 1960s at the rate of say three hundred a year, whereas the number of vacant chairs in sociology in the entire country was only five. Curiously enough, many of those who go into fields where little special professional training is required to get in a program pay little attention to job opportunities until they have such large investments in what they are trying to do that they cannot bring themselves to give up their quests. For a sociologist or a historian to retool himself for journalism, archival work, or business results in a trauma, if not sheer disaster. Universities have great difficulty in adjusting their output of specialists to the demand of the market--they are inelastic on both the supply and demand side of the equation.

Another characteristic of the "cycle"of university life is the supply of new funds. In the period of which we are speaking both foundations and the federal government were falling over themselves to finance new programs or special investigations. Private foundations had a fetish for the "new"—something that would push the boundaries of ignorance a little further away, even though the removal of those boundaries sometimes did not seem so very urgent. That they should support anthropological research on how the women of a given Western European nation face the menopause seems peculiarly quaint, at least to me. Furthermore, foundations preferred to provide "seed" money in order to start a program, and then after five or ten years to pull out and leave the financing of the new enterprise to the recipient of the original grant. The temptation to receive moneys of this kind and to pray that the future would take care of itself was too strong for most to resist. The result was, at Columbia, that the University came to be loaded with very expensive undertakings for which the student demand was limited. The day of reckoning came with a vengeance in the "university depression" of the 1970s.[2]

The intrusion of public moneys into higher education also had its complications. The Federal government or its agencies,

[2] Note should be taken here of the fact that in Western Europe foundations of the American kind are almost nonexistent. Governments created grant-giving bodies to assume the functions performed by American foundations. The experience of these bodies was not unlike that of foundations in the United States.

especially the military, began or extended a practice of making contracts with universities to undertake certain research. This was true of departments in physical science, particularly departments of physics, chemistry, and engineering. These contracts were obviously short-term (their length was determined by the task involved, but staffs usually had to be expanded and equipment purchased to carry them to completion).

Funds from such sources became so large that they might constitute as much as fifty per cent of a university's budget and even more of those of departments directly involved. Professors who devoted time to these projects were given remuneration in addition to their regular salaries and this practice tended to skew pay scales throughout the system. Then, when a project was finished or funds dried up for whatever reason, the university was placed in a financial bind that could be embarrassing.

Why more caution was not used in extending such services is an obvious question. Trustees, who are usually successful businessmen, might have been expected to exercise more foresight in these matters. Like the administrators in universities, they undoubtedly were moved by a desire to help their nation and were tempted by opportunities to see their institutions grow. One needs to remember, also, that trustees are for the most part very fully occupied persons. They receive information and recommendations on matters about which they must decide from administrators whom they appoint and upon whom they must rely. They are prone to accede to the wishes of those who are more intimately acquainted with the details of issues involved than they possibly can be. In the appointment of top administrative personnel or in moments of crisis they, as a rule, exercise their own judgments.

When a depression comes to a university, that institution has to make economies which frequently are very silly. Housekeeping, for one thing, is reduced to a minimum. At Columbia janitorial service did not include cleaning or dusting the books in one's office and it was ludicrous to witness a distinguished professor like, say, Alan Nevins, taking time to clean the dust from his books. This was especially so when one compares it with the changing of a light bulb or light tube. In these cases one had to advise the janitor of the need for service. After he had come to ascertain what was needed, he called an electrician to do the job. He came with an assistant to carry the tube or bulb and to set up a ladder. This is featherbedding with a vengeance. Moreover, the attitude of the people engaged in service work was that they had the upper-hand and would do what was requested of them in their own time and at their own convenience and in as condescending a manner as possible. Even their immediate superiors seemed to be in awe of the unionized workers and had little authority over them. But budgetary considerations were overriding and the University did such things as to let the windows get so dirty that artificial light was required even on bright days.[3]

Fortunately for me, I reached the upper levels of the academic hierarchy in the upswing of the university business cycle. Students were numerous, for the most part well prepared, and highly motivated. Funds, especially Fulbright fellowships, were available to help get students to their source materials, and job opportunities were enough so that I could almost always place a person who had passed the orals and was well along with his dissertation in a post that paid enough to support two people.

One of the service jobs I did in the department in those years was to chair the committee on placement, which meant that my duty was to seek out openings in the profession and to recommend students to fill them. In the performance of this task I had to know the students well, which resulted in spending a great deal of time with them. Secondly, it meant that for every opening I had to consult with my appropriate colleagues to get their ideas for the recommendations. I had to attend meetings of professional societies, like the American Historical Association, in order to discuss with selection personnel from other universities the candidates whom I

---

[3] In the older buildings air conditioners were installed in windows of professorial offices, incidentally years after they had been installed in the offices of the janitors. The installation was such that the upper and lower sashes of the windows would not meet, which left a band the width of the air conditioner, say two feet, that could not be washed at all. Each professor's window in my building had a black band across it as though the place were in mourning.

was proposing; and I had to write literally thousands of letters both about openings and about candidates. I took pride in this work and although I received no special compensation for it, save for the assistance of a secretary once a week, I derived much satisfaction from it. I took pleasure in witnessing the reaction of students when they were appointed to a good post and realized that at long last they, too, were launched on their careers. Only rarely did students turn down posts that were offered to them, although it did happen. I must admit that in some of these cases I was often irritated much to my later chagrin, for I may have spent hours in my efforts at getting an offer for an individual only to see a blithe refusal on his or her part. It also meant that I could not propose another's candidacy in such cases, for the next person would obviously be my second choice.[4]

This service job brought me into contact, as I have said, with almost all our more advanced students and I am sure that they frequently registered for my classes so that I would know them better.[5] I also was drawn closer to students by doing still another service job—advisor to students in European history. When persons in graduate history arrived at Columbia, they were to consult with me about their programs, especially about their seminars. This was particularly important because the seminar instructor would normally become the sponsor of the student, that is, he would see him through all the steps involved in getting an advanced degree. Then, lastly I was for years advisor to the Graduate History Club, which was a student club aimed at getting professors from other universities to speak before it. From such speakers they heard different points of view and got new ideas; and they also received some degree of comparison with their professors at Columbia. In addition, these club meetings provided an opportunity for students to meet their professors in at least a semisocial setting, to talk about professional

---

[4] To be sure, we sometimes recommended more than one person for an opening, but rarely were two individuals absolutely equal.

[5] Eventually this work became so burdensome that I was responsible only for students in fields other than American history. Another staff member handled these students.

problems, and to make suggestions regarding the conduct of the department, including course offerings.

One of the results of these various service jobs was that I became swamped with students who wanted to work for their Ph.D. degrees with me. The situation became such that I had some thirty-five candidates every year whom I was sponsoring for the degree. I attended some thirty-three oral examinations each year; I participated in ten to fifteen examinations of dissertations, which meant the reading of the dissertations with the care that an editor in a publishing house would give to a manuscript that he was publishing; and I averaged four candidates a year, who received their degrees, for whom I was the sponsor. In addition, I always had a few persons who were working for the M.A. degree and whom I took on because of some special competence or interest in the field in which they were working, like Belgian history.

Obviously, I was carrying a very heavy load and by the end of each May was completely exhausted. In fact, toward the end of my active career on Morningside Heights there were times when I passed out (once in class and once in the street) from sheer fatigue. These "spells" were at first diagnosed as heart attacks, but subsequently as the result of overwork. It became clear to me that to save myself I would have to be relieved from teaching from time to time. The only way to do this, so far as I could see, was to get a leave of absence in order to do research. The first of these "leaves" was a sabbatical, which came due in 1947-1948.[6] If I remember correctly, Gordon Wright was engaged to give my courses in the French field that year.

The writing project which I had in mind for my leave from teaching was a very ambitious one—the rise and fall of civilization. For a long time I had been interested in this very broad view of the past. I had studied with care *The Decline of the West* by Oswald Spengler, which had appeared after World War I and which had a renewed appeal in the aftermath of World War II, and I, along

[6] Years of service did not usually count until one had a tenure post. When I agreed to remain at Columbia, I was given credit for some years in a nontenure post.

with many others, was drawn to the attempt by Arnold Toynbee's effort to find a formula for explaining the phenomena of the appearance and then disappearance of great cultures.[7]

I was not, however, at all satisfied with the analyses made by these two writers. Basically Spengler argued that the rises and falls of cultures were determined by social attitudes and that falls were preceded by beliefs in an essentially socialistic society. Toynbee, for his part, thought that cultures had "challenges" and that their futures were determined by the "responses" which they made to these confrontations. This statement seemed to me to be almost tautological; it said nothing about what challenges under what conditions might elicit what responses that would lead upward and which would lead downward. Similarly, his cliché that cultures have periods of "withdrawal and return" was also tautological, rather than analytical, and hence unsatisfactory. Furthermore, neither Spengler nor Toynbee made an explicit statement of what attributes made a society more civilized than another and thus provided no criterion by which a civilization could be measured for its degree of advancement or retrogression. Frankly, I thought that I could do better than they had and decided to make the attempt.

My philosophy about changes in society through time was, as I have stated earlier, greatly influenced by the *histoire du synthèse* school in France and especially by Lucien Febvre.[8] I was of the opinion that the course of a society might be altered by factors in any aspect of human experience and that the historian interested in the large phases of societal changes had to take within his purview the totality of man. I thought that changes might come about by changes in population, health, economics, politics, or social stresses and strains or from any combination of these segments of human activity.

---

7 I suppose that my interest in this macro-historical endeavor really dated from my student days when I read Edward Gibbon's *Rise and Fall of the Roman Empire* and Montesquieu's *Considerations on the Grandeur of the Romans and their Decadence*.

8 This school eventually became virtually dominant in France. It had such well-known adherents as Fernand Braudel and other members of the *Centre des Recherches Historiques*.

I also believed that changes were always imminent; and that they might come from within or from without the society (endogenous or exogenous changes).

The task of the historian in the study of change was then, as I saw it, to examine all types of factors at work in society--their character, their magnitude, and the timing of their coming together. My views were strengthened by my connections with and activities in the Social Science Research Council. The Council was, as we have seen, dedicated to the proposition that in studies of societal behavior all of the social sciences should be employed--a proposition of which I was convinced. Furthermore, I was involved in the work of the Committee on History of the Council and this committee undertook two studies that influenced me greatly. One concerned the philosophy of history, which resulted in the publication of a small book entitled *Theory and Practice in Historical Study* (1946). Essays in this volume were written by such persons as Charles A. Beard, John Herman Randall, Jr., Sidney Hook, and Merle Curti, and exchanges with these scholars had a great impact on my thinking. The other study was published as *The Social Sciences in Historical Study* (1954) and contained a long essay by me on the subject of change. My research for this contribution did much to widen and sharpen my views. Furthermore, I was fortunate at just this period to become well acquainted with Alfred A. Kroeber, who was a visiting professor at Columbia. Kroeber had recently published a study, *The Configurations of Culture* (1944), that contained many concepts that were in harmony with my own and were given sanction by a great mind.

With this background to the book I wanted to write, I went to an editor at McGraw-Hill, Lois Cole, to discuss the nature of the study that I was about to undertake. I had in view a relatively short volume designed for a wide reading public. I suppose that writers invariably hope to reach a large audience, if they have a message, and that was my case after I had experienced how restricted the market was for scholarly works. Moreover, the words of my early master in France, Henri Sée, still rang in my ears— "all masterpieces are short" —and I hoped that this book might be a masterpiece.

McGraw-Hill proved to be interested in my proposition and so I went to work with the assurance that what I would produce would be published, but of course, with the usual condition, "if the manuscript were acceptable to the publisher!"[9] I even received a small advance, which was new to me, but which I thought was important in eliciting interest and support from the publisher.

During that academic year I worked very hard. I had a small cubicle in Butler Library at Columbia, with no telephone, no sign on the door to indicate who was inside, and with no way of anyone's finding out my location except through me. Moreover, I had immediate access to the excellent collections of the Library with the privilege of taking books to my cubicle while I was using them.

At the beginning I had intended to include cultures of the East (especially China and India) in my survey, but I soon discovered that existing economic histories of these areas were not reliable enough for my purposes and also that my knowledge of these portions of the globe was so inadequate that I could not hazard even informed guesses. So I restricted my work to the West and its well-known antecedents.

The result of my labors was a short volume of some two hundred and eighty pages of text and was published by McGraw-Hill in 1951. It sold well by my standards (10,000 copies in the first year), was very favorably reviewed, appeared in Great Britain, and was translated into French, German, Italian, and Spanish.[10] Much to my surprise McGraw-Hill did not publish a second edition, for the editors thought that the original sale had exhausted the market.

[9] This proviso used to seem to me very one-sided, but once I was on the other side of the business, I realized that publishers had to protect themselves against sloppy, even no-good manuscripts which came to them from authors in whom they had put their trust.

[10] By the time the book came out, Lois Cole had left McGraw-Hill for T. Y. Crowell's. Book editors are indeed a very peripatetic group. Her successsor was a pleasant person, but in an attempt to improve a paragraph he combined two sentences which resulted in making a novelist out of a very prominent poet—much to my chagrin when the reviewers caught it. The moral is beware of changes made by editors to smooth one's style!

Fortunately, the Columbia University Press acquired the rights to it and kept it in print.

This is not the place to report my findings at any length, for they were expressed very succinctly in the book. Suffice it to say here that I did try to define civilization; I did try to identify peaks and troughs in the cultures of the West; and I did try to analyze the dynamics of change. Civilization, I held, "refers to achievements in such aesthetic and intellectual pursuits as architecture, painting, literature, sculpture, music, philosophy, and science and to the success which a people has in establishing control over its human and physical environment." In my analysis, I placed great emphasis on explaining those factors which lead to the economic rise of a culture. I found that a high correspondence has always existed between periods of high productivity of goods and services in a culture and its periods of greatest achievement in controlling human environment and creating aesthetic and intellectual works of a high order. In addition to economic factors I found that other forces are extremely important, such as art forms, social goals, and ideologies of various kinds, whether borrowed from others or created by the culture itself. The selection of standards which would lift cultures to higher levels of civilization seems to have been most successful where the exchange of ideas and art forms was the most active (commercial centers, for example), where economic growth was taking place, where competition among individuals was keen, and where people wanted to improve their physical well-being. Factors leading to a culture's decline are just the reverse of those leading to its rise. Here is a finding which should be a guide to statesmen.

I also concluded from my study that cultures which reach high levels of civilization not only borrow heavily from others, but they also "export" to other cultures much that has made them great; or if they do not export it, what has made them great is stolen or borrowed from them. This is almost axiomatic in the realm of the diffusion of technology. Once people understood that a given technique, like making pottery on the wheel, has lessened the labor input, improved the product, and contributed mightily to prosperity, then other cultures soon adopt it. Styles of art are diffused also, as can be seen in the spread of Greek building forms to the Italian peninsula where today are to be seen the best "Greek" remains. The dispersion of ideologies is also great, as can be observed in the spread of Christianity or of Mohammedanism. Cultures do not appear to have been successful in maintaining for themselves what has made them great.

I was of the opinion that I had clarified the processes with which I was dealing. I was so convinced of the value of my contributions to the subject as to request an opportunity to read a paper regarding my subject to the International Historical Congress held in Rome. My request was granted and I was pleased to learn that Arnold Toynbee would chair my session, for I thought that his presence would guarantee a large attendance. Much to my chagrin, however, the meeting was very sparsely attended, for the organizers of the Congress had scheduled a free visit to the Catacombs at the very time I was to speak. Apparently many of the world's historians preferred something that had been dead for over a thousand years to my "choice pearls," which I wanted to spread before them. Be that as it may, Toynbee was much impressed with my paper, especially the section having to do with diffusion and led a lively discussion about it.

This appearance in Rome and the book itself brought me a certain amount of notoriety. I was sought out by agents who arrange lectures; I was asked to speak at several institutions; and I was put up for several clubs in the city and even for the Social Register! For the most part such advances left me very cold. Lecture tours to remote cities in the dead of winter in overheated trains or planes, stays in underheated hotels, and meals of a nondescript quality did not appeal to me, unless the fees were very good, which they were not. As for lecturing in general, I had all that I could swing at the University. And so far as club life went, I did not take to it. I had lived in the Cosmos Club in Washington during the war and knew what it was like. To be sure, it gave one an opportunity to meet persons in journalism or radio or television or publishing, who would have been an asset to one in my profession, but my penchant was to devote myself to research, to my students, and to my sons, of whom I was very proud. So I turned down nearly all the things that might lead me into other paths than the one I wanted to follow.

In the meantime the stream of students continued, and my university load seemed to get ever heavier. Consequently, I began to cast about for a way to get another leave of absence. The Fulbright teaching fellowships were at this time in full swing and so I decided to apply for one of them. I thought that my chances would be good because I knew French and Italian well enough to lecture in them, and I could manage to handle German if I had enough time for preparation. Thus I applied for a Fulbright that required that I teach at the Institut des Sciences Politiques at Paris in September and October of 1951 and at Grenoble in December and January. I proposed that at the first two institutions I give a course in French economic history, essentially the course that I had been giving at Columbia. I made arrangements with the school where my younger son was enrolled to take a leave (the principal assured me that the boy would get more out of the trip than he would at school in New York) and I saw to it that my elder son, who was then at Cornell, would be well taken care of. My wife got a leave of absence, and Columbia engaged Leo Gershoy to take care of my classes. Thus the stage was set for another trip abroad.

Just before I was ready to leave for Paris, however, I had a letter from the director of the Institut des Sciences Politiques to the effect that the Institut had courses in French economic history but none in the economic history of the United States. He was sure I knew the economic history of America and that I would not mind switching to that subject. Of course, his assumptions were not exactly correct, particularly regarding what I would like to do, but by this time all arrangements had been made to leave and there was little that I could do but to accept the change.

Thus it came about that my wife, my younger son, and I took off for Paris in early June. Our first task was to find a school for my son. I thought that this would be easy, given my connections and employment, but when I applied at the public Lycées which I knew in the Latin Quarter, I was given the brush-off, sometimes rather brusquely. I finally did find an opening at Henri IV, in the third grade, which was the appropriate grade, but I was told that my son would have to compete for the place with thirty French boys and that the competition would be in the form of a written examination in French!

So, I went looking at private schools. I hoped to get him into L'Ecole Alsacienne in the Montparnasse quarter, but that was filled, too. Finally, I located L'Ecole Frédéric Le Play in the Champs de Mars quarter and we went there for an interview. I imagined that this would be a very conservative place, if it were inspired by Frédéric Le Play, and I turned out to be correct. The school was, however, small and the people understanding. I thought that my son would be given special attention there, which also turned out to be the case. What convinced my wife that this was the school for the boy was a curious thing. While we were waiting to see the headmaster, the boy had to go to the bathroom. My wife went with him and when she returned she said that she had decided that this was *the place*. When asked why she had come so suddenly to that conclusion, she replied that the toilet seat was covered with rosebud decals and that an institution with such finesse was the right spot for her son.

Once the question of a school had been determined, we looked for a place to live and found a good pension on the Avenue Frédéric Le Play. It seemed that we were chasing the old boy rather diligently. Then we acquired a car in which we took off for a seaside resort at Le Moulleau, south of Arcachon. Our route took us to Tours, Poitiers, Périgueux, the Valley of the Dordogne, and Bordeaux. Thus I was given an opportunity to tell my son about the fight between the Christians and the invading Moslems and the exploits of Roland. We discovered that many of the restaurants and hotels which had been destroyed during the war were being rebuilt and trying to regain their clienteles by providing excellent food and lodgings at low prices. We profited from that circumstance. We stopped at one place, the Chateau of Mercuès, where we had a suite in the tower. I am sure my son thought that he was a knight of old.

Le Moulleau turned out to be a very good choice. It was on a bay and thus the waters were protected from the surf of the

Atlantic. The bay is a famous place for the cultivation of oysters and our son soon made friends with a boy whose father had an oyster bed. Sometimes the lad would bring us a two-quart pail full of oysters; at other times the father would invite us to go on his boat with him to "turn" oysters, that is, to roll them over so that they would grow round instead of flat. On such occasions we could eat our fill. Quite appropriately the little boy's name was Roland.

Our living arrangements at Le Moulleau were very good. We ate in a hotel where the food was excellent, but we had rooms in a villa which the hotel rented. This was a house where D'Annunzio had lived with some of his lady friends when he spent his summers in France. The place was near a beach where there were many children with whom my son could play and from whom he could learn French. We decided, however, that in the mornings he should go to an organized beach group where he could get instruction in swimming and where he would be under the supervision of an instructor. It turned out that the man in charge was wonderful--he was an aspiring singer who moonlighted by supervising children at the beach.

I had brought a lot of books on American economic history with me from the States and I spent much of my day reading them and organizing my lectures for the fall. I decided that since I had to get up a set of lectures, I should do so in such a fashion that they would make a publishable manuscript. My wife was also working on a book, so she spent long hours in the villa with me. The only American visitors which we had at that time were the Gershoys, who had been at Tarbes where he was working on the biography of Barère, a member of the Committee on Public Safety during the French Revolution. He and I got our exercise by trying to introduce baseball to my son's friends on the beach, but we had only minor success. We did better with swimming.

Finally the summer drew toward its close and we left to continue our Tour de France. We went down to Biarritz, but I was turned off by the place after I ran into a large, dead rat while in swimming. We then went to St. Jean de Luz where we had Basque friends. They took us to a festival of Basque dances and gave us many lectures about the necessity for Basque autonomy, if not independence. Our friends, who had a fleet of shipping trawlers, had established a tradition of sending some Basque every year to study at Cornell, a tradition which, I believe, continues to the present.

We went on from St. Jean de Luz to St. Jean Pied le Porc, a quaint market town, by Barzun les Bains, whence a card was sent to Jacques Barzun, which he seemed to resent, and thence via the Routes des Pyrenées, over the famous Col de Bisque and le Col de Cauterets. How the bicyclists on the Tour de France manage to get over these mountains is beyond me. Even our little Quatre Chevaux had its troubles. Here we also barely avoided disaster when I made a sharp left turn in front of a large car coming up at high speed. I suppose that I had not looked sharply enough,for the traffic was extremely light.

On this trip we by-passed Lourdes, for I thought that it would be too depressing and then after Bagnères de Luchon decided that we had had enough of the mountains and turned north. Soon we arrived at the town of St. Gaudens, which I had to visit for no other reason than the fact that the sculptor St. Gaudens had been a friend of my family and a frequent visitor at our house. The town was, however, a delight. The upper stories of many houses in the old section had been built out over the streets, which gives the effect of arcades.

Eventually we arrived at Carcassonne, which my son proclaimed to be his favorite town, and then proceeded on to Albi to see the red brick cathedral and the paintings of Toulouse-Lautrec, many of which are located in the museum of his home town. From there we took off through the Massif Central—through Le Cantal, which made me think very much of Vermont (most areas I like very much make me think of Vermont), into Le Puy-de-Dome to the Mont Dore, La Bourboule, which is a health center especially for children, to Le Puy itself with its dramtic church on top of a mountain, to Clermont Ferrand, Riom, and finally to Vichy. I felt that I had to see where the government of France was during World War II and also where the "people of Vichy" were tried after the liberation. Neither place was particularly attractive to me.

On this trip I had one of the most enjoyable meals of my life. After La Bourboule, we began looking for a restaurant at which we could have lunch. Much to my surprise we went through village after village and through a vast area with nary a public place to eat. It got later and later; we became hungrier and hungrier; and as we became famished, even sweet tempers began to sour. Finally, we came rather suddenly upon a country inn in an otherwise desolate region. Out of sheer desperation I decided that we should eat there. The proprietor told us that we were very late, that he did not have much, but that if we would be patient he would scrape up something. Similar introductions by American innkeepers would have turned me completely off; and in this case I must admit to having had some dismay.

No sooner had he spoken than some wandering minstrels who were working a street fair in a neighboring town appeared. In an entirely impromptu manner they began to play, sing and rehearse some of their "acts." They were Italians and some of their songs or stories were in a neat mixture of French, Italian, and Provençale. They were absolutely hilarious and kept us well entertained until the food came. First there were *hors d'oeuvres* of smoked ham, radishes, scallions, butter, and, of course, fresh baked bread. Then came perch which a boy had been sent out to catch—a fish which would melt in one's mouth. This was followed by *la daube provençale*, which, when properly prepared, is a most delectable dish (it is a kind of *boeuf bourguignon*). Then came a lettuce salad of a tenderness seldom equaled, cheese (one of the cheeses was cantal, which made me think of Vermont cheddar), fruit including fresh almonds, coffee, and appropriate local wines all along the line. This meal put us behind schedule, for after it all of us had to take a nap.

From Vichy we went into Burgundy. At Cluny I was able to give the family a lecture on the Cluniac reformers of the Church and to see the monastery and Church. The next stop was, I believe, Beaune, where we visited the hospital, still furnished with the equipment used in the Middle Ages, and saw the remarkable Last Supper by Roger Van der Weyden. We also visited the wine cellars, which stretch along the main street. One of the characteristics of "tasting" in cellars is that the alcohol hits one when one comes into the open air, which I knew about but which my wife did not! Then to Dijon to see the castle of the Dukes of Burgundy.[11] Then on to Vézelay with its magnificent Romanesque church where the first crusade was preached and where many crusaders took off for the Holy Land. Then we headed for Paris with stops at Auxerre and a longer one at Sens, to spend some time in the Cathedral and to speculate on the source of some of Paris' water supply from a nearby stream.

Finally we arrived in Paris, travel weary but much better informed about France south of the Loire than I had been before. There is nothing like a "Tour de France" to get to know the country. And to do it by small car is much easier than by bicycle, which I had attempted earlier.

As we were unloading the car before our new abode at the pension Avenue Frédéric Le Play, a strange thing happened. With these cars baggage space was so limited that baggage had to be piled on their tops. My wife was not one to travel lightly. She had nine valises to one for me and one for my son. Among her valises or boxes was a hat box with twelve hats, not one of which she had ever put on her head since we had left Paris three or four months earlier. Now when the Parisian street cleaners clean the streets, they turn on fire plugs (they are not high hydrants like ours but are flush to the ground) and let the water flow along the gutters. With willow brooms (long small branches of the willow are tied to broom handles) they sweep whatever has to be swept into the gutters and it flows away into the sewers. For reasons which I shall never understand, although I plead complete innocence of any malice, that hat box broke open and twelve hats inside went miraculously into single file, like a family of ducks, in the gutter and floated along toward the sewer. By quick action and at the risk of getting my feet wet and with the, one might say, insistent urging of my wife I rescued some of the head gear. But I noticed in the future that the baggage had much less in the way of hats than it had had on this trip.

---

[11] Besançon was the normal capital of Burgundy, but the Dukes moved to Dijon when Besançon was taken from them.

CHAPTER X

A Yankee Fulbrighter Abroad

Soon after our arrival in Paris, I made my way to the Institut des Sciences Politiques to make final arrangements for my lectures. I was committed to giving twenty of them, and according to the French system I could give them as fast as I wanted to. Also according to the French system, students could attend my lectures or not, as they pleased, but for a certificate they had to pass examinations in a number of fields of which one was American economic history. My schedule was set up and the date for the inaugural lecture was fixed. I did not know exactly what an inaugural lecture was, but I soon learned that I was supposed to be exceptionally brilliant, that I should invite all my friends, cousins, uncles, and aunts and that the administration would turn out in force.

In due course the great day arrived. I reached the Institut in plenty of time to size up the situation, as I always do when I have any apprehension about what is about to take place. In good season the very large room began to fill. I suggested to the *bidello* [1] that he bring in some extra chairs, which he seemed loath to do.

[1] A *bidello* is a man who sees to it that a professor's room is in order. He erases blackboards, picks up papers, opens or closes windows, and is more or less useful and agreeable, or disagreeable.

"Mais monsieur le professeur, maybe you need some chairs for *this* lecture, but you will never need them again." He turned out to be absolutely correct. When I began my lecture, I recited this little episode and then I invited all the young ladies who were standing in the back to come forward and sit on the edge of the platform. "I like to have young ladies at my feet" (mild reaction of the audience). Then I made excuses about my poor French and warned the audience that I might make some colossal errors, as I once did at the pension in the Rue d'Assas. Then I recounted the story about putting my trousers every night under my mistress. This brought the house down, but I sensed a bit of uneasiness on the part of the Director of the Institut.

The lectures went on at the rate of two a week. As the *bidello* had suggested, my audience dropped very rapidly to a basic thirty-five. I hired a young lady to help me put the English lectures into French, so that I wound up with an English manuscript and a French version of the same, such as it was. I thought that the lectures went fairly well, but I realized that I was not getting close to the students as I had managed to do at Columbia. I tried everything—taking them to lunch, to have *apéritifs*, to have informal conversations—but nothing worked to my satisfaction. I did my stint and finally the time for the examinations, which were oral, arrived.

The procedure for these tests was for the professor to meet students individually and quiz them for a certain number of minutes. My colleague André Siegfried was able to find out enough about an individual in three minutes to give the candidate a rating. I could not find out enough to satisfy me in less than fifteen minutes, and one was paid for the examinations by the number of students one had. I had twelve students who stood the exams (remember that thirty-five were in attendance at the lectures). Of these twelve, five had never been to a single lecture and two had not attended even half the lectures. When I asked those who had never attended how they expected to pass, the answer was that they had read the articles on America in the Encyclopedia Britannica and believed they were well informed on the matter at hand. I failed all those who had never attended my class and one other, who did not seem to know much of anything. Having failed half of those who stood the exam, I was called on the carpet by the Director, for the percentage seemed by comparison with that experienced by French professors to be very high. I explained the circumstances and he congratulated me on the standards which I had maintained.

Our stay in Paris was by no means all work. One learns a great deal about a country by just living there. For example, there was the time when I received a ticket (*contravention* in French) for a traffic violation. This was at the time when Paris was becoming a great parking lot and one put one's car wherever one could. In my case I had put it under some trees along a boulevard where what the birds did to it should not be mentioned here. I did not know what I had done wrong until I got to the police station, where the sergeant was very friendly. He almost fainted when I told him what my mission was, for most of the French at that time were scofflaws about such summonses. Then he told me that I should have had my parking lights on (I had never seen the lights on French cars) and that I should in the future obey French laws. Also I should have a brass plate with my name on it installed in the car—a detail that the seller of the car had never mentioned. So much for Parisian traffic control. Aside from this, that traffic was sheer anarchy, if not mayhem.

Our period in Paris was withal very pleasant. We had a great number of friends and led an active social life. Our friendship with the Crouzets and the Fourastiés deepened and we enjoyed them very much. We often went on excursions to the environs of Paris for Sunday outings. Then we had a very close friend from Columbia, Irwin Edman, of whom we saw a good deal. He was a Fulbrighter at the Sorbonne, but unlike me did not go around to his Dean to see about his lecturing schedule. Finally, after he had heard nothing from his institution, he did call on his Dean, only to learn to his chagrin that he had been completely forgotten. I should add, however, that the Dean had a viable excuse—his professors had been threatening to strike! At any rate, Irwin got his schedule straightened out and did his lecturing, much as I was doing.

Our relations with Edman were very pleasant. He was lonely and often sought our company. He liked to play games with French words and idiomatic expressions, which was fun for me. I remember that we had quite a time trying to find the French word equivalent for "back seat driving," but finally did find it, thanks to Mrs. Fourastié. It is "La mouche du coche," at least for back seat driver, an expression which comes from one of La Fontaine's fables in which a fly riding with the coachman would go down and bite the rear of a horse that was not going at the pace the fly thought desirable.

Irwin liked to dine with us and reciprocated our invitations by taking us out to dinner. I recall one such outing at La Reine Pédauque, a restaurant which he liked very much because of its name. On the occasion in question, I was sitting on the bench when the lady next to me went into hysterics. As the waiters escorted her to the manager's office, I looked down to try to determine what had caused her outburst. At the end of the bench near the wall I saw a very large rat, which the headwaiter spied at the same instant. Whereupon he explained, "Even the rats of Paris know the best restaurants."

My son, who stood in high favor with Irwin, did well in his school—rose decals and all. His French improved rapidly and his accent was far superior to my own. He even appeared in a play given by the school in a theater in Montmartre.

My ambition and my energy seemed to have no bounds that year. I prepared the English version of my lectures for the publishers—this time it was for Thomas Y. Crowell—and I also worked on the French manuscript and got that to a point where it was accepted for publication by the Presses Universitaires de France. My command of the French language was not all that the Academy would have liked and I later learned from the copy editor of the book that he had a time whipping my manuscript into shape for the printer. But he did the job and the book had a mild success on the Continent, which at that time had relatively little on American economic history. In fact, the English version was translated into some ten foreign tongues and those in Far Eastern sold well.

In addition to this, I arranged for a trip to Belgium and Germany for a series of lectures after I had completed my work at the Institut des Sciences Politiques. My friend Charles Verlinden made preparatons for me to lecture at Ghent on my philosophy of history; my friend Paul Harsin arranged lectures at Liége; and the American cultural atաché at Berlin obtained a lecture at the Meinecke Institut at the Free University at Berlin. The lectures in Belgium went very well, especially one before a group of bankers and economists at Liége at which the president of a medium term bank asked me my opinion about the future of his type of bank. I replied that when medium term loans remain too risky for regular commercial banks, medium term banks will always have a place in the banking community. I learned that he quoted me the next day at his annual meeting of stockholders. I might add that I was royally entertained at both Belgian cities, for I was well-known because of my study of the Flemish movement.

From Liége I went to Düsseldorf where my sister Barbara was working in the Quaker Hilfe educational program. She helped me obtain the services of a German professor to go over my lecture to be sure that my German text was correct and also that my reading of the lecture was comprehensible. Unfortunately my German is not so good as my French or Italian. While I was with her, she had an offer to become the headmistress of the Northfield School for Girls at Northfield, Massachusetts—a post which she accepted.

My stay in Berlin was interesting. I was put up in a house for visiting professors and for regular professors who had not yet found housing in the city. There I made some very interesting contacts. The lecture went well, althought I was happy when I had discharged my obligation.

When the lecture was over, I took the opportunity to visit the city and East Berlin. I wanted to see what the old University of Berlin looked like (it was now called the Humbolt University and was communist) and I wanted to see the Französischestrasse where I lived as a student. The destruction was so extensive that I could not even find the Französischestrasse to say nothing of the apartment building where I had my digs. How the Germans were able to endure the bombings that they suffered will always remain a mystery for me. The Humbolt University was a great disappointment to me, for it had been turned into a Marxist institute and a communist agency, at least so far as the social sciences were concerned.

My companion was an English girl, who was a friend of my sister. She had a station wagon and had offered to take me to see the sights of East Berlin. And see them we did, especially the colossal billboards with the faces of the communist great with the obvious purpose of covering ruins that had not been cleaned up.

When our sight-seeing was ended we made our way to the Brandenburg Gate. There we were stopped by the newly created Volkspolizei. The English Quaker worker had in her station wagon old clothes which she had been gathering for the poor. They were in the wagon when we entered the East, but we had no proof of that and were told in no uncertain terms that it was against the law to take goods from the East to the Western part of the city. We were under temporary arrest. During this very embarrassing period one of the policemen asked me, "Sind Sie Amis?" The only translation which I knew for "ami" was friend, and inasmuch as this English girl was one of the homeliest persons I had ever seen, I wondered if he were kidding me. I put up some cock-and-game story, which only made matters worse, until the English girl explained that "Ami" was German slang for American. When this became clear we had little difficulty in settling the matter of the clothes!

Shortly after this episode, I left Berlin and was happy to be out of the city. I felt terribly oppressed—a real case of claustrophobia. How the Berliners were and still are able to stand it, I do not know, but apparently one could get used to it. Nevertheless, I met many who had the same reactions as I, especially among the students with whom I spoke. In fact, I learned that several to whom I lectured finally made it to the United States.

When I got back to Paris, I was informed that the Société d'Histoire Moderne was about to celebrate its fiftieth anniversary and that the officers wanted me to speak, as a representative of foreign scholars. I accepted this invitation with alacrity and prepared a paper on the migration of features of one culture to another—a theme which was based upon my *Rise and Fall of Civilization.* I spoke at the same session as George Lefebvre, the famous historian of the French Revolution, with whom I had already had several contacts. This opportunity was in itself very flattering, but Lefebvre went out of his way to praise my paper.[2] Naturally I was very pleased with this bit of glory.

As soon as this event had taken place, it was time for us to move on. Our next stop was Grenoble, which was part of the schedule which had been worked out with the Fulbright people. I looked forward to being at Grenoble, for it was the home of Stendhal, for whom I have geat admiration, and it would provide, as I knew, excellent skiing. I left Paris alone in the car to find a place for us to live and a school for my son to attend. I went down via Le Creusot, which I had never visited and of which I now saw little because of fog, then on to Saulieu, Dijon again, and Lyons. Once at Grenoble, I busied myself with finding a school at La Tronche, a suburb, and then a pension, which turned out to be an excellent one for our purposes. The school was a girl's school, which took boys in the early grades. It was very *bourgeois* and very Catholic. The children wore a uniform and white gloves each Friday, when they received their weekly report cards.[3] My son was very happy there and continued his excellent progress in French.

At the University (I was in the Faculty of Law, for it is there that economics is taught in France), I repeated the lectures which I had given in Paris and with just about the same reception and results. The one big difference was that my colleagues could extend to me and my family much more social intercourse than had been the case in Paris. My colleagues were very agreeable and did everything in their power to make our sojourn enjoyable.

Grenoble is situated in a plain that is surrounded by Alps. The skiing is superb in the mountains and it did not take me long to get equipment for my son and myself and to initiate him into

---

[2] I had read a paper previously that year before a regular meeting of the Society on the history of American agriculture. It was essentially one of the lectures which I had delivered at the Sciences Politiques.

[3] Before he went to this school, he spent about a week at the école communale of La Tronche. The teacher was a communist and made life miserable for the little American capitalist in his charge.

the joys of the sport. We went to all of the places around—Alp d'Huez, Mégève, Uriage, Villard de Lans, and Chamrousse. Skiing in Europe is quite different from that in the United States. Instead of working one's head off, one takes it easily. Two hours for lunch is not unusual—and instead of a hamburger one has a hot dinner of at least three courses. Furthermore, I never used a rope tow in Europe; in fact, I do not recall ever having seen one. The entire sport is conducted in a much more relaxed and civilized way than anything which I had ever experienced in America.

In the course of time, both my son and I became fairly adept at the sport. Inasmuch as I could take off more easily than he, because his schedule was limited by his school,[4] I sometimes skied alone. At such times I frequently went to Chamrousse, which was somewhat more difficult than my son enjoyed. The descent from La Croix, the very top, was spectacular. The scenery changed continuously, for the fall was somewhat precipitous.

On the return from one of these solitary junkets I had an experience which showed me that France was not so free of racial feeling as most people maintained. On this occasion I was returning from Chamrousse somewhat late, so I took a short cut through the quarter of Algerians in Grenoble and just at the hour when workers were returning home. At one point I saw a man on a bicycle coming toward me and inasmuch as he was weaving I slowed to a crawl. Unfortunately *he* ran into *me* and in such a manner that his head hit the corner post of the car and opened a wound which bled profusely. Immediately my car was surrounded by Algerians who assumed that I was French, and for a moment I feared that I would be mobbed. At the critical moment one of the more intelligent ones in the crowd said to me in a very loud voice, "You are Moroccan, n'est-ce pas, Monsieur?" In an equally loud voice, I agreed that I was. At once the crowd was stilled and I went on my way after exchanging documentary information.

When I related the incident to my friends in the town,

---

4 French schools give the children Thursday afternoons and Saturday afternoons off. This makes the weekend short and father and son excursions limited.

they immediately cited many instances of clashes between whites and North Africans. Algerians did the menial tasks—ditch digging, sewer cleaning, and the like; the white workers had skilled jobs, carpentry, masonry, electrical work, plumbing, and so on. Algerians could not get into white unions, as a rule, and social intercourse between the two was almost unheard of. In fact, when a white girl in my class fell in love with a Moroccan of very high social and economic standing, the reaction of the French was not unlike that of Virginians a generation ago when a black and white contemplated marriage. Toleration of ethnic differences will come, if at all, very slowly.

On another trip to the mountains, my son and I left the slopes earlier than the crowd for the purpose of avoiding the traffic. As we went down the hairpin turns one could hardly see the cars coming from below because of the snow that was piled up on the side of the road. I proceeded with great caution, but at one place I saw a car coming up at considerable speed. I crept over to my side until I was partially in the snow bank and stopped. The oncoming car maintained its speed and after it had made the turn skidded and hit me. Although the damage was not great, my book of instructions from the insurance company instructed me in case of any accident to obtain a "*constat*", or report from the gendarmes (national police). It turned out that the car which had hit me was a gendarme car, and when I demanded a *constat*, the gendarme inside was furious. Whereupon he tried to catch me in some contravention of the laws. He tried, or made me try, the horn, the lights, the windshield wipers, etc., etc. I met all the tests, but then he thought of making me work the windshield wipers by hand, which the book says you should do if the mechanism that ran them failed. This I did not know how to do, but as the policeman wrote out the ticket, I read the book of instructions and before he handed me the ticket, I was working the blamed things. This made him more angry than ever and he said things which he was to regret. Anyhow, the report went in and the next morning before I was up the policeman's commanding officer came to the pension to apologize for his man. Such is life when one follows the rules.

Our stay in Grenoble was enlivened by the life at the

pension in which we lived. *La femme à tout faire* was a *paysanne* of the countryside, who literally did everything. She was a very hard worker and I saw her actually break ice in the town public laundry trough and scrub out clothes until they were snow white. The lady of the house was an excellent cook, who did her shopping on a bicycle that she rode to market three miles away. Her husband was a blind engineer, but he was an avid speculator on the stock market and I learned a lot of the market's language, if not wisdom about investing, from him. The other *pensionnaires* were largely students who were convalescing from one thing or another. They took as their goal the teaching of the latest French slang to us poor Americans, and I must say that they did a remarkably good job.

The countryside of La Tronche was beautiful. As spring approached, the snow disappeared and skiing became a thing of the past. One of the ski instructors informed us that there is always something interesting to do in the Alps and he suggested that we come to his slopes to pick flowers. This shift from skiing seemed rather tame, but we tried it. Much to my surprise vast fields were covered with daffodils and jonquils. Just the sight of them was a delight.

Moreover, my son had a bicycle and received great pleasure from it, especially for short trips in La Tronche. On one occasion, he ventured out on an important road leading from Grenoble and was nearly killed. There were no speed limits in France, and the Swiss with large cars burned up the asphalt on the road in question. My son stuck his hand out to signal a left turn, but as he did so, he found himself in front of a Buick going at a fantastic rate. I witnessed the entire scene and shall never understand how the car missed him, but by sudden braking in a loud screech and veering into a ditch, the car avoided him. In the future, he did not travel that road.

Our time to leave Grenoble eventually arrived and we went on to Turin, where I was to give some lectures at the university there—this time in Italian. I spoke largely about the history of American agriculture and in the process made some friends who have remained loyal to me over all these intervening years. At that particular time the Italian universities were anxious to have American lecturers to catch up on what scholarship they had missed during the war, or during the Fascist period.

After Turin we went to Florence where we took quarters in a *pensione* at San Domenico, a small town on the way to Fiesole. The place was run by a real beauty by the name of Dudy Bertolini, who was the spitting image of the Venus in The Birth of Venus by Botticelli. Fortunately she had young children the age of my son and in playing with them he began to learn Italian, as he had learned French at Le Moulleau. His progress was very rapid and he had a good time to boot. As for myself, I rewrote my economic history of the United States in order to make it more readable and more fluent.

When that task was done, we moved on to Rome. We thought that we would go to the neighborhood of the Villa Borghese, so that my son would have a place where he could ride his bicycle in safety. Much to our surprise the traffic between the Via Vittorio Veneto and the Villa Borghese had so increased since our last visit that the poor boy could not even get across the street with his bike. So we went looking for a place within our means and our budget with a garden where the bike could be used. Finally we found a place and my wife went in to make the arrangements, for her Italian was without a tell-tale American accent. She came back and quoted a price which seemed to me to be impossibly low. So I went in to confirm the arrangements and to see the rooms. Everything seemed fine and the first night at dinner the food was excellent and we were waited upon in a manner to which I would like to become accustomed by two young men who were dressed like admirals in the navy. I could not believe it.

Neither could I understand how the madame was able to provide what she was serving for what we were paying. So being curious by nature, not to say suspicious, I opened my eyes a little wider to see what the explanation for the situation was. Not to my surprise I noticed that we were not the only people in the place, but that others came and went in couples and that there was a high correlation between their ages and the length of time which they remained in the place. When I was quite sure of my ground, I went to my wife and said, "We are living in a *bordello* and we must leave." To which she replied, "We are staying right here because I feel so much at home." And stay we did.

My wife was working on a book about futurism which came out under the excellent title of "Looking Back at Futurism," and Rome had many of the former Futurists with whom she could consult. I did work on Italian economic history in preparaton for a course which I was to give at Columbia and I gave some lectures at the University of Rome on American history. My son went to a school run by Jesuits but by that time was getting tired of being buffeted from place to place by the migrations of his parents. Ultimately we spent some time at a beach on the Italian Riviera, Sestri Levante, which was much to his liking. Finally we made our way to Le Havre, where we left our car for the Leo Gershoys, who had purchased it. The year had been an active one, but we were glad to be going back to America and to be with our elder son. He was taking a program in nuclear engineering at Cornell University and was finding the going very rough.

When I returned to my work at Columbia,I soon found out that my load was as heavy as ever, if not heavier. Furthermore, I was becoming intersted in a new field for me. I had become impressed with the fact that historians and for that matter all social scientists were making value judgments at every turn but I observed that they had few if any implicit or explicit assumptions to guide them in their decisions and the rightness or wrongness of what they judged. To help clarify my own mind on this subject, I established with Otto Klineberg, a social psychologist then at Columbia, a University Seminar to study the problem. As I have stated earlier, such seminars allowed us to invite kindred souls from other institutions to exchange ideas with us on the matter under consideration. One of these guests was John P. Gillin, on leave from the University of North Carolina and Visiting Professor of Anthropology at Columbia. Our attenton began to focus upon the basic values of a culture as the guiding force in making judgments, and Gillin and I developed a plan to collaborate on a book on this subject. His experience in studying other cultures proved to be valuable, and my travels in Europe had given me some insights into the way different people judged various social phenomena.

I felt the need of more experience with other cultures than our own and of areas of our own culture that I knew little about. Moreover, I thought that it would be valuable to consult with European scholars of the phenomena which interested us. Fortune played into my hand. The Department of State asked me to go to Latin America, especially the Argentine, to give some lectures along the lines of my *Rise and Fall of Civilization.* This opportunity allowed me to visit a large part of Central and South America and to get some feel for the civilizations of the Aztecs and Incas. I was royally received in Buenos Aires and worked hard to make my mission a success. Unfortunately my Spanish was not adequate to lecture in the language, but I had the services of a simultaneous translator by the improbable name of Murphy who was a genius. He improved so on what I had to say that I was tempted to adopt him for life. If I had a story to tell or an anecdote to relate, he would have the audience rolling in the aisles.

I returned to the States via Rio de Janeiro, just at the time of the Mardi Gras. The celebrations were so extravagant that I really was put to it to reconcile them with Christian virtues. After Rio, I went on to Port au Prince, where the French is astonishingly good, then to West Palm Beach to visit my mother, who had moved there for the climate, and so on home.

Hardly was I back at my last than I had an opportunity to have a NATO Research Fellowship, for my ideas on a study of basic values for Western Civilization much interested those in charge, particularly Paul Henri Spaak. Almost simultaneously I was asked by Donald Young, who was then the director of the Russell Sage Foundation, if I would be interested in writing a history of European philanthropy in modern times. That seemed to be an attractive subject amd I said that I would be interested in such an enterprise and suggested that I make a preliminary investigation to see if it were a subject of enough importance to warrant a full-length treatment. To this suggestion he readily agreed.

Thus it came about that I had sources of support to undertake two very interesting investigations. As a first step, I went to Europe with my younger son to interview persons who would have ideas or knowledge of both subjects. Together we visited eighteen countries and interviewed literally hundreds of persons—scholars, journalists, statesmen, and leaders in business.

Of the two studies which I had in the works, the one on basic values was completed first. Although the contemplated collaboraton between Gillin and me did not materialize, for he became involved in other enterprises, his ideas provided much of the framework for the study which I prepared.[5] The book was published in 1960 under the title *Basic Values of Western Civilization* by the Columbia University Press.

My findings helped to clarify my own basis for making judgments in my profession as a historian, and I hope that they have been helpful to others. Let me state the essence of my message by quoting from the book:

> *Basic values reflect in essence the choices which men have made out of a wide range of possibilities as to the way they want to live, the wants and desires which they try to satisfy, and the ardor with which they strive to achieve recognized goals. . . .*
>
> *The total galaxy of ways of doing things and looking at things, weighted according to their respective standing in culture, constitute the value pattern of the culture. . . .*

I went on, following Gillin's views, that a distinction should be made between "ideal" values and "modal" values, that is, ideals which the culture considers the most desirable and modal values which are compromises with perfection or acknowledged

[5] John Gillin became tied up in the revision of his textbook during the preparation of this work and eventually became Dean of the Graduate Faculties at the University of Pittsburgh. He invited me to join him there, but I decided not to accept his flattering offer because to do so would have meant that my wife would have to give up her post at Hunter College in New York.

deviations from perfection. Then I endeavored to state what our ideal values are and to give illustrations of some compromises with them. For example, we have an ideal of the sanctity of the individual or of life, but under certain circumstances, like war, we sacrifice the individual for the good of society or the totality of individuals in the culture. I used as evidence of my findings laws, even those of an international character like the charter of the United Nations, the writings of scholars in the fields of the social sciences, and public opinion polls. I discovered that polling organizations had made surveys in nearly all Western countries in which such questions as the following were asked: What profession would you like your children to enter? What have been your greatest mistakes in life? Whom among statesmen do you admire the most? What part of your religious observances do you consider the most important? And so on. To each of these questions the interviewed was given a multiple of choices in his replies. In my view these polls were extremely revealing.

It was and is my contention that cultural values change very slowly, but obviously they do change, as for example, in the attitude toward marriage and the family in the United States. Then, individuals display aberrations from norms of basic values, as in the case of Adolf Hitler. I also contended that these basic values condition the behavior in a culture and are supported by many institutional devices—churches, schools and government—to keep individuals from diverging from them.

The reception given the book by scholars was most favorable. Perhaps historians were the least favorable of any professional group to it, for as one of my colleagues remarked to me, "Basic values are things which one takes for granted, like love, and do not need to be analyzed." Lay readers reacted to it in a variety of ways. Some thought that it was a wonderful statement of a very tough problem; others, who gave the book a superficial reading, thought that my naming of "ideal" values was naive. As for myself, I was pleased with what I had done, for the analysis gave me a better foundation and understanding for making value judgments (which is what I was after originally) than I had ever had before. At all events the book continues to sell even now after several years on the market.

The other study which I had in hand—a survey of European philanthropy—turned out to be extremely interesting. I discovered very early in my investigation that Europeans had not established large, wealthy foundations on the scale that Americans had. To be sure there were European foundations, like the Nobel Foundation, based upon moneys from the dynamite business; the Carlsberg Foundation in Denmark, financed from the beer industry; the Rothschild Foundation in France, supported by earnings from banking; the Gulbenkian Foundation in Portugal created by an Armenian who had a cut in the earnings of the Iraq Petroleum Company; the Welcome Foundation in England, built by an American pharmacist from moneys earned in the anti-toxin business, and devoted to medical education; the Gini Foundation in Italy (principally active at Venice), brought into being by earnings from supplying public works projects; and the like. In some countries, especially Spain, there were many foundations, so-called, devoted to religious ends, like the support of some saint or monastery. Most of these had been established for a long time (many since the sixteenth century) and for the most part had very small financial resources, barely enough in some instances to provide funds for the annual dinner of the executives of the fund.

One of the common characteristics of these European foundations seemed to be that the moneys which supported them had been made very rapidly and for the most part by persons who were not accustomed to having large sums for their own living. Yet the European foundations were small and few compared to American foundations, and the essential explanation for this fact seemed to be the working of income tax laws. The English income tax laws limited very markedly deductions for charitable or educational ends nor did they permit the placing of the stock of a company in a foundation exempt from inheritance taxes, which would allow a family to continue control of a company by controlling the foundation. Inasmuch as European countries followed English practices when they adopted income tax laws, all of Western Europe put real impediments in the way of establishing foundations. It became clear to me that American foundations became as numerous as they had not only because their founders wanted to indulge in good works but also because they sought to reduce their income taxes. In some cases, they wanted in addition to maintain family control of their businesses by placing voting stock in the hands of charitable foundations which their members would continued to dominate.

As a result of my investigations, I came to the conclusion that a full-scale study of European philanthropy would not be worthy of the effort.I did, however, lecture widely on the results of my findings and my efforts won high praise from an organization that groups foundations together, a kind of professional or trade society.Some of the lectures were published in various journals and my final report was given to the Russell Sage Foundation, where, I trust, it still reposes.

By this time in my career, I realized that I was pretty much committed to hopping around in my interests. I had found it difficult to concentrate my attention on one area or one short time-period. Part of this jumping seemed necessary for reasons of making a living. For example, if I had stuck to Belgian history, I would have found few opportunities to teach it, if, indeed, any. French economic history had greater possibilities, but it had to be combined with general European history to provide employment. Futhermore, I discovered that an intellectual *Wanderlust* led me from one interest to another. Sometimes I would think that what I knew about a certain subject, let us say the Fascist period in Italian history, was sufficient to satisfy my curiosity and would move on to something else. This characteristic of my professional life was also fostered by the fact that in my seminar, I would allow students to follow their own interests rather than to force them to work within the limits of my own. This meant that they were getting me interested in certain subjects that led me afield.[6] In retrospect, this procedure may have been a mistake so far as advancement in my career was concerned. I am convinced that if I had concentrated on one subject, like the

[6] I should add that I did not sponsor students whose interests were completely out of my areas of some competence. I kept them, at least, within areas where I knew the languages and the literature involved and the general history of the period.

French Revolution, I might have acquired more fame and fortune. Also in retrospect, however, I am glad that I did what I did, for I never got intellectually bored, fed up, or saturated. A professional rolling stone has more fun than a moss-covered one.

This lack of concentration in any one small area had peculiar ramifications that I should mention here, although some of them will get me ahead of my story. One of these was that, being active in so many fields and succumbing to that American trap to establish a professional society and journal for each, I became a "founding father" of several.

My first excursion in this direction was helping in the creation of the Economic History Association (1940) with its *Journal of Economic History*. This editor of this publication was E. A. J. Johnson, then of New York University, and I was the associate editor. The meetings of this group were at first very enjoyable and congenial. After World War II, however, a schism developed among the membership. A new element, deriving its inspiration from the application of mathematical techniques to their analyses, put in an appearance. They were the Cliometricians. They were pretentious about what they could do with their methods—of what they could extrapolate from a paucity of data. They twitted us "old school" economic historians for not knowing statistics nor econometrics, nor economic theory. They went ahead and published some atrocious stuff, which clearly showed that they did not have much evidence to go on. Futhermore, they tried to intimidate the rest of us with their techniques and to get control of everything concerned with the discipline. They did get control of the Economic History Association and dominated it for a while, which made the annual meetings rather unpleasant for the rest of us.

I was, much later (1968), elected president of this organization, although the Cliometricians had kept me from this honor for some time. The annual meeting at which I delivered my presidential address was held at Brandeis University. We made serious efforts to hold our gatherings at universities and to make use of their facilities for housing and eating in order to keep our expenses down. On this occasion we had plenty of trouble, for one institution which had extended an invitation to us backed out at the last minute and we had to make an emergency switch in our plans.

The meeting did come off, however, and I took advantage of the opportunity afforded me to trace the history of economic history in the period of my professional life. I noted that economic history had begun as an adjunct to political history, that it had gradually developed a *raison d'être* of its own in dealing with the way men provided for their material needs and desires and the problems they encountered in doing so, and that it had to include considerations from man's social, demographic, political, and intellectual sides as they impinged on our economic lives. I concluded by saying that quantitative methods had been employed from the beginning of the discipline and that the Cliometricians were simply adding techniques at providing evidence that had to be employed along with other empirical data. I saw no reason why the two branches of the field should not enrich each other rather than denigrate each other. The chastisement was mild enough, but I think that it did some good. At least, I had many compliments from both camps.

I became president of the Society for French Historical Studies in 1964, and also of the Society for Italian Historical Studies (1972). In these positions I did not have to deliver presidential addresses, but merely to preside over the meetings of the trustees and then of the business meetings of the respective groups. These were not necessarily easy tasks, for even among scholars there were always the prima donnas, the empire builders, and the authoritarians.

I was, however, invited to speak at the annual banquet of the Society for French Historical Studies in Chicagoshortly after I had been president and as I was approaching retirement. On that occasion I spoke about my career in French history—how I came to be interested in the field, where I studied and with whom, how I did my research and writing, how I conducted my seminar and colloquium, how I stood up under my load of work, and how I managed to live with my colleagues. I stressed the fact that the greatest pleasure and satisfaction which I received from my profession came from seeing my students develop, in helping them get established in the profession, and from watching them become productive scholars. My pitch proved to be very apropos, for when I had concluded my statement, my students presented me with a copy of a *Festschrift,* entitled *From the Ancien Régime to the Popular Front*[7], which they had prepared in my honor. No sooner had this presentation been made than it was announced that my students and friends had amassed a fund for the creation of a Clough Prize to be awarded annually toward the publication of the best dissertation in modern European history at Columbia. Indeed, the professional autobiography, which I had presented and which included some of the stories and tidbits contained above, could not have been better timed.

It was on this occasion that I gave some statistics on my activity as a teacher. I estimated that I had faced in my teaching life-time some 5,000 students, given 9,600 lectures, sponsored two hundred and fifty candidates for the M. A. degree in history, attended 1,000 Ph.D. examinations for the degree, carried to the end 100 candidates for the Ph.D. degree, and attended at least, or so it seemed, 100,000 committee meetings of one kind or another. I believe that I saw more people through to the Ph.D. degree in the field of European History than anyone else in America. This was owing in large part to the fact that undergraduate and graduate faculties at Columbia were separated, that Columbia attracted a great number of students who were interested in European history and who had the appropriate language equipment, and that my program for the instruction of graduate students was efficient.

I might add in concluding this chapter that I was never a serious candidate for high office in the American Historical Association. I served on a number of its committees, but I was defeated once for a seat on the Council, which was the stepping stone to the presidency. By the time that I might have been a candidate, I was old enough so that the honor did not fire me up. Besides I refused to solicit support for the post, as was the case with many of those who won it.

7 The title signified the range within modern French history in which my students had published. It was edited by Charles K. Warner and published by the Columbia University Press in 1969.

Chapter XI

The Late Fifties And Early Sixties

In the late 1950s and early '60s, I became conscious that certain changes were taking place in my life. I realized that one of these was in my family—the part that I held most dear. My elder son finished his degree in nuclear engineering at Cornell and came to live with us in New York while he did graduate work in physics at Columbia. He was entering what I call the mating stage. Physically he had been in it for some time, but now he was prepared both psychologically and economically (almost) for the momentous step. He had known several girls during his preparatory school and college days, but he now began to concentrate on one, whom he had met while he was doing his military service. He was a frequent borrower of my twelve cylinder Lincoln, which I had foolishly acquired for $400 because it seemed like such a good buy. Only a blind man would have failed to see that he would soon leave the family nest. He was married June 23, 1956.

My wife was also showing signs of "withdrawal." She began to lose interest in the farm on the ground that "it was too much," although I had always employed a girl to work for us full time during the summer and even brought capable maids from New York to lighten the load. If my memory serves me correctly, my wife went to the farm for only one complete summer after 1960.

She was an excellent teacher of languages—and was proficient in Italian, Spanish, and French. I have never encountered in my career anyone who could teach languages as well as she. Thus, when we were in this country, she could easily find a post for the summer. For the most part in the 1960s, she was employed to teach Italian at the Middlebury College language school. This was only a hundred miles from the farm, so that she "visited" us at least once per summer. On one occasion she even brought twenty-four others with her! If we were in Europe, she would leave me to pursue her own interests. Then one winter semester she took a group of girls from the college where she was teaching to Europe. Furthermore, as I have said earlier, she did not accompany my younger son and me when we went to the country on weekends, as she had once done. The result was that my younger son and I were often left to shift for ourselves by ourselves. This was difficult for both of us. The moral of the story is that if one wants to keep a family intact, its members must remain together.

Under the conditions which I have just related, life at the farm had its problems, but I did my utmost to cope with them. For one thing, my younger son suffered very badly from hay fever, which meant that he could not work in the fields with the farmers as had his older brother. In fact, for parts of the summer his malady kept him from many bucolic pleasures, like fishing. Swimming and boating were all right, but the lake to which we went was far enough away so that he could not go without me to drive. Hence he was confined to the farm and even to the interior of the house.

I had the good sense at least to find him an occupation. I hired him as my cook. In order to teach him the economics of the home, I allotted him a certain sum a week with the understanding that anything that he could save out of it was his. The result of this arrangement was that *I* was taught a lesson, which was driven home with a vengeance in the very first week. In those seven days we had the cheapest hot dogs, the poorest hamburgers, the most tasteless bread, the thinnest orange juice, and the weakest coffee that was ever faced by man. Talk about a college education to make one smart! At all events we soon worked out another arrangement with a minimum of expenditures and a maximum of what he could gain per week. With that we sailed merrily on. What was particularly gratifying to me was that the boy became a great cook, yes, a great chef, and has remained so even to the present day.

Passing the summer alone with me was not, however, all joy for him. I set aside my summers for writing, and writing requires that one has to be alone and undisturbed for long periods of time. This meant that the boy had little companionship during the day and was even shooed away if he came to my study. He could, of course, do a great amount of reading and this he did, but I knew that he was lonesome. Of an evening I would read aloud to him, perhaps *Tom Sawyer* or *Huckleberry Finn* or *David Harum*, but he craved younger company and took to going to the neighbors after supper. Then I was the one who was lonesome.

I tried many devices to alleviate the strains and one thing was successful (in addition to cooking). I bought him a model A Ford that was in poor enough condition so that it was necessary for him to work on it most of the time. In order to make it presentable, he had to do a lot of body work on it and to have it go, he had to make interminable repairs. Because he was too young, he could not get a driver's license and so driving was confined to the land of the farm. He learned to drive well and also learned how to avoid, or get out of, all manner of scrapes. On one occasion when he parked, he failed to set the brake; the car took off; and he had to rescue it from the top of one of Vermont's ubiquitous stonewalls. Another time, he got stuck in a soft spot and had to jack it a little at a time and insert boards under the wheel until he had enough under it so that he could drive off. And still another episode of the same nature resulted from getting the car wedged between the barn and a tree. Experience is a good teacher, if one is willing to learn, and he was willing. He never gets stuck any more and can fix almost anything about a car.

The summers at the farm were, however, memorable ones and did a lot to shape his life and mine. My work at Columbia was as heavy as I have earlier described it to have been, and maybe heavier. I was sponsoring students for the Ph. D. in both Italian and Spanish history as well as in French history. This meant that I had to be up in two areas. This having been the case, I was always on the lookout for opportunities of employment that would take me away from Morningside Heights—and to Europe. Such opportunities did arise from time to time and ultimately one that I thought highly desirable came along. I was invited to go to Turin, Italy, to teach as a Fulbright professor in the Institute of European Studies, which was associated with the University. Columbia was disposed to let me accept this job, for it was always possible to find a replacement for some of my work and at less salary than I was getting, strange as that may seem.

The Institute of European Studies was supported by local industrialists, particularly Adriano Olivetti, and was devoted to the study of post-war problems. It was staffed by professors from all parts of Western Europe, many of them very distinguished scholars, who were appointed for lengths of time which varied from a week to a month. Students came from various NATO countries and a few from Yugoslavia; all had fellowships which covered their board and rooms. In addition, there were a couple of full-time professors, of whom I was one, who tried to tie the lectures of the visitors together and who gave the examinations at the end of the terms. Finally, there was an administrative group, led by a real organizer, Gustavo Malan, that assembled both professors and students, solicited the necessary funds, and attended to the myriad details involved in such an enterprise.

Thus it came about that I, my wife, and younger son arrived in Turin at the beginning of summer to start another year abroad (1955—1956). We came as early as we did in order to make the necessary arrangements for our living and the boy's schooling. We found an excellent pension in Piazza del Castello, within walking distance of the Institute, and a school, San Giuseppe, which was not far away. With these details settled we looked for a place where we could spend the summer and the boy could perfect his Italian in preparation for the school year. My wife wanted to go to Lake Como, for she was at the time translating *Il Piccolo Mondo Antico* by Antonio Fogazzaro, one of the most famous of Italian novelists of the nineteenth century. She wanted to get to know the "Fogazzaro country" and hence Lake Como. We spent some time in looking for a place and finally took quarters at Dongo, which was not exactly the center of Fogazzaro's activity, but, on the other hand, not far away. Dongo had become famous as the place where Mussolini had been taken prisoner at the end of World War II when he tried to flee to Switzerland.

We remained in this place only one night, for the quarters which we were considering turned out to be over a bus stop and a filling station. What between the peculiar stage bus horns all night and gas pumping and automobile repairs all day, the place was terrible and we went looking for another spot. We thought that we had found a satisfactory one down the leg of the lake toward Como rather than toward Lecco, but when we went in for a swim, we noticed chicken feathers all over the place. Upon inquiry we learned that a poultry slaughter house was located nearby and that the wastes from that place were unceremoniously dumped into the water there and because of this fact and that there is no outlet on that leg of the lake, the water was highly polluted. And lastly, we learned that most of the water used by people around the lake came from the lake itself, albeit from a depth that is supposed to be free from the surface pollution. At all events, we were turned off from Italy's lake country, dramatically beautiful as it may be, and we headed for the Mediterranean, where the sea water would be less contaminated. We ended up at Marina di Massa, where we settled in for what turned out to be a very pleasant summer.

In the fall we went to Perugia for a session at the university for Fulbrighters. This consisted of courses in Italian literature, art, language, and politics and I became a schoolboy again. I cannot say that I enjoyed that experience, for I had been in the academic driver's seat too long. Moreover, the Fulbright organizers placed us around the town in families. We were put in a house which was located next to the town dump. Here refuse burned continually and gave off an acrid smoke that was awful. Then, too, the water supply system of Perugia had been destroyed during the war and repairs had gone so slowly that the town was on short water rations. On waterless days, we had to fill the bathtub before seven in the morning and then dip it out even to flush the toilet. Lastly, Perugia is a hill town, that is, the center of activity is on top of a hill, and we were located at the foot. For all our business affairs we had steep streets to climb.

Eventually this ordeal came to an end, as do all ordeals in one way or another, and we went on to Turin. The town is located between mountains and plains, which is an admirable situation. The students were interesting and colleagues from great universities were inspiring. There I made lifelong friends with individuals like Erich Schneider of the University of Kiel, Herman Wold of the University of Uppsala, Henry Laufenberger of the Law School of the University of Paris, Robert Pelloux of the University of Lyons, Carlo Cippolla of the University of Pavia, Jan Tinbergen of the Netherlands, and many more. To discuss Europe's problems with men like these was very useful for my own understanding and for my teaching at Columbia.

Life in Turin was also very good. The Italian radio and television monopoly, RAI, sponsored a symphony orchestra that was excellent; traveling theatrical groups appeared frequently; and the Academy of Turin provided lectures by leading statesmen from various countries.

Perhaps, however, the greatest thing about our winter was the skiing that my son and I were able to do. Every weekend that the weather permitted we took off for the mountains, trying out one place after another. We finally concentrated our activity on Sestriere, for the town had abundant facilities for lodging and eating and all levels of ski-runs. My wife seldom joined us on these junkets, for she did not ski. For her part, she was engaged by our cultural attaché at the American Embassy to go around the country lecturing about America and the American woman. She was gone so much that my son and I shared a room and my wife had another room for the short periods which she was with us.

My son made great progress in Italian and received good marks at school, but for the first time I began to realize, at least in part, that what I thought were great opportunities for him to learn foreign languages and to get to know foreign lands had their disadvantages as well as their advantages. He was moved about so much that he had little chance to make close friends, just a mass of acquaintances.

During the Easter recess, which was long by our standards, we planned a trip to Greece. My wife was to make the arrangements, but failed to do so with the result that I had to make them at the last moment and without very much information as to travel possibilities. The final itinerary was to go to Brindisi by train and from there take a boat, the "Angelica," which made a trip through many of the islands for a week. The "Angelica" turned out to be a very ancient vessel that had been built for the Alaskan run during the Klondike gold rush. In the course of time it failed to meet the United States' Maritime Service standards and was bought by a Greek shipper. The ship was not only of an early vintage, but it had all the odors of all its years and acquired new ones with every docking.

At first things went well enough. Our first stop was at Corfu and I learned that this area was a favorite stamping ground of the late Hohenzollerns, a choice which raised that family in my estimation for taste. From there we went to Athens via the Corinth Canal and I saw where the ships in ancient times had been dragged overland across the peninsula—a no mean feat. The canal is cut through stone and was barely wide enough to accommodate our vessel. We finally arrived at Piraeus, the port of Athens which is a place teeming with activity. I had difficulty in believing that only a century and a quarter previously Lord Byron had written that he had ridden his horse down to the beach at Piraeus from Athens, then with a population of some 6,000, for a swim.

Athens and, indeed, all Greece turned out to be quite different from what I had imagined it to be. The capital is a modern city with very few remians from antiquity except for the Acropolis, which was blown up during the siege of the city by the Venetians in 1688, and the Agora, or ancient market place (it was in the process of being restored when we were there). The Acropolis is especially beautiful with its Parthenon and the Erechtheum with its porch of Caryatids. There one feels the presence of the ancients. Their greatness was driven home to us by a representation of *Seven against Thebes* by Aeschylus, which we saw in the theater of Dionysius close by. Although we did not understand the language of the play, the power of this work came through to us, in part, perhaps, from the knowledge that this was where the Greek theater developed.

I was greatly impressed by the fact that the influence of Byzantium, which was dominant in Athens in the first part of the Middle Ages, was so much in evidence. Constantinople's style of architecture, particularly in Greek Orthodox churches, is more frequently encountered than remains from the ancient period. I was also amazed by the amount of Venetian influence to be seen, particularly in fortresses along the coast, which stem from the period of Venetian domination from the end of the fourteenth century to the coming of the Turks in 1456.

Subsequently we went to Delphi, which has a charm of its own, but which requires considerable study in order to reconstruct the ruins in the mind's eye and to know enough of ancient history to comprehend the importance of the place in ancient times. On the way to Delphi the road is very narrow, runs through mountains, and has innumerable precipices which the driver seemed to cherish as a means of showing how close he could come to the edge without going over. If this were not enough to make one believe that the end was near, the travel authorities served meals en route that always began with raw shell fish and which always remained on the tables for some time, because we were always behind schedule. My son and I got deathly sick from eating these things, which curtailed our sight-seeing most severely. But we did manage to get to the theater at Epidaurus with its extraordinary acoustics and to get into the countryside where we witnessed threshing by driving rollers over the grain—rollers drawn by oxen—spinning with the spinning stick and pottery making on the wheel, just as one sees them on ancient amphora.

Our visit to Athens was made especially difficult by the fact that my Greek was almost nonexistent and when I spelled out painstakingly the name of some street with my knowledge of the alphabet limited to the letters of college fraternities the name was usually Plato Street, or Churchill Square, or something equally simple. When one travels, it is a good idea to know the language of the country in which one is or to have some one close by who knows the language.

After our visit to Athens had come to a conclusion, we embarked once more on the "Angelica" and went to Knossos, Crete, where we visited the remains of the Cretan civilization, which contributed so much to Greece. We, like everyone who visits the place, became intrigued by the suddenness with which this civilization came to an end. Then we visited several of the Greek islands, many of which had been temporary stopping places of Ulysses. In fact, after seeing most of them, we could understand why he kept on going.

As we docked and took on cargo and passengers at one port after another, the odors became ever more varied and pungent. The peak of our odoriferous experience was reached when at the same stop snails for the Paris market and goats for God knows whom were stowed next to our cabin. In the case of the goats, they were stabled with their sterns toward us. Not only was this unbearable, but my wife hit the ceiling and I thought would kill the captain. But she did get the cabin changed! A British physician whom we had met on board, jumped ship at this point. He could stand it no longer.

We arrived back in Turin somewhat the worse for wear, but we survived and I completed my assignment by late spring. We enjoyed the spring in the Alps again with their blankets of daffodils and jonquils. We left eventually for Rome, where I had to have an operation for a hernia, which I had acquired from putting a heavy valise on top of our car. Having an operation in a foreign land is an event itself. The first thing is to find a private "clinic," for middle-class people usually go to such establishments for their surgical needs. These institutions are small, have limited facilities, and are usually run by religious orders or medical entrepreneurs. The one I chose, San Domenico, was managed by an order from Piedmont, which made me feel at home. Once the clinic is selected, then one goes about the problem of choosing a surgeon. From investigating clinics, I had learned who were the surgeons operating in the most selective of all the institutions. I deduced that the one most employed by them must be all right. So I settled on such a one and the date was set for the event.

Going to a hospital like an Italian clinic is different from anything which I had experienced in America. When I arrived at the hospital, the Mother Superior visited me to talk about this and that. When one topic was exhausted, we moved on to another and finally we discussed finances. When that subject had been covered, the conversation went to questions of how I would get along at the clinic. In this area the Mother Superior asked me whether or not I smoked, and when I replied that I did, she said, "Professor, here we do *not* smoke." To which I replied, "Reverend Mother, here are my cigarettes." I have not smoked from that day to this, which meant that those authoritarian words from the Mother Superior resulted in enough savings in one year to cover the expenses of the operation many times over. Moreover, the reform meant that I had much less throat trouble than I had had for years.

The stay in the hospital was in itself interesting. Everything was à la carte, European Plan. Towels were so much each. And for other than standard food or wine which was served, a supplementary charge was made. The pay-off, however, was the following. As most people know, a patient is usually constipated after ether, and I was no exception. When the measures taken proved to be of no avail and more time than I thought appropriate had gone by, I asked why they had not given me an enema. The reply was quick and certain: "We did not think that you would want to stand the expense."

Similarly on cold days, I asked for heat and they said that I could have it if I paid so and so much! That I was willing to do. As to the surgery, however, I thought that it was excellent. As to the costs: When I sent the bills to the Blue Cross-Blue Shield organization, they were disallowed on the ground, they claimed, that I had had the condition for a long time before I was insured. This statement was made without any evidence. Fortunately, I had been required to have a physical examination before I took the Fulbright Fellowship and the hernia had not shown in the report. With that evidence Blue Cross-Blue Shield made the payments, but their earlier ruling had weakened my faith in their mode of operation.

After I had regained my strength, I turned my attention to my next writing project, which was intended to be an economic history of Western culture. I made a publishing contract for it with Thomas Y. Crowell, through the auspices of Lois Cole. The *Economic History of Europe* which I had done for Heath with the brother of Lois, Charles W. Cole, needed revision and my collaborator did not want to do his share of the work. So we agreed to let the book die, and Heath indicated that this was all right with them. So I went to work and worked very diligently. As the writing progressed, I realized that the story which I was producing was largely the economic history of Western Europe. I tried to introduce the economic history of the United States, Canada, Latin America, and Eastern Europe, but this seemed ancillary in comparison with the innovative developments in Western Europe.

I made good progress with this book, which was considerably different from the one I had done with Cole. It began in ancient times, took in more of the world, came down to the present, and introduced new subjects like population growth. When I returned to the States, I continued with it and finally submitted it to Crowell. By that time Lois Cole had left Crowell and the new editor very cavalierly turned the manuscript down. The work was mine, however, and I took it to McGraw-Hill, who accepted it with alacrity. It soon became the standard of its kind, was translated into several foreign languages, and went through many editions.[1] I could see that it would be valuable to me after retirement as a source of income. Fortunately my estimate of the earning power of this work turned out to be accurate.

My work at Columbia went on, as I have already

---

[1] It was first published in 1959 under the title of *The Economic Development of Western Civilization.* The edition which came out in 1975 was revised by Richard T. Rapp, and published as *European Economic History.* The editors of McGraw-Hill wanted me to take on a young man as a collaborator in order to keep the book up-to-date after I was no longer able to do so. The choice of Rapp was an excellent one, but he soon left teaching for the investment business!

described it, and I continued to look for periods of relief. Eventually the time came for another sabbatical and I applied to the Rockefeller Foundation for a grant-in-aid to allow me to be absent from teaching for an entire year. Sabbatical leaves were granted for a half year at full pay or a full year at half-pay. My project this time was to write an *Economic History of Italy*, for I wanted to go to Italy in order to be where my wife wanted to go for her studies. The Rockefeller Foundation granted me the money which I requested and we prepared to be off again for 1961-1962.

Before we left I had an opportunity, which I thought that I should not ignore. John Walden, an editor from D. C. Heath in Boston had been after me for a long time to write a textbook on Western European history. The books which they had on their list in this field were not going very well and their former editor of a series—Alan Nevins—did not seem to be willing to get new titles. I kept stalling on the matter, but one day of the spring of 1961, Mr. Walden said to me: 'How are we ever going to get any good textbooks if you experienced scholars refuse to write them." This stunned me—it gave me a pause. After some reflection, I asked him if he would be interested in a book written by a group of scholars whom I would choose, provided that I planned the book and saw to it that my authors actually turned out good manuscripts. I thought that in this way I could help a group of young scholars who had studied with me, or at least had been at Columbia, for young people in our profession need recognition by writing and most of all need more money. I had, also, the further thought that in this way Walden would get his textbook without my surrendering my research plans and I would have an added income when I reached retirement. So it was agreed.

I selected my authors with care and chose those who had shown in their graduate work that they were capable of producing. They included Nina Garsoian, then of Smith College; David Hicks of New York University; David Brandenburg of American University; Peter Gay of Columbia; and Stanley Payne of Wisconsin.[2] I figured how many classroom hours there were in a normal college year and planned that there would be a given number of pages (a chapter or a half chapter) for each of these hours. I thought that there should be enough maps so that students would not have to buy an historical atlas; that there should be introductions to each section and at their conclusion, summaries; that the bibliographies should be adequate to meet the needs of graduate students but that the level of sophistication should be what was wanted in the first or second year of the better colleges; that the book should be in paperback and priced so that we could beat all competition on price; and that the book should come out in one, two, or three volumes so that the teacher could use it at least for part of his course. The ancient and medieval parts constituted one volume, the period from the Renaissance to Napoleon, another, and the nineteenth and twentieth centuries, a third. Lastly, I made an arrangement for royalties which was very favorable, with the percentage going to authors increasing with the volume of sales. Each author's share was to be determined by the number of chapters which he wrote and each chapter had a limit on the number of pages to be devoted to it.

My choice of authors turned out to be a happy one, for finished manuscripts began to come in very shortly. They were of a high calibre and followed my general philosophy of history in that they attempted to integrate economic, political, social, and intellectual history of the Western World into a related whole.

As soon as the details of this enterprise had been completed, my wife, my younger son, and I took off. My plan this time was to go to Northeastern Italy, which I knew less well than Central Italy, and to work closely with Carlo De Cugis, an assistant to Gino Luzzatto, the Dean of Italian economic historians. In fact, Luzzatto was engaged in writing in the same period as I and had agreed to share information with me. Inasmuch as Luzzatto lived in Venice and De Cugis spent the summers at the Lido, I decided to go to the Lido at once and to Milan in the fall. This did not meet with the

---

[2] We added other authors later, Otto Pflanze of Minnesota, Robert E. Frykenberg of Wisconsin, and G. Wesley Johnson of the University of California, Santa Barbara. As can be seen, I tried to get geographical distribution in the list and aimed at persons teaching in places where the text might be adopted in large numbers.

approval of my wife, who wanted to go to Rome and did. As for the younger son, we planned that he go to Innsbruck to add German to the French, Italian, and Spanish, which he already commanded. This did not meet with *his* approval, for he was in love with a young lady from whom he thought he could not be absent. So the year of leave began very inauspiciously from a family point of view.

Our flight to Europe was on a Columbia University charter that was exceedingly crowded, but was very cheap. We arrived in Paris, and my wife left immediately for Italy. My son and I took possession of a Volkswagen, which I had ordered in New York, for I had fallen for the propaganda that here was a car to end one's automobile trouble. He and I were to go to Innsbruck via Nancy, Strassburg, the Black Forest, and Lichtenstein. We had covered only some hundred and fifty miles, when my son, who was driving in the hopes that this would take his mind off his girl friend, reported that he was losing the brakes. The first breakdown of the Volkswagen! We limped into Nancy and to the Volkswagen garage. Upon investigation, the mechanic decided that the tube from the brake fluid reservoir, which was plastic and located under the front hood, was loose and in characteristically nationalist tones remarked, "These Boches don't know how to put the parts of a good car together." He pushed the tube on the reservoir a little more firmly and then filled the reservoir with new brake fluid.

We took off again, quite merrily. All went well until we approached Strassburg and the brake pedal began to go soft again. Once more we limped to a Volkswagen garage and related our former experience. This time the mechanic probed more deeply and discovered that there was a hole in the plastic reservoir for brake fluid. So he replaced the thing, and sent us on our way rejoicing, more or less. Anyhow after that the brakes held, but the Volkswagen was a disaster. It had to be tuned up every thousand miles or it sounded like a coffee grinder; the motor had to be overhauled at 6,000 miles because some part was defective; and eventually an accident to the front end resulted in an expenditure of over $250.00 because the steering apparatus cannot be straightened—it has to be replaced.

After Strassburg we had no more trouble with the brakes. We went to Freiburg-im-Breisgau, which was a charming town before the war, but which had been badly bombed at the very end of the conflict, and then on to Lichtenstein. I enjoyed this enclave in Europe very much, for it seemed so free of international tensions. There we bought a fancy camera for my son, for he was an enthusiastic photographer. Eventually we reached Innsbruck and made arrangements for his summer. I found an old friend, Mrs. Reut-Niccolusi, the widow of a professor at the University, who was running a pension for students, which I thought would be a good place, but my son did not like it. I then found a private room for him and helped him to get a job taking care of some boys, which I thought would aid him in learning German. Unfortunately this did not work out well, nor did the whole summer. He made the acquaintance of a young lady who wanted to learn English and spent most of his time escorting her around. I only discovered this later on when not enough time was left to do anything about it.

From Innsbruck, I drove on to Venice and took a room in a small hotel at the Lido where I could walk and swim. This was a good arrangement and I worked well. Both De Cugis and Luzzatto were of great assistance to me. I was uneasy, however, for I missed my wife who insisted on staying in Rome and I worried about my son.

After a couple of months at the Lido of Venice, I went to the Villa Serbelloni on Lake Como. This is a beautiful place on a promontory that partially divides the Lake in two. The property commands stunning views of the Lake and of the not-distant Alps.

The Princess Serbelloni, an American by origin and without issue, had willed this property to the Rockefeller Foundation with the proviso that the Foundation should maintain it in its previous condition in perpetuity. The Foundation had a white elephant on its hands, but did the best it could with it. The place was used for meetings of scholars and for writers who wanted a spot where they could work without being disturbed.

I knew the name Serbelloni, for one of the ancestors of the late Prince had served Napoleon after his first invasion of Italy.

The Serbellonis were of the house of Thurn und Taxis, which had had a monopoly of the postal carrying service in the Holy Roman Empire. Much to my surprise they continued to have a franking privilege in many countries because of this fact. I was glad to go to the Villa because my very good friend Garrett Mattingly, who was desperately ill, was there. It was the last time I was to be with him.

The Villa was a good place to write, but it was an American enclave and not ideal for one working in Italian affairs. Furthermore, my wife refused to join me at the Villa and I was very upset at her action, and the Villa and Foundation were very put out about it, for they had reserved a space for her.

I went up to Innsbruck a couple of times to visit my son and discovered that he was not profiting so much from his opportunity as I had expected that he would. There was little that I could do about it, and he assured me that he was learning the language. On those trips I usually went through the Brenner Pass, but on one occasion to vary the route I went over the Stelvio Pass, which is the highest wagon road in Europe (9,049 feet). In the middle of August there was so much snow at the summit that the National Ski School was doing a land-office business. I was glad that I had taken this route in spite of a terrific number of hairpin curves, for it allowed me to visit for the first time the charming town of Merano. I would not, however, recommend the Stelvio except to the stout of heart.

When the summer was over my son went back to New York to begin his college education. He had decided upon Columbia as the place to go. I feared that he had chosen this place because he knew that I, as a faculty member, would not have to pay tuition for him. To free him of any consideration of this kind I had made it clear that he might go anywhere and that any sums which he saved me by going to Columbia would be given him upon graduation to go to graduate school or to go into business.

Undoubtedly I made a mistake in leaving him on his own that freshman year, but I felt that he was ready to assume responsibilities of this kind. Indeed, I now am of the opinion that parents frequently give their children responsibilities before they have the experience to assume them with profit.

As for myself, I moved to Milan in the fall and worked very hard on my economic history of Italy. My wife remained in Rome and I thought that our marriage was nearing the breaking point. With the issue at a climax, my wife came to Milan and pleaded with me to continue our marriage. She seemed sincere and I agreed to try once more to make a go of it. By this time, I had finished what I had to do in the north and moved to Rome with her.

My intellectual life in Rome was very pleasant. I had come to know well several leading historians, economists, and political scientists—Rosario Romeo, Leone Valsecchi, Guglielmo Negri, Luciano Morando, Salvatore Villari, Amintore Fanfani, Ugo Papi, Charles Verlinden, and many more—and they went out of their way to help me, both in my work and in my social life. In addition I came to know Max Hartwell of Oxford very well and he criticized my manuscript as I went along—and so, too, did Rosario Romeo.

We also had several friends visit us from the States. Among these was Grayson Kirk, President of Columbia, and his wife. When his cable arrived saying that he wanted to see me, I was certain that something was in the air. It turned out that he wanted me to become the director of the Casa Italiana at Columbia, which had been under a cloud during the war. I was not at all sure that I wanted to assume this task, for I was aware that members of the Italian department at Columbia had been divided about the administration of the place. Kirk proved to be persuasive, however, and I agreed to take on the assignment.

During the summer we went to a beach not far from Rome, Lido di Lavinio, where we had very good accommodations in the Villa delle Sirene. This was the area where Ulysses is supposed to have been lured ashore by the Sirenes—hence the name of our place. Here I wrote from morning to night, except for an occasional swim, and finally had a manuscript to show publishers. Rosario Romeo helped me to place it with Cappelli of Bologna and I was successful in making arrangements with the Columbia University Press to bring it out in the United States.

One incident marred the rather idyllic stay at the

beach. Along the shore of the Mediterranean in this particular region there is a very poisonous fish, which buries itself in the sand and sticks a dorsal fin straight upwards. If one happens to step on this fin, one gets a shot of poison that is similar to the venom of a cobra. I had made fun of the Italians who told me about the agonies occasioned by this fish. Pride (or a superior stance) goeth before a fall! One fine day I stepped on this miserable fish. Immediately I knew what I had done and immediately went to the *bagnino* (life guard) for the well-known remedy of ammonia.

I thought that I had done all that was necessary and kept on swimming. Soon the pain came on—a pain the like of which I had never known. Bee stings, burns, broken bones were nothing compared to it. I had enough sense to go to my room, but once there I was in real agony. The only remedy which was at hand was whiskey. I took a good slug of that, and when it had had no obvious effect, I took another, and then another. At last a call went out for a doctor, for the pain was such that I cried out when it hit the peak of spasms. When he came, he gave me shot of something, without asking any questions. Whatever it was that he administered turned out to be incompatible with whiskey. I was soon unconscious and remained so for hours. When I finally returned to some semblance of consciousness, I had an urgent need to go to the toilet. My wife helped me get there, but once inside I passed out for good and opened a mean gash on my forehead. According to later accounts three persons were necessary to get me back to my room. Eventually the pain wore off (and also the medication, if one can call it that) and I seemed none the worse for my experience. I had, however, an enormous appetite that remained with me for days. I do not, however, recommend wounds of this kind as an appetizer. Martinis are to be preferred.

The following year was a difficult one. The directorship of the Casa Italiana turned out to be more unpleasant than I had imagined possible. One of the members of the Italian department had wanted the post very badly and did not make things easy for me. Furthermore, my instructions were to get some cultural activity into a house that had remained dormant for some time. I did that, but the life of an impresario without funds is a tough one. I did manage to raise some money through gifts; I put on concerts for which I could charge a fee; and I held an auction of works of art contributed by Italian artists. On this last occasion it stormed severely the night of the event, so few persons turned up. I had to do a considerable amount of bidding and buying myself to prevent the sale from being a disaster. My wife put on plays with her students; I received the collaboration of some singers for concerts (Lisa Albanese of the Metropolitan Opera was most gracious); and Columbia University's symphony gave a Vivaldi concert that attracted so many people that I had to pipe the music to adjoining halls in order to accommodate everyone.

I also had a great number of lectures, and some of them were real tests of my equilibrium. The first that I sponsored was by Achille Lauro, the then Mayor of Naples, owner of the Home Lines and of the Neapolitan football team. I thought that he would be an excellent drawing card and I gave his talk considerable publicity. By the appointed hour the house was full, including the Dean of the Graduate Faculties, who was to receive him. But no Mayor appeared. An hour went by, during which I tried to hold my audience, most of whom were accustomed to the lateness of Italians, being of Italian descent themselves. Two hours went by and no Mayor, and my efforts at providing diversions were exhausted. Two hours and a half late the man appeared in tow of the Italian Consul General, who later confided to me that the reason for the tardiness was that he was showing the Mayor Columbia University!

The next lecture was to be by Max Ascoli, who at that time was editing a journal of political opinion and who had married a very wealthy American woman. I was anxious to get Max interested in the Casa, for not only was he a man of culture but a person who could be very helpful financially, if he wanted to be. Unfortunately he had been a resident at the Casa, which at its beginning had provided visiting Italian students with rooms, and had had a feud with Giuseppe Prezzolini, the first director of the Casa.

In order to have everything go smoothly I had Max and his wife to dinner at the Faculty Club before the lecture. We had a very good dinner and made our way to the lecture hall of the Casa in good spirits. When we arrived, the place was full, but in the front row with venom in his eye was Prezzolini! Max took one look at him and said to me that he would not enter the same room in which *questo matto* sat. Max's wife and I went to work and finally convinced Max that this was exactly what Prezzolini wanted—to discourage the appearance of his enemy. So Max gave his lecture with his hands shaking quite perceptibly. Prezzolini took notes assiduously with the apparent intention of writing a scathing newspaper article about what was said. Indeed, Prezzolini wrote for *Il Borghese* in Italy, which was a sheet of reaction with vile diatribes against anyone it did not like. So far as I know he never wrote such an article against Ascoli, but he did about a colleague whom he described as "a sausage casing filled with mud," which gives some idea of his style. Max escaped from such a wrath, but he never came back to the Casa.

Then there was the time when Benedetto Croce died and I thought that it would be a good idea to have an evening at the Casa devoted to the thought and influence of Croce. I invited Irwin Edman to give a brief sketch of Croce's esthetics. I got Leopold Arnaud, a former director of the Casa Italiana and Dean of the School of Architecture, to give a brief statement of Croce's ideas of art. I asked Prezzolini to speak about Croce as a statesman. And I volunteered to say a few words about Croce's philosophy. All went well and the house was full. But, the next day I received a communication from Prezzolini to the effect that I had made a mistake in saying that Croce became anti-Fascist at the time of the Matteotti murder. He insisted that the change came *after* that murder. I did not think that I was so wrong and wrote him to that effect. He replied that as an historian I should have a sense of time, that the change came *after* the murder. This went on for some letters until enough had been written to prompt Prezzolini to propose that we publish our dialogue in a small book. To this idea, I replied that the exchange had not interested me, that I could not believe that it would interest any number of readers, and that we should bring the whole episode to a conclusion by burying or burning our letters, whichever he preferred. I still have my collection, but the public has never seen them. What he did with his, I do not know.

After a year and a half at the Casa, I decided that I should retire from that job at the end of the second year, and I did. I had made some good friends in the Italian community of New York, which was compensation enough for the efforts which I had expended. I also heightened my interests in the history of Italy. My *Economic History of Modern Italy* came out in 1964 (with an Italian translation) and was a big success in both the United States and Italy. This prompted me to prepare with a former student, Salvatore Saladino of Queens College, *A History of Modern Italy, Documents, Readings, and Commentary*, published in 1968. It also did very well but was priced so high by the Columbia University Press that it did not sell widely and could hardly be afforded by students as a text.

Also as a corollary to my stint at the Casa, I was decorated by the Italian government as a Cavalliere of the Order of Merit of the Italian Republic. The "ceremony" at the Consulate in New York was a curious affair. I simply went to the office of the Consul General with no one in attendance except my brother Reginald and the decoration was slipped to me almost under the desk as though it were a dirty picture. I think that the consul was dressed down for this, for subsequently a large reception was given me at the Italian Center of Italian culture, presided over by the cultural attaché.

The decoration itself is a curious thing. The rosette in Italian colors has a design on it that looks for all the world like a crown, but is actually a castle of the Renaissance with its towers which stand up like points on a crown. The story goes that the design was made by a former monarchist and that he slipped this over on a wager. The first time that I wore this in Italy, where it was not well known, a street salesman of glassware spoke to me in English and when I remonstrated with him that I was an Italian and could he not know this from the insignia which I wore, he replied, "Oh, I thought that was the insignia of the Home Lines" (a shipping line of Naples). I was terribly deflated.

The other corollary of my sojourn at the Casa was that I established at the end of my stay a "university seminar" in modern

Italian affairs. It brought together scholars in the fields of history, government, and economics from universities from Harvard to Rochester, New York, and to Washington. We met once a month and had papers read and issues discussed. On one occasion we had an international congress with distinguished colleagues from England and Italy. The papers given on this occasion were edited by Edward R. Tannenbaum and Emiliana P. Noether and published under the title *A History of Modern Italy* (1968).

Chapter XII

More Of The Nineteen Sixties: Southern Italy And The Near East

Soon after I had finished my term as Director of the Casa Italiana, I was offered still another appointment to teach abroad, this time also in Italy. In my many contacts with Italy, I had a particularly warm friendship with Luigi De Rosa, then on the staff of the School of Commerce and Economics of the University at Bari. He invited me to come to Bari to teach and made this financially possible by arranging a N.A.T.O. fellowship for me and by getting the University of Bari to provide me with living quarters and other prerogatives.

This was a great opportunity to get to know Southern Italy, and especially La Puglia. I had discovered that my early urge to travel had waned for areas with which I was already acquainted but could easily be brought back to full vigor by going to regions new to me. I retained my curiosity to get acquainted with things that were foreign to me and my interest in other cultures had been whetted by my writing *The Rise and Fall of Civilization* and *The Basic Values of Western Culture*. If I were at Bari, I reasoned, a trip to the Near East would not be too much to envisage and travel there would provide knowledge that would be useful in the next revision of the textbook I had with D. C. Heath.

Not only did the acceptance of the offer seem

attractive professionally, but I thought also that it would not create any family disruptions. My elder son was married, as I have said, and had a job with long-range stability as a basic research physicist in the Air Force. My younger son had a position in the "back office" of a brokerage house in Wall Street, which seemed to assure him of a lifelong profession. My wife was teaching, to be sure, but I knew that for any chance to go to Italy she would arrange a leave of absence and would be with me. Thus I decided to accept the post offered me.

My sojourn in Bari was most delightful (1966-1967). The guest suite at the University which I had was very comfortable. I was given the privilege of eating in the professors' dining room of the university's commons, which was cheap and good. I had full use of the library which was in the same building as my suite. Lastly and not least importantly, my duties were not onerous.

It is *de rigueur* in an assignment like the one I had, as I had found out in Paris, to give an inaugural lecture. Such was arranged for me; and I spent a considerable amount of time in the preparation of it. I even had my Italian text checked by a local professor to be sure that I had no mistakes in it. A big crowd turned out for the event and all went well until I left my prepared manuscript and began to speak extemporaneously in the hopes of being more effective. Unfortunately, I used a colloquialism which I had learned in New York and which had a hidden meaning of which I was quite ignorant. I wanted to say that I came to Bari as a scholar and not as a propagandist for the United States or to stir up trouble. What I actually said was "Non vengo per rompere le scatole," which is literally "I come not to break boxes," but which has another sense of not breaking maidenheads. One can imagine the hilarity and my own embarrassment, although at the moment I did not understand the error which I had made.

My inaugural lecture made me well known throughout the Faculty and for that matter, throughout the town. After the *gaffe* which I made, I had a good attendance whenever I lectured. These lectures were mostly in the regular classes of professors, who were always glad to have me available, for they were frequently forced to be absent because of other duties.

These "other duties" were usually giving oral examinations to individual students. In fact, these tests were the way in which students in Italy moved up the academic ladder. The process is written into law and professors have no chance of circumventing it. With so many persons going to universities (in part to enjoy rights, privileges, and prerogatives granted students), and with students having a legal right to try the exams several times, professors are swamped. Moreover, professors often have other employment than at a university to eke out their existences, which makes them less available to students than they otherwise would be. Lastly, many instructors do not live in the towns where they teach, but commute from distant places, which takes a lot of travel. For example Professor De Rosa, who lived in Naples, taught not only at Bari but also in a university which was being established at Pescara. I went there once to lecture for him and was worn out by the long train trip.

I enjoyed my work at Bari very much, the people whom I met, and the Puglia in general. Professor De Rosa and others were most hospitable and were forever taking me to see the sights and to enjoy the excellent food of the region, especially the seafood. The town of Bari, which was growing very fast as part of the Italian "miracle" of the time, has a few architectural gems, especially the Cathedral, the Basilica of St Nicholas, and other mementoes of St. Nicholas.[1]

During the spring recess, my wife and I went on a trip to the Eastern Mediterranean, as I had hoped we would. Many of my former students were scattered around the Near East and I let them know that we were coming. Meeting them and being entertained by

---

[1]The remains of St. Nicholas are buried at Bari. To him is attributed the saving of a ship carrying boys across the Adriatic and thus he became the saint of voyagers and of the giving of gifts at Christmas time. I enjoyed particularly the churches at nearby Andria, Molfetta, Trani, and Barletta. Near Andria is the famous castle of Frederick II, Castel del Monte, which commands an excellent view, and to the south of Bari is the picturesque town of Alberobello, whose characteristic form of architecture is the *trullo,* (houses, a church, and even a hotel), which has as a roof, a cupola ending in a point, something like a Persian type of tent. It is said that this form of building goes back to prehistoric times, but whether or not this is ture, the *trulli,* painted white, give the town a very distinctive air and one that is exceedingly beautiful.

them made our trip more pleasant than it otherwise would have been.

Our first stop was Istanbul, where we were to be the guests of Pierre Oberling, now at Hunter College. He was then the director of the American Research Center and well known throughout the city. He and his wife were most gracious in their hospitality and rolled out the red carpet for us. As I have said, visits to new places gave me a thrill, and Istanbul was certainly a city that was entirely new to me. The town is situated on the route from the Mediterranean to the Black Sea and is consequently very cosmopolitan. In the harbor one sees the flags of many nations and on land one encounters people from every part of the world.

Some of Istanbul's sights were not what I had expected. For example, the Golden Horn, that I had envisaged as a most beautiful spot, was more like the Bronx River at its worst, than anything else I could bring to mind. Fortunately, a rather attractive place was not far away, a section known as "Pierre Loti," after the French novelist. This reminded me that the influence of Turkey had been very strong on the culture of France in the Romantic period, especially on Pierre Loti and on Delacroix.

We "experienced" Turkish food and drink; we visited many mosques; and we learned how solicitous Molems are for sick animals, as witness the area in front of the Süleymaniye Mosque which is filled with sick birds.

The most beautiful structures of the city are, in my judgment, the Aya Sofia, which antedates St. Peter's in Rome by a thousand years and is one of the architectural wonders of the world, and the Blue Mosque, which is close by. I came to know both of these structures very well because the American Research Center, where we stayed, was just below them. Nowadays muadhdins, the ones who call the faithful to prayers, do not climb the tall minarets to perform their functions but turn on loud-speakers from down below. Such was the case in the Blue Mosque and in Aya Sofia, and also in several other places close by the Center. The result was that the calls to prayer went on incessantly, or so it seemed, and were disturbing to both work and sleep.

From Istanbul we flew to Beirut, which had been

praised to the skies by my colleague at Columbia in Near Eastern economic history, Charles Issawi. Beirut is located on a narrow plain by the sea, against a back-drop of high mountains that rise abruptly behind it. The place has no artistic treasures of any great note, but it is interesting, or was then, as a banking and commercial center. From Beirut we went to Damascus. The route took us up the high mountains to the east along a road that was a series of hairpin turns, So sharp were they that several trucks had overturned before our arrival. Such accidents occur, to be sure, because the Lebanese pile freight on them until the trucks are very top-heavy.

At the height of the mountains we found very good skiing (this was April) and beyond that a very fertile and lush valley which was in sharp contrast to the more barren land that we had seen hitherto. We went on to Baalbek, which is famous for its Greek ruins, and then to Damascus, a not very noteworthy city, and yet full of sites of Biblical lore and famous for its Grand Bazaar. A bazaar, incidentally, is a collection of many small, individually owned sections or shops placed under one roof. It is characterized by its noise and smell. We would have liked to go on to Palmyra to see the remains of many ancient civilizations and to the Krak de Chevaliers, which was built at the time of the crusades and which, it is said, was large enough to take in 5,000 men and horses. Unfortunately our available time did not permit these excursions.

From Beirut we flew to Jerusalem to the part controlled by the Moslems, which at that time (just prior to the Six Day War of 1967) contained most of the sites which we wanted to see. We landed before Easter and there was a crush of Christians going to the city, which meant that all travel facilities, especially air lines and hotels, were jammed. Then, to make matters worse, Easter almost coincided that year with the date of the Hegira, when faithful Moslems make their visit to Mecca. I did not realize that the second most holy city for Mohammedanism was Jerusalem, but it is. Mohammed ascended into heaven from *The Rock* there, from a spot on which today stands a very imposing Mosque. Accordingly, when Moslems make the trip to Mecca, they do their utmost to include Jerusalem in their itinerary. Futhermore, when they travel, they carry all manner of things under their flowing robes which they may need on the long trip to Mecca. These may include wash basins, cooking utensils, stoves, and even chamber pots. So what with both Christians and loaded-down Mohammedans on the move, we had trouble with our accommodations. They were hard to get and at times very odoriferous.

In spite of some inconvenience we arrived in Jerusalem, but had great difficulty in getting a room and just as great trouble later in getting a flight from Jerusalem back to Beirut. We were fortunate, however, in finding a very pleasant Mohammedan taxi driver. He really took us under his wing to act as guide, counsellor, and chauffeur. He invited us to breakfast to ensure that we had a typical Moslem meal; he took us to his house so that we might see how his people lived; and he drove us to all the Holy places, which he knew we wanted to see. These included the Mount of Olives, the Garden of Gethsemane, the Sacred Way, the Holy Sepulchre, Bethlehem, and the Dead Sea. He failed, however, to get us into the Dome on the Rock, the great shrine of his own religion, for the place was so crowded that access was being limited at the time to the faithful.

The visit was a whirlwind affair because, when we finally were able to get plane reservation to Beirut earlier than planned, we thought that we should take it. Our flight took us back via Amman, the capital of Jordan, which we were pleased to see.

Hurried though our tour of the Holy Land was, we learned a great deal. The animosity that existed between Christians and Moslems was brought home to us with a vengeance, for nearly all the local people were extremely bitter about the existing situation. We saw and talked with many Palestinian refugees. It seemed that they wanted to live in misery to demonstate to the world the injustice that they felt had been done them when they were pushed off their land to create a homeland for the Jews. They and most others insisted that there could be no peace so long as Israel existed.

I was impressed by the aridity of the country and the low level of agriculture of the area near Jerusalem. I was reminded of what one of my teachers had once said about the land of milk and honey, that there was so little vegetation in it that only goats and bees could get a living from it. Also I recalled what William Westermann, professor of Ancient History at Columbia, had said about the so-called Fertile Crescent, a term popularized by his colleague at Chicago, J. H. Breasted—that it was neither a crescent nor fertile. I thought that Westermann was right.

Once back in Beirut, we took off immediately for Cairo to see the wonders of Egypt. We were certainly not disappointed by the country and recommend it highly for cultural travel. We found in Cairo the mosques to be extremely impressive,[2] the Pyramids of Ghizeh and the Sphinx to live up to all their claims, and the treasures in the National Egyptian Museum, including many from the Tomb of Tut-tank-Amen, to be as good as advertised. Inasmuch as I have a special interest in the technology of the ancient world, I devoted much of my time at the Museum to studying it. The displays of boats show how close the ancients came to developing the hinged rudder from the steering oar—the crucial step was missed by a very small margin. The examples of smelting and forging metals, of making pottery, and of agricultural techniques are very good.

In those days the presence of President Gamal Abd El-Nasser was evident on every hand. He built broad avenues in the new parts of Cairo and an especially wide one from the airport to the center of the city. Enormous posters of the President beamed down on one in a most impressive manner.

Yet, it was apparent that Nasser had not changed the country very much. We were able to witness "military" maneuvers from the windows of our hotel, which overlooked the Nile. One day some soldiers were being taught to row landing boats, but they made such a mess of it that I concluded that Egypt would fare poorly if it embarked on another war with Israel. Unfortunately it did engage in such a war very shortly afterward (the war of 1967) and my prognosis proved to be correct.

---

[2] The two in Cairo which I liked best were Ibn Tulun and the Mosque of Sultan Hassan.

From Cairo we went up the Nile to visit Luxor, Karnak, and the Valley of the Kings. We took rooms at a most amazing hotel in Luxor, the Winter Palace, that had been built during the period of British domination. I think that, if I were an Egyptian, it would have made me, by its elegance and arrogant demeanor, anti-British.

We wanted to go on to Aswan to see the new dam, but the small Russian planes, which at that time carried people up from Cairo, were heavily booked up and we could not get passage on them. It was also difficult to get a hotel reservation back in the capital. I had taken the precaution previous to leaving Cairo to engage a room at the Nile Hilton, where we had been, and had been assured that a room would be ready for us on our return. I even phoned the hotel from Luxor to be sure that a place would be available. So, we went back to Cairo and to the Hilton. Once there, I was informed that no room was reserved for us. When I insisted that I had engaged a room before going to Luxor, I was told that there was nothing in my name. When I said that I had confirmed the reservation by phoning from Luxor, I was asked to show a receipt of the conversation! When I inquired just how one obtained a record of a phone conversation, I was faced with a stare of amazement. At all events, the Hilton clerk said that he knew where I might get a room and he referred me to the Omar Khayyam on an island in the Nile. He told me further that it had been the town house of the father-in-law of King Farouk. This information, together with a desire to get away from the Americanism of the Hilton, decided me to give the place a try.

The Omar Khayyam turned out to be delightful. It was a wonderful building and had a lot of chalets (cabins) in its park. We were put into one of them. The first evening we had an excellent meal in the main hotel and during it learned that a very large wedding celebration was to take place at the hotel that night. We were informed that we might find it interesting. And interesting it was.

We took up an observation post on the terrace of the hotel where we could get a good view and waited. And waited. It was a cold evening, as evenings usually are on the edge of the desert (they are even colder on the desert itself),and we began to imbibe cognacs to keep warm. The brandy was almost at the point of taking over altogether, when the fun began. It consisted at that point of a wedding procession for all the world like those seen on Grecian vases. First came the flower girls strewing real flowers along the walkway. Then came musicians playing trumpets. Then the dancing girls (or was it vice-versa). Then the bride and groom. The relatives of both, and friends. Finally, there was the hoi polloi. Apparently anyone could join that group and my wife suggested that we become part of the crowd. I was hesitant to move, for I was not exactly accustomed to crashing parties. But my curiosity got the better of my judgment or my manners and we did fall in. The procession made a turn or two through the park and then entered a large pavilion, which made me think of a circus tent except that it was made of wood instead of canvas. I hesitated to enter, for that would really have been crashing a party, but again my curiosity got the upper hand and in we went.

Inside the pavilion people were seated at tables. At one end of the place there was a fairly large stage. Next to it on its left side was a lodge or box and in it were the bride and groom. By the time we were seated, the moment seemed propitious for another drink. Momentarily I forgot that the Moslems were non-alcholic drinkers. They did have coke, however, which is a favorite beverage in North Africa.

By the time that I had received my coke, dancers appeared on the stage. They were, of course, belly-dancers! And they were something in their contortions, at least for an innocent from Vermont. They worked the bride and groom over for what seemed a long time, although I doubted that they needed that treatment, and then they took on the entire gathering. Just to drive their message home, the head belly-dancer ultimately came down on the floor and worked on individuals. For some reason, she came directly to our table and twisted herself to such an extent that I feared that she might lose part of her anatomy. When she had spent herself, she leaned over the table and whispered in my ear in perfect Brooklynese, "Toots, what'cha doing after the show?"

The next day we took off for Libya, where another former student, Mustapha Baiou, dean of the University at Bengazi, had invited me to give some lectures. As we were waiting at the airport for Nasser's guests to a summit Arab meeting to pass through, we read in a local English newspaper that Mustapha Baiou had just been named by King Idris I to the post of Minister of National Education. We concluded, and rightly so, that this promotion would make our visit even better than we had expected it to be.

The flight to Bengazi gave us a good view of the terrain in which most of the North African fighting took place during World War II. Not only is the distance from Cairo to Tripoli very great (some thousand miles), but the land is arid and cut by many, many wadi (great gullies, ravines, or valleys). The thought of fighting in that area made my hair stand on end.

When we arrived at Bengazi, we had a note from Mustapha Baiou, asking us to meet him at Tripoli and to stay on the same plane that we had come on. We did, but when we arrived at Tripoli, we found another note telling us to return to Bengazi, whence he had been called by the King. So after a short sight-seeing visit in Tripoli, we boarded the plane on which we had come and went back to Bengazi. There we finally met our host and were put in a modern hotel which was very comfortable. Our first order of business was to settle upon our program. It consisted first of an archeological trip by car to the famous Greek and Roman ruins of the area. Then I was to give some lectures at the University of Bengazi. Finally we were to go to Tripoli for a longer visit; and from there we were to return to Bari.

Libya, in those days, was a very interesting place. It was beginning to show the effects of the income from the oil which had only recently been brought into production on a large scale. The oil resources had actually been discovered by the Italians during the Fascist period, but Mussolini had decided that Italian finances were such that the capital necessary for development was not available because of his military plans.

What the Libyans were doing with their newly acquired income from oil was most astounding. Much of it was put into buildings in the two capitals, Tripoli and Bengazi, and into the construction of still a third capital, El Beida, for King Idris, further east.

The process of modernization created many anomalies, such as very modernistic structures among real hovels in seas of mud or clouds of dust, depending upon the seasons. In Bengazi a "sports city," on the scale of an Olympic Games establishment, was going up amid slums and unpaved streets. Builders from many parts of Europe were engaged in the work, from Scots to Bulgarians. I met the manager of a large Scottish firm, who told me that working in Libya had some very queer aspects. The government demanded speed in construction, but the mores of the country were most deleterious. For example, every time that he had large batches of concrete ready to pour, the *muadhdhins* would call the faithful, including his workers, to prayer and the concrete under the hot sun would soon set and spoil. He related that he was spending a small fortune in bribing the *muadhdhins* to delay their calls until the concrete had been taken care of. A Presbyterian paying off an Arab seemed funnily incongruous.

The archeological tour, which was given us, was extremely informative. We were put in charge of a professor of archeology of the university who had studied at Dropsie College in Philadelphia. He was, incidentally, an Egyptian, for trained Libyans were not in great enough supply to fill all the posts that were being created by the development of an educational system. He was a learned man, but did not want us to miss a thing. He was so insistent in the performance of his duties that my wife became very irritated with him. He was wearing us out to a point at which we could not enjoy what he was showing us.[3]

The manner in which the Romans were able to manage the sparse amount of water available amazed me, as it has thousands of other visitors of the region. They built water-level aqueducts in

[3] In the Eastern region of the country we went first to Cyrene, where we rescued an American woman in shorts in a Muslim graveyard. She was the target of a Moslem who considered that she was desecrating a holy place by showing her bare legs and he was throwing small stones at her. Then we visited Tulmeitha and Apollonia. In the Western region we went to Leptis Magna and Sabratha on our return trip to Tripoli.

several places to carry water [4] and many cisterns in which to store it. In one place, they had chiseled a channel down the face of a cliff by which to bring water down very gradually. They accomplished this feat by having the descents at very moderate degrees and using many hairpin curves to get from one level to another, much as they did in constructing roads to get up or down hills.

The Romans were great builders in almost everything. Indeed, the area abounds in the ruins of Roman roads, amphitheaters, temples, and statues. There was also much evidence of their success in holding the desert back by building wind-breaks and the planting of trees, bushes, and hardy crops. By contrast, modern efforts to accomplish the same end, especially those of the Fascists, were noteworthy for their failure.[5]

One social phenomenon of which I was only vaguely aware became apparent during our sight-seeing, especially in places near the fringes of cultivated areas. In them nearly all menial work was done by blacks from Sudan or from other parts of lower Africa. I was informed that this had been the case from time immemorial and that it had much to do with "black" slavery in the Mediterranean basin. From the practice, the slavery of blacks reached America.

For the most part I did not find Libyans to be industrious or enterprising, but I did find them very friendly. This characteristic was illustrated by an experience we had on our return from our archeological trip along the coast. When we reached a main road, our chauffeur informed us that we were nearly out of gas and that neither he nor our professor-guide fancied getting marooned in the bush. We looked for a gas station but could not find one nor even a human habitation where we might secure a small provision.

I suggested flagging down one of the few trucks which were still on the road, but this proposal met a negative response

---

4 They did not have pipes or tunnels strong enough to stand pressures which develop if water is contained in them.

5 Fascist policy was to reclaim land and to settle immigrants on small holdings, as they did in certain places in Italy. Most of these "colonies" in Libya were not economically viable and were soon abandoned.

because it would cause a loss of face. At last, a truck did stop near us to meet certain needs of the driver. As soon as he was at liberty, I addressed him in my best pigeon English-Arabic. When I had finished, he replied, "O.K., Joe, I'll help you out." He explained that he had worked for Americans during the war and that they had saved his life. So, much to the amazement of our guide and his chauffeur, the driver siphoned some gas from his tank and gave it to us. He would not even take any money for it.

We got back to Bengazi all right and I then began to prepare for my lectures at the University. Of course, there had to be a mix-up. My first encounter with students was scheduled for New Year's Day, Moslem style, because some one had been confused about the day on which this event took place. The result was that the students were for the most part on vacation. Somehow, however, an audience was dragooned into a lecture hall and I let them have my message. During the discussion period after the formal presentation, I was asked many intelligent questions, which led me to belive that they had understood what I was trying to get across. In a few minutes of fraternizing with the students, a young man came up to me and asked if my wife and I would be interested in attending a party at his brother-in-law's house to see the old year out and the new year in (Moslem style). He explained that his sister had studied in the United States and that his brother-in-law was adjutant general of the Libyan army. We accepted his invitation with alacrity.

The New Year's party was something to write home about. The sister of the young man was a pretty girl, but a little on the heavy side. In the hallway, as we entered, there was what I thought was a basketball and this led me to inquire about her children who played basketball. I was quickly informed that she had no children and that the ball was a medicine ball, which she threw around her grounds because her husband would not let her go out in public to get any other form of exercise! As the guests arrived only one or two wore veils, but for the most part the men and women kept apart. Most of the women spoke no Western language and the few that did displayed at once their lack of general education. I realized how recent the "liberation" of women was in North Africa.

The entertainment part of the evening consisted of eating a little something standing up in the dining room, and then of conversing for awhile in the salon. The guests were mostly professors, military people, and diplomatists from Arab countries. There were no alcoholic beverages, even for Westerners, but vast quantities of carbonated waters of various kinds.

This made the party quite distinctive, at least for me, but as midnight approached something else happened which made me feel as though I were in a quite different world from the one to which I was accustomed. We were ushered into the dining room and seated at assigned places. At each place there was the head of a lamb (boiled, I think) in its entirety, except for the wool. One began eating the eyes, for, we were told, they were considered the greatest delicacy. I thought that I might manage the tongue and the brains, but somehow the eyes repelled me. Then to make my case more difficult, my lamb had one eye cocked up, as though it were saying, "Guess upon whom the joke is now." Clearly the joke was on me! Luckily, we managed to beat a retreat before we were completely embarrassed.

Before we left Libya, a banquet was held in our honor. The guests were all men, except for my wife and the daughter of one of the Egyptian professors who was a product of British culture. The food was as good as I had had, but it was not distinguished except for the lamb, which is excellent in North Africa. It was quite different from the roast camel, which we had tried. That was so tough I thought that it must have been grown especially for the rigidity of its tissue. Later I saw a herd of camels being driven to a slaughter house and understood the situation. Obviously camels, like horses, were too expensive to raise for meat and were eaten only after years of service or after an accident which required doing away with them.

At all events, the banquet was an honor and in the one speech made, also different from similar events in the West, pleasant things were said about me. I did, however, miss wine with the food and developed an especial aversion to carbonated drinks. I can belch, if need be, to show my approval of food without coke or ginger ale!

Eventually we made the trip back to Italy via Libyan Airlines, which were managed by personnel from Air France. The service was not bad, but the French permitted the stewards to sell various products (I imagine for the steward's profit) and these individuals were very obnoxious in their eagerness to get rid of their wares.

My duties at Bari were soon ended and we were ready to return home. On our way back to the States we visited De Rosa and his family at Naples. I had not spent much time there since the nineteen twenties and was impressed by the cultural improvements, particularly the art galleries, and the growth of the city. After Naples we went on to Rome, where I lectured at the University, and to Florence, where I performed again in the Faculty of Economics. I arrived in Vermont just at the season to plant my garden.

At this time I was at the height of my career and began to receive honors of various kinds, and along with them new duties. Undoubtedly the most interesting of my obligations derived from my appointment in 1960 to the Board of Directors of the International Economic History Association. I had been associated with this body from its very inception, but its administration had been directed largely by Michel Postan and Fernand Braudel. As they grew older, they turned their attention to other matters so that the task of running the international body fell upon the Board. In this group there were representatives of communist as well as capitalist countries and some of them were my friends of long standing.[6]

Our main tasks were to choose officers of the Association and to prepare for meetings, which were held every two or three years. In the performance of these duties both personal and international rivalries (and ideologies) played a very strong role. The Russians were very difficult about these matters, or at least one of the two on the Committe was. Apparently the Russians have a policy of

---

[6] These included François Crouzet, Le Roy Ladurie, and François Furet of France, Peter Mathias of England, and Charles Verlinden of Belgium. I also made many new friends, especially Cristof Glamann of Denmark, who has the distinction of being a member of the board of Carlsberg Breweries in Copenhagen (in my view the best beer in the world), Herman Kellenbenz of Gemany, Jean François Bergier of Switzerland, S. P. Pach of Hungary, who invited me to Budapest to lecture at the historical institute, and Witold Kula of Poland.

appointing one real scholar and gentleman to such boards and a second man who is a "politico-scientist." The latter is usually very objectionable.

The objectionable character we had maneuvered himself into positions that got him a place on programs, even though he promised not to keep on doing so. He always gave the same line—that Marxism was the wave of the future and that those of us who could not see its virtures were thick-headed. He tried his best to become President of the International Association, but we fought off the threat by making Witold Kula of Poland the President on one occasion and the Russian Vice-President and then when the next time came for an election, we stymied the Russian by giving him another term as Vice-President.

In these contests some members of the Eastern bloc were quite frank in saying that they could do nothing about it—they dared not oppose him. Even members from the West were hesitant to stand up to him, largely for fear of destroying our entire enterprise. For the most part, I found the representatives from Russian satellite countries to be scholars or interested in real scholarship, but the Russians to be very painful propagandists.

At all events, membership on the Board of Directors of the Internatonal Association allowed me to go to places which I otherwise would never have visited, or not have visited so well as I did. These places included Stockholm, Copenhagen, Warsaw, Leningrad, Budapest, Moscow, and Tashkent. Most of these capitals I enjoyed, but travel in Eastern countries leaves much to be desired as to comforts and food.

I have a theory about travel that I can always find accommodations and so when alone, I usually make no advance reservations. On one occasion I arrived in Warsaw and barged up to the tourist office at the airport and solicited its help in finding a room for the night. I encountered a very pleasant young man who took on my case as though it were his national duty to solve my problem. He began to telephone around, but much to his surprise, could find nothing. Every room in the city was taken because of a lot of trade union meetings being held at that very moment. And to cap the climax the international Olympic games committee was holding its sessions there. In fact, Avery Brundage, then president of the Games, had arrived that very morning with a plane load of dignitaries and had "mopped" up all the rooms.

At last the young man decided that the only thing to do was to go ringing doorbells and he commandeered the Tourist Bureau's car for that purpose. We saw most of Warsaw in the next two hours but found no accommodations at all. I feared that in desperation he would have recourse to places to which I could not go. He did persuade the Marine on duty at the American Embassy to let me sleep in his bed, if nothing else turned up. At the moment when we were about to abandon our search, the chauffeur of the car thought of a hotel that the Teacher's Union had constructed and that I would qualify to get into as a teacher. It was still free because the price was so high that no Pole could afford it. Even at thirty-five dollars a night it looked good to me. It was on the top of a high building and provided an excellent view of the Vistula River. I remained there several nights in order to visit the city with my friend from the Tourist Bureau.

Warsaw is a pleasant city. It was badly damaged during World War II and its old city completely destroyed. Its population was badly decimated and its Jewish section wiped out. I had enough time on this occasion to explore the city in detail and to see the great effort made in the restoration. The old city had been rebuilt to give the appearance that nothing had happened. In the Jewish section an impressive monument to those lost in the holocaust had been erected. In some instances entire churches had been moved to improve the flow of traffic and to enhance the beauty of the town. I was impressed, however, by the strong control of the government over everything, the anti-Russian feeling of the people, the paucity of consumer goods in the stores, and the oppression of authorities over the students and their professors.

On another occasion, my wife and I went to Leningrad for an International Economic History Association meeting and then to Moscow for an International Historical Congress. These conferences gave me a good opportunity to get better acquainted with these cities. After the meeting in Moscow, I decided that we should take a trip to Tashkent in the Uzbek Republic, famed as the crossroads of trade between India, Russia, and China. Marco Polo had passed through it; so, too, Genghis Khan with his hoard of invaders.

I was amazed at the distance covered on the flight out. It was much greater than I had anticipated and the journey brought us nearly to the borders of China. Nor did I realize the size of the Kyzyl-Kum desert—it seemed to stretch on forever. The pilot of the plane went to some pains to show us what was being done to reclaim some of this vast wasteland. How caravans ever managed to cross it remains a mystery to me. Seldom, nowadays, does one see any camels, for the air plane has taken their place.

Tashkent itself is an attractive city with its mosques and gardens, its newly designed avenues, and its new buildings, constructed since the earthquake of 1966. Some of these are extremely well designed and in their detail surpass much of what I had seen in New York. The city is also interesting for its bazaar, where merchants seemed to be carrying on trade, especially in fresh garden produce, for their own profit. In fact, I was told that communism had taken a much less strong hold there than in Western Russia.

In the Old City, we went to a Moslem school of higher learning, a madrassa, attached to a mosque. There we met students, who live in individual quarters, not unlike cells in a monastery. Their studies were exclusively of theology, as has been the tradition for centuries, but they travel widely in the Moslem world and thus are less provincial than one might think. More technical education was left traditionally to the guilds, but now more and more is reserved to modern universities in the Western manner.

The general public hygiene of Russia leaves much to be desired to an American accustomed to high standards in such matters. Public toilets, except in very large cities, consist of two open trenches, one for men and one for women, over which one squats. In Tashkent, hygienic facilities were especially poor. At our hotel, we did have a toilet attached to our room, but it was so filthy that it was unusable. Although I complained about it to the floor supervisor, and was sent plumbers, no cleaning was done until I went to the Intourist office in the hotel (in every hotel there is such an office to take care of and to keep an eye on foreign tourists). In the presence of a large group of Americans, I yelled that I wanted the s . . . in my bath room cleaned up at once. This time I got action.

Our trip to Tashkent was to have included side excursions to Bukhara and Samarkand, but somehow they were eliminated. Intourist is not above such one-sided changes. We did, however, want to go to these cities, famous for rugs and mosques, so we organized a special excursion to them. It is not easy once in the USSR to do a thing like this, but we did it. We were glad that we had, for the cities were worth the trouble. Both are beautiful and exotic. Among other things we went to a native tea house and had tea on couches that looked flea bitten, but were not.

Upon the conclusion of our visit to the Uzbek Republic, we returned to Moscow. The trip was not very pleasant, for the Russians have a practice of having their planes loaded and *then* towed by tractor into position for take-off. This procedure may take an hour, which means that during it the air-conditioning system is not working. When one sits in a closed plane in a desert with the sun beating down with all its force, the passengers inside the cabin literally cook. This was the case in this instance.

Our stay in Moscow on the return was without incident, except that I had an errand at the University, which took me once again to the unimaginable, architectural monstrosity that houses it. Unfortunately this style prevailed for enough time so that a university building in Warsaw was modeled after it.

At the airport on our departure from Moscow, we were inundated with propaganda leaflets on the virtues of Russia and its economic system. I saw nothing on Russian taxes, so I asked the girl—a very good looking one—for an information booklet concerning them. She feigned not to know what I was talking about. When I explained what taxes were, she exclaimed, "Oh, we don't have any such horrible things as that in Russia." I thought that I might suggest to her that there is a tax tacked on all prices, but on second thought I decided that such an effort would be a waste of breath and time.

Another incident worth noting was that on the flight out of Moscow the zipper on my trousers stuck. I tried to explain in German my predicament to the Russian hostess aboard. Her German was not adequate for this crisis, so I had to demonstrate what had gone awry. I was somewhat embarrassed, but she was not. Anyhow, she could not help me and I had to wait until we landed in order to make repairs.

Finally we arrived in New York and I took up again my work at Columbia. I was about to embark upon my last years of teaching and to make plans for my retirement. Both periods were to be more eventful than I had imagined possible.

Chapter XIII

Student Riots of 1968

Once back in New York, I returned to my teaching at Columbia, and my wife returned to hers at Finch College. Both of us were extremely busy, for students flocked to us in our respective institutions. I had a particularly large number of candidates for the Ph.D. degree—my absence had done little to reduce the load which I carried. Dissertations created a lot of work, for they had to be read, criticized, rewritten and reread several times before they were ready for examination.

I had expected that the last years of my teaching career would be happy and serene, but such was not to be the case. They were fatiguing and turbulent. I expected the work-load which I had, but I did not anticipate the student trouble which developed. Without any warning that I knew about, a small number of those enrolled at Columbia began to display a hostile attitude both toward the very institution which they had chosen to attend and toward members of the teaching staff. Their resentment was not directed at me personally, but I was perforce subjected to their outrageous behavior.

Many have been the attempts to explain the revolutionary spirit which grew up among the students in the 1960s and, for that matter, among some members of the staff. None of the efforts to analyze what took place has seemed to me to be satisfactory. I should like here to record what I think were some of the major factors involved in the movement which made my last years of teaching the bitterest of my life.

Much of what I consider to have been responsible for the changed behavior of our youth is based upon the premise that in our society our fundamental patterns of conduct stem from our fundamental values. The behavior of the individual is, in turn, controlled by institutions which have grown up over time and were traditionally very powerful in regulating social intercourse. Unfortunately many of these institutions have been greatly weakened since the beginning of the twentieth century and some have been almost obliterated.

Probably the most serious change in our social arrangements has been the breakdown of the family. Time was when an individual spent most of his formative years within the confines of his own home. This was my own experience. Goals in life were established there. Much of one's deportment was determined there and controlled there. Much of one's economic existence centered there. And a large amount of one's social life and to some extent intellectual life was concentrated there.

In a relatively short time, however, the family lost much of its importance in forming one's life. The family became less of an economic unit than it had been when men were engaged primarily in agriculture. Members of the family went in many directions in the search of education and employment. Members of the family pooled their resources or earnings less and less, but used their earnings as each individual thought best. Members of the family were together for shorter and shorter periods of time, so that the interaction of its members was reduced. Then, as women left home to become wage earners, no one remained in the household to create a nucleus of family existence—not even to greet members as they returned from their dispersed activities of the day. Parental influence diminished, especially paternal discipline.

Some of the controls and formative features of the family were supposed to have been taken up by schools, and undoubtedly were to some extent. Teachers could not, however, provide the love that parents should have given their offspring, nor did they have their charges enough of the time to have the formative influences which children need. In due course the influence of the schools was lessened. Children began to display that independence which they were practicing at home and teachers, like parents, began to lose the respect of their charges and their control over them. With mass education, the children of the stabilizing middle classes associated more and more with the less disciplined children of the lower classes. Teachers had to spend more of their time and energies to keeping order and less to forming and imparting knowledge to those for whom they were supposed to be responsible. To save face, they tried to hide behind a pedagogical philosophy of *laissez faire* and of permissiveness. English instruction went so far as to encourage students to speak and write as they "felt." Students did not "diagram sentences," learn the parts of speech, get instruction in the nature of a paragraph, or get to know what constituted a sentence. Students who did not meet even the most bland set of requirements were pushed ahead into the next classes by "social promotions." Little encouragement was given to achievement.

The above paragraph gives, of course, a somewhat exaggerated picture of the true situation, but there is much truth in it. My eldest grandson confided to me that he did not know what adverbs and adjectives were until he was in a freshman English class in college; a "hired girl" whom we employed and who was in the second year of high school could not figure out what her wages should be if she worked eight and a half hours and was paid $2.50 an hour, for she was totally allergic to fractions; the principal of the academy in a nearby town indulged regularly in mixed metaphors, split infinitives, mixed tenses, and dangling participles; and the writers for the local paper and broadcasters for the local radio station were so illiterate that what they did with the language was unbelievable. For example, one of the broadcasters pronounced victuals like "vik-tu-alls" and another referred to the English philosopher as Thomas Hob-ess. Not only were the schools promoting undisciplined young but illiterates as well. To me, the intellectual future of our country in the humanities looks grim indeed.

In addition to the family and the schools in the formation of our youth, there were also the churches. Not only did our young traditionally go to church and Sunday school, but they looked up to church leaders as examples to follow in their behavior. Gradually, however, churches began to lose their influence over our youth and leaders failed to be models to be followed or respected. I think that some of the beliefs of the churches, especially the fundamentalist ones, were so palpably untrue that the youth lost confidence in the teachings of these institutions. That Jonah should have been swallowed by a whale or that the world was created in seven days belied common sense and were not very important anyway. Furthermore, attractive alternate employment of Sundays began to develop—the auto ride, golfing, motor boating, camping, and the like were added to a long list of nonreligious social activities.

Not only did the major institutions which controlled behavior begin to break down, first in the urban areas and then in the more rural ones, but also individuals were able more easily than previously to get out from under what restraining influences remained. The automobile permitted them to remove themselves quickly from the presence of friends and acquaintances, and trains and airplanes added to the possibilities of seeking distant opportunities of behavior that would be contrary to usual norms. Even the sheer size of urban areas was almost a guarantee of being hidden from the scrutiny of those whose opinion one might fear.

Models of behavior were no longer leaders in the church, or school, or society at large, but were movie actresses and actors, or those to whom the youth were constantly exposed, such as television personalities and professional athletes. The lives many of these people lived were not those representing our traditional basic values and our moral standards. Permissiveness of every kind was flaunted right and left; permissiveness contributed to hostility toward all authority and even to violent opposition toward it; consideration for others was replaced by an attitude of grab all available, whether legal and socially desirable or not.

In the nineteen sixties the trends noted above began to reach a climax. World War II, then the Korean War, and finally the Vietnam War played their roles in removing people from the controlling influences of the neighborhoods in which they lived. Not only was this the case of men in the services, but also individuals in civilian life. A large percentage of the population was torn from its moorings for some kind of employment connected with war work. The discipline which the armed forces provided was not of the kind to keep men and women from taking advantage of the lack of usual, behavioral restraints. The dramatic rise in divorce and crime rates were ample evidence of this point. Moreover, men were taught various forms of violence—after all, violence is what war is about. When they returned to civilian life, the new permissiveness was mixed with violence to an unprecedented extent. Lastly, the extreme economic activity of the period made possible an excessive license to act in ways that were not usually in our society. If one were dismissed from a job, one could find another very readily. If one were bored, one could find immediate, if temporary, solace in drugs.

That the new modes of behavior found their way into academe is not surprising. College and even graduate training were so extended that all types of students, the qualified and the unqualified, the poor and the rich, ones from backgrounds of culture and those with no culture, were accepted. Returning veterans went to school because G. I. grants for education were available. Others were so enamored of college life that they perpetuated their existence in it as long as they could persuade their fathers to pay the bills. Many new colleges were founded to take advantage of governmental bounty; and many more upgraded their offerings to graduate school levels whether or not they were equipped to give students adequate instruction or research opportunities.

Colleges competed with one another for students in order to keep their doors open. In fact, I once heard an administrative official say in regards to admissions, and not entirely in jest, that the only condition for getting into his institution was that "the body be warm." Under such circumstances, even though I have perhaps exaggerated the case for purposes of emphasis, the environment of colleges and universities changed dramatically in the half century following World War I. This was the very period of my experience in higher education.

There is no question but what there were flaws and faults in the system, but they were not of proportions to warrant the extensive and violent reaction of students to them. Just where and when the first reaction occurred is somewhat beside the point here. The fact is that violence against university authorities was general in the late nineteen sixties. Some of the early centers for it in America were the University of California, Berkeley and Columbia Univeristy in New York, but it also took place in both Germany and France. In each place the circumstances differed to some degree. In the United States students were usually hostile to the Vietnamese war, for they were the ones who risked their necks; they were the ones who were being torn from training in their chosen profession; and they were the ones who had little to lose by the use of violence against the war.

I, too, was against the war. I thought from the first that we had little chance of winning it, that Indo-China was not a viable part of our sphere of political, military, or economic influence, or that the horrors of war were justified by whatever had taken place there. I did not have, however, enough courage of my convictions to come out strongly in public against the war. Nor did many of my generation do so. The generation of students at the time did have such courage, and this is to their credit. There is, however, little question in my mind that the opposition which they showed to the war contributed to their violence against university authorities.

In Germany and France, conditions were obviously different. German students lived in a society still suffering from a defeat in war; they lived under shortages of many of the good things of life, especially of housing; and they considered their futures with uncertainties and trepidation. In France, students were generally hostile to the Vietnam war or were smarting from the horrors of trying to keep Algeria under the control of France or from the remorse of losing it and the rest of overseas France. Then, in both of these countries so many individuals were being trained in certain fields, like sociology and history, that chances of finding positions in their specialties were exceedingly slim, if not nonexistent.

As is usual in cases in which large numbers have gripes, students (also their elders who shared their feelings) sought rationalizations for their positions. Some had recourse to various concepts of change in society and some of these involved the use of force, as in the case of the French and Russian Revolutions. Others thought that they were denied some kind of "natural" rights, and although they were usually not aware that this concept was man-made and from the eighteenth century at that, they realized that it was a principle for which many men had fought. Others sought refuge in some kind of anarchical philosophy which was basically to destroy the institutions that exist, for whatever grows up in their place could not be worse than what presently existed. Still others thought that they had some legitimate complaint about the way a university or its officers had treated them and I am certain that such instances existed. I realized only too well from the experience of my younger son and my long period of anxiety about him how some students felt. In a large institution it is inevitable that there will be individuals who will shirk their responsibilities, although I believe that the great majority of teaching staffs were conscientious in the performance of their tasks and made real efforts to help their charges far beyond the limits of ordinary expectations.

Be that as it may, we at Columbia were faced with a special set of circumstances. The Univeristy is situated on the edge of Harlem, which is almost solidly "black," and its inhabitants began anew in the 1960s to display a growing hostility to its neighbor on Morningside Heights. This was part of the fight of ethnic groups for a higher status in American society and more civil rights than they had so far enjoyed. Some of these struggles enlisted the support of white leaders, and some of the black leaders, like Martin Luther King, won large white followings in demonstrations in defiance of authority, like the civil rights marches. In fact, the first serious trouble at Columbia was accompanied by the occupation of Hamilton Hall, which is the main classroom and administrative building of Columbia College, by a group of blacks known as the Black Panthers.

The first violent disturbance did, however, come from undergraduates. The University, in answer to a long and urgent demand, had decided to build a gymnasium in a section of Morningside Park, which is a public park. This section was essentially a rocky cliff and completely unused. Permission to build there had been cleared with the city and with some groups in Harlem. The University agreed that part of the gymnasium could be used by the youth of Harlem under the supervision of college physical education personnel and that still more of the building could be so employed when the college was not in session. A similar arrangement had already been worked out for a playing field in another part of the park and was functioning smoothly, so a precedent was set to allow a reasonable hope that this plan would be satisfactory to everyone. Although much controversy existed about the new gymnasium, especially in University circles, construction began.

One night in the spring of 1968 a group of hot-headed students began to tear down a fence that had been built to protect the machinery and equipment of the contractor who was building the gym and to keep people away from the construction site. Then, as had been indicated above, the occupation of buildings of the University first by blacks and then by students began. At this time I was at Penn State to give some lectures and did not learn in any detail of what was going on until my return two days after the trouble had started. Upon my return from Penn State, I had several private matters to which I had to attend and I remember that I rushed, even ran, to my office from my bank to keep an appointment with a young man named Snow who wanted my advice and help in getting a fellowship and introductions for work in France. Much to my surprise he was not at the appointed place at the specified time and as I left the building I saw him with a placard, behind which he tried to hide, urging students to keep away and to help take over the offices. I took pictures of him and his co-workers, pictures which I have to this day. I was particularly astonished at this person's behavior, for the University had awarded him a fellowship of $5,000 a year for four years, three of which years he could spend anywhere his work might take him. His lack of appreciation for what had been done by the institution he was trying to ruin was bewildering to me.

This was only one example of what was taking place. A young instructor in French history and the history of the French Revolution appeared and seemed to be trying to play the role of Robespierre in giving counsel to the students. He was definitely on trial as a member of the staff and I was chagrined that he was throwing his chances away, for I had been instrumental in having him appointed. Another case which shook me was that of a young lady in one of my classes who had been doing very well. She held, moreover, a fellowship like Snow's. I saw her manning an information booth in front of the administration building from which she gave students directions of where to go and what to do to help the "cause." I went up to her and said that I was amazed to see her there and asked her if she did not think that her behavior would jeopardize the continuation of her fellowship. She replied that she was not worried, that, if need be, she could get a larger grant from another place, and that when she arrived there she would tear that down, too. I reported this incident to the *Wall Street Journal*, and I remember that it became the object of an editorial in the *Journal* by Vermont Royster.

In these first days no one seemed to realize the seriousness of the situation, and observers were prone to toss the whole matter off as a springtime exuberance. The authorities tried to negotiate with the occupiers and refused to use force to free the buildings for their regular use. I thought that force should be employed, but my friends in positions of power feared that physical harm would be done to students and that the University would suffer from adverse publicity.

Soon the authorities came to realize that the students did not know what they wanted and kept altering their demands. More and more buildings were taken over or "freed," as the saying then was. Entry and egress were forcibly prevented by the occupiers. Obviously considerable damage was being done. Fires were set in corridors of the buildings and in some cases filing cabinets were emptied to provide fuel for the blazes. One of my colleagues lost a manuscript upon which he had been at work for at least seven years.

A fire was set in the building in which I had my office and did considerable damage, but it did not reach my own possessions. Students paraded through the campus in troop fashion yelling one slogan after another. The cry which most aroused fears in most of us was, "Burn it down, burn it down."

The "revolutionaries" had no central organization or leadership and no generally accepted set of demands. They did keep in touch with one another via the University's telephone system. Individuals seemed to vie for power and endeavored to establish their positions by haranguing crowds on the Plaza in front of Low Library, which is the administrative building at Columbia. These "speakers" decked themselves out with bands around their heads to look like bandages and with red armbands to resemble figures of French revolutions from 1798 to 1848, as portrayed by David or Girodet, or to make one think of the "heroes" of the Finland Station revolt at St. Petersburg. When individuals did not make the Sun Dial, the most prestigious center for speaking, they appeared on the steps of buildings to try to get the attention of enough of their fellows so that they would get a "seat at the peace conference." They were extremely imitative and every detail of the troubles at Berkeley or Paris or Berlin was reproduced on the Columbia campus. If some slogan were yelled, they all yelled it. If one group decided to put banners out the windows of occupied buildings, all groups put them out. If some one started to wear arm bands, they all wore them. They followed the leaders like sheep, but always moved in packs like hyenas. So far as I could ascertain, they showed no individual physical courage.

Some members of the teaching staff were favorably disposed toward what was going on. There were those who were overtly supporting the rioters and preaching to them from steps of the University's buildings. They were mostly younger men, who were going through the throes of being tested, which is always a trying experience—the *Privat-Dozents Periode*. Then there were the "Concerned Professors" who organized meetings in Philosophy Hall and appeared at first to be trying to bring order out of chaos. I attended some of their meetings in hope of establishing a group that could mediate between the University and students. I soon came to the conclusion, however, that this effort was dominated by a political scientist who apparently hoped that he could improve his position in the University and, I was told, perhaps become the President of a "reformed Columbia." He had the support of a few professors, particularly from the departments of Sociology, History, and Anthropology. Finally, he had behind him also individuals from the neighborhood who had no connection at all with the University. He would, as chairman of the meetings, recognize those who were his henchmen and refuse to recognize any others; he would not even call the meetings to order until he was sure that the session was dominated by his men.

Still another group, led by Theodore de Bary and Fritz Stern, both from the History Department, took shape. They began their activity when the rumor got about that a number of undergraduates, among whom were several members of Columbia's athletic squads (these athletes had probably the best record of behavior of any during the crisis) were going to throw the occupiers out of the buildings by force so that classes might resume. The de Bary group feared that such strife would lead to injuries on all sides and to much destruction of property. They held a famous meeting of students and faculty members to try to stop any recourse to physical action. I was sympathetic to their position and spoke at the meeting. I endeavored to add some humor to the session in hopes that tensions might be lessened and I urged that students leave the use of force, if force had to be used, to the police who were trained for such business and knew the legal responsibilities involved.

The University authorities were becoming more and more concerned about the situation. They called a meeting of the faculties, but it amounted to nothing except to show how divided the staff was. Finally, they did ask for the protection of the police, who appeared on the campus in large numbers. They continued to try to negotiate with the students in the buildings, but to no avail. At last, they asked the police to intervene—to free the buildings. This was done, but the students in many cases had to be carried bodily from their barricades. Many arrests were made and many, including a few professors, were carried off in "paddy wagons."

As one might imagine, the buildings in which the students had been were a shambles. I believe that the condition of Low Library was the worst. Here the students had broken into the files of the President and destroyed some of the famous works of art that were hung in his office. They had had little or no food, except what was smuggled in and remnants of lunches were strewn about. Water and lights had not been cut off, but the housekeeping left much to be desired. I met Jacques Barzun as I went into the building after it was freed and both of us encountered on the way in Vice-President David Truman. As we surveyed the mess, Barzun turned to Truman and said, "I guess that you know on which side I stand." This remark might indicate that where he stood might be uncertain, for there had been bad blood between them when Barzun lost his administrative post as Provost and Truman took over as Vice-President.

I went to my office and found no damage and few things disturbed, although the people who had been there had made free with some sherry and whiskey which I had in my files! Other offices had, however, been ransacked, windows broken, and fires lit at their doorways The sight was, indeed, a sad one. Then to make matters worse, access to buildings was not controlled (outside doors had been ripped off and first floor windows broken) and looters were running off with typewriters, adding machines, and books. At the height of the trouble, fears arose that a mass attack might be made upon the University by blacks from Harlem, and it was certain that they would be aided by students and a number of sympathizers who had flocked to Morningside Heights from far and near. The police were concentrated on Morningside Drive and awaited an attack. Fortunately, the attack never came.

At what seemed like at "long-last," (I would think about two weeks) the time arrived to try to get back to some degree of normal university life. This turned out to be much more difficult than had been expected. A meeting of the faculties was held to get some consensus of what moves should be taken. The divisions which had risen during the troubled times appeared. The administrative authorities made an attempt to explain the step of police intervention, which had been taken so reluctantly. In his presentation, Vice-President Truman broke down and cried. Well he might, after what he had been put through and after he had had a chance to gauge the attitude of his colleagues. In general, one had the impression that the professors present had great sympathy for the students who revolted, although this appraisal of the situation may be inaccurate. Many who were hostile to those who had participated in the uprising absented themselves from this assembly; and besides the sympathizers with the students were much more vociferously conspicuous than their opponents.

It became apparent to me in this session that the policies to be urged and eventually those adopted would be toward pacification and that there would be no severe punishing of anyone. It became evident, also, that some effort would be made to give student representatives more of a voice in University affairs, although I sensed that students would have little real power and that they would soon tire of having the responsibilities connected with the day-to-day management of such a large institution. I sensed, too, that there was some sentiment in favor of getting rid of both Grayson Kirk as President and David Truman as Vice-President, although feelings of this sort were expressed almost surreptitiously. Most professors were not yet ready to take firm stands for fear, I thought, that they might be caught on the wrong side of the fence.

Whatever the long-range measures were to be, many issues were in need of immediate action. One was, should classes be continued and should students be required to go to classes. Another, very closely connected problem was, should students be given credit for the work of the second semester, even though they had done nothing from the inception of the trouble. Professors were given the option of continuing their classes or not. I decided to continue mine, for the reason that I knew students had paid good money and a lot of it for their instruction and that they had a right to get it. My smaller classes (a seminar and colloquium or reading class), which normally met in my office, I decided to hold in my own apartment.

The building in which my office was located

(Fayerweather Hall) was a shambles and enough students were hostile to me for the stand I had taken that they made life very uncomfortable for me when I went on campus. I think that most of those enrolled in the colloquium came to the sessions which I held at home and about half of those in the seminar continued to attend. I decided also to continue my lecture course and in this case I held it where it had originally been scheduled to be. This was the Law School, which had not been invaded by the ruffians. I suppose that about a third of those registered for this course continued to attend my lectures. I think that I was one of the very few, at least in the Faculties of Philosophy and Political Science, who tried to carry on.

The problem of credit to be given students for the abbreviated semester was even a more onerous one to solve than that of continuing classes. In graduate work at Columbia there was a rule that a student might enroll for a certain amount of lectures, but not do the work assigned by the professors. This was called "courses taken for attendance credit." The theory behind this practice was that a student might make better use of his time by work in the library or travel or whatever than listening to lectures. I was a critic of this procedure, for I discovered that students in applying for jobs might say that they had had a course with me, which implied that they knew something about the fields which I taught, but then their prospective employers would learn that they were completely uninformed about the subjects in question. I had taken a stand, as a consequence, that any student who took a course with me for attendance credit must attend the lectures for at least two-thirds of the sessions. In fact, I had made this point very strongly at the beginning of the semester and none of the students had indicated that this was unfair.

Soon after the liberation of the buildings, students who had been in my lecture course began waiting on me to inquire what my policy was about giving credit under the existing circumstances. I informed them at once that I had established a policy at the beginning of the semester, that this was a policy that I had adopted some time ago, that everyone involved knew exactly what that policy was, and that if they had chosen to risk their attendance credit by not attending, the risk was all theirs. They felt that this was not fair and I agreed to meet them in a body in my office to discuss the matter. They came at the appointed time, their number increased by several so-called leaders, who were not registered for the course but were supposed to have strong powers of persuasion. I refused to meet with anyone not in the class and after much delay those not involved departed. I held my ground with the others, for I thought, and still think, that I was right. Finally, they, too, left.

They then went to work on the "authorities," and the up-shot of the matter was that the latter left the decision up to me. The then chairman of our department, John Mundy, who was one of the most determined of the pacifiers, joined the struggle against me and so hounded me that I finally took the following position—that I would not change the grades myself, but that if they were changed, I would not make an issue of this unprecedented move. I learned later that Mundy did have the Registrar change the grades for those students who had not attended my classes to "attendance credit." In fact, some of these students gloatingly came to me to congratulate me on having come around to their position and to shake my hand. I refused to shake with them and made it clear that it was not I who had changed the grades.

As time went one, a debate as to the "causes" of the trouble was begun. For reasons which I find very difficult to explain, a feeling, even a sort of consensus, seemed to emerge from all the talk that the University was at fault and that those in authority had mismanaged the crisis. There was almost no blaming of the students for all that had happened. Indeed, a year later, when I was in Paris, Fritz Stern, a well-balanced historian and one who certainly did not side with the students, gave a talk about the entire episode and left the impression that those at fault were from the University side. When, in the discussion period following his remarks, I pointed out that the students appeared to have been without blame, he was quick to admit that, of course, they were the instigators of the excesses and that any legitimate complaints could have been handled in a less violent way. I cite this event only to show that the climate of opinion in the near aftermath of "'68" was that the students were not the real sinners. This is not meant as a statement in criticism of my good friend Stern.

The attitude which I have just expressed had much to do with what happened in the months after the occupation of the buildings. In the first place, very few students were punished in any way. I believe that of the many who were arrested only a handful were actually indicted and, if my memory serves me correctly, they were let off scotfree. Also to the best of my knowledge the University took no disciplinary action against any one. Payments on fellowships and scholarships to those who had yelled "burn it down, tear it down" were continued without a hitch. No professor was called on the carpet for any reason whatsoever, although it is probably true that some without academic tenure may not have been reappointed if they had made notoriously bad records for themselves.

Then I was particularly roiled by the fact that President Kirk and Vice-President Truman were made the scapegoats for the disturbances. During the ensuing summer both resigned their positions under pressure. Truman became President of Mt. Holyoke College and Kirk was given a good "settlement," including a fancy house in the Riverdale section of the Bronx. This was a very small recompense for what he had gone through.

Andrew Cordier, who had been Dean of the School of International Affairs and who had made a good reputation for himself in this post, was appointed Acting President and then President. He belonged to a religious sect that opposed violence of any kind, had been Deputy to Dag Hammarskjold at the United Nations, and before that a teacher in some Midwestern academic institution. He pursued policies of pacification in every way and spent money very liberally to get the University back to some form of normal operation. He ran up enormous deficits that I thought were more than the finances of the University could stand, and I believe that I was right. Although the University survived, it suffered very greatly.

I thought at the time that Cordier's policies were wrong, and I still do. The next winter the occupation of buildings was again attempted by students and again no one stood up to them. The new attack came about noon time with the students entering Fayerweather Hall as professors, including myself, were going to lunch. Most of the newcomers were entirely unknown to me and I suspect many were rabblerousers from high schools or other colleges in New York as well as from Columbia. I wanted the University police to make some effort to withstand the new occupation, but they apparently had orders to engage in no violence. I took a black jack from a student's hip pocket but was told by one of the police to stop that sort of thing before I was killed. Cordier thought that the best thing was to sit out this uprising, which was perhaps wise, for students were beginning to tire of these escapades. Cordier had the patience of Job.

In the ensuing months efforts were made to satisfy student demands for changes in the administration of the University. The chief reform semed to be the creation of a University Senate, which was to be composed of representatives of various groups, including students. The role of the Senate was largely advisory and came far from meeting what students had been demanding. They had hoped at one time to play a role in the selection and promotion of teachers and administrative officers and they even aspired to have a voice in making the budget. Such aspirations were not realized and, I have been told, students soon found that the responsibilities of managing a great university were more of a burden than they wanted to assume.

Cordier endeavored to assuage hurt feelings by naming new people to high posts, the most important of whom was an economist, Peter Kenan. He did not last long and was followed by Theodore de Bary, a specialist in Chinese history and culture. He proved to be an excellent administrator and a man of dignity and sense. After a couple of years Cordier gave up the reins of the University and returned to the Deanship of the School of International Affairs in order to help pay for an extravagantly expensive building for which he was responsible. His place was taken by William McGill from the field of psychology.

Although the University wound up with good administrators, the destruction which the "sixty-eighters" had advocated had been very largely accomplished. Although the place had not been burned down, it had been badly scorched. Many very excellent professors left Columbia for other posts. From European history we lost Orest Ranum to The Johns Hopkins University and Peter Gay to Yale. Charles Wagley of Anthropology went to the University of Florida and Herbert Hyman of Sociology went to Wesleyan, and there were many more who refused to live under the tensions which had been created within their departments. Furthermore, recruiting staff to take the place of those who left proved very difficult. Few wanted to get into the messes which existed, as we soon found out in History.

Also, the University discovered that the prestige of the place had suffered a severe set-back. Fewer students than formerly sought admission to either the College or the graduate schools, and the summer session enrollment, which depended mainly on teachers around the country, fell off drastically. This was a test of what they thought!

To make matters worse than they might otherwise have been was the fact that the ecology of Morningside Heights was deteriorating very rapidly. Respect for authority had declined so fast that the place became an eyesore. The campus, which Kirk, with the financial help of the Rockefeller family, had tried so hard to beautify, went to the dogs. Many of the public rooms of the University, like the ones in the Library and the corridors of the Law School, came to look like subway stations. The entire area, especially because of its proximity to Harlem where the incidence of crime was higher than anywhere else in Manhattan, became seriously blighted. Conditions were so bad, indeed, that I was very uncomfortable on the streets, and going to the theater with a return home fairly late at night involved a real risk. My apartment was robbed five times, a member of my household was mugged by being hit over the head with a window weight, and my wife was robbed in the street. Both Morningside Park and Riverside Park became practically unusable except in broad daylight and by two or more persons going together.

Efforts by the University and other institutions of Morningside Heights to acquire property for institutional building were stymied by the outrageous prices demanded by slum-landlords and the opposition of dwellers in apartment houses whose rents were kept down by rent control laws. The place became so unattractive that potential donors to the University frequently took the position that there was no point in giving money to a sinking ship and potential students and staff did not want to live in such unattractive surroundings. Moving to a new site had been considered but discarded because of the enormous expense, which would have run into billions of dollars. Lastly, the University was beginning to feel the competition of the tax-supported institutions of the state and city. The outlook for Columbia was, indeed, bleak. What a sad state for an institution that had a scant twenty-five years earlier been one of the great universities of the world.[1]

The blow that was dealt Columbia appeared to me as a great calamity. I was heartbroken by the events of 1968 and by the policies of supineness taken by the authorities. I had, however, only one more year of active service before I would be subject to mandatory retirement because of age. I thought that I could stick it out, and I did. I held my seminar and colloquium the following year at my apartment and went to the University only for a lecture course and my office hours. Things being as they were, I had no urge to continue my teaching and no desire to live in the shadow of the University. Retirement came, unfortunately, as a great relief.

---

[1] In 1979 a committee of the faculties of Columbia published a survey of the University. It presented a serious appraisal of the damage which had been done to the institution by the students in 1968 and 1969. The conclusions reached were every bit as pessimistic as my own.

Chapter XIV

From "In Retirement" To "In Memoriam," Almost

From what I have just written about life at Columbia University in the years 1968-1970, one can readily understand that I had little appetite to continue my work there. Even if I had wanted to go on, the University's retirement policy was adamant: voluntary retirement at age sixty-five and mandatory retirement at age sixty-eight.[1] In any case, teaching after retirement age usually means "more work for less pay." Thus it was that I looked forward to the end of my university career with pleasure.[2]

What I did in the ensuing years was quite different from what I had imagined I would be doing. I had never fallen for the line taken by insurance and annuity companies that I would settle down on a balmy beach, get a tan, and watch the years go by. I had thought that I would keep on studying, reading, and writing, although at a leisurely pace, and that I would do more outdoor work at Peacham than I had had time for previously. How wrong my

---

[1] As President Butler approached the age of retirement, he changed the rules to allow administrative officers to continue in office after the above ages. President Eisenhower changed the rules back again!

[2] Incidentally, I postponed a sabbatical leave so that it would be a "terminal leave" and make my retirement come a little early.

predictions turned out to be!

So far as my writing projects went, I planned to go to Paris with my wife in my first year and to begin another economic history of France. The book I had in mind was to be quite different from my *France, 1789-1939*, published way back in 1940. The new book was to be more of an economic study in the tradition of my *Economic History of Modern Italy*. I thought that it would be a good idea to conclude my career by returning to Paris where I had originally decided upon a life of scholarship in European economic history. My wife agreed with this plan and arranged for a leave from Finch College, for she had a couple of more years before her own retirement.

Thus it came about that we left for Paris in the summer of 1969. We took an apartment in Reid Hall, which I described earlier, and I went to work. My first step was to go to visit my friends and to discuss with them my plans. I learned at once that, while I had been concentrating my efforts on Italian history, much had been happening in the French field that I knew little about. Fortunately I could go to such experts as Fernand Braudel, Ernest Labrousse, François Crouzet, Pierre Léon, B. Gille, François Furet, Jean Fourastié, and literally a host of others for advice and help.

From them I learned that Braudel and Labrousse were sponsoring a multi-volume economic history of France, which was to be written by France's leading experts. Here was competition with a vengeance! I knew that I could not match such competition and tried to console myself with the thought that I would be producing a one-volume synthesis of the period from the end of the eighteenth century to the present. So I persevered.

Competition was not, however, necessarily my chief difficulty. I soon became aware of the enormous amount of literature that I would have to wade through before I was adequately prepared to turn out the book which I had in mind. Nothing daunted, I plunged into the task with energy. I was able through my friends to get into a section of the Bibliothéque Nationale where I could always find a seat and into the Salle des Professeurs of the Sorbonne Library where I had access to books that I needed and some limited privileges for borrowing. Then, I also had at my disposition the library of Reid Hall, where I could find such things as dictionaries, very general works, and encyclopedias.

I began with the period at the conclusion of the eighteenth century, the Revolution, and the Napoleonic periods. I made fairly good progress, but the end of the tunnel looked discouragingly far away. Undoubtedly I made slower progress than I might have because my wife and I had many friends who invited us frequently to dinners, to receptions, the theater, art shows, and concerts. This was all very enjoyable and part of our plan for retirement, but it did eat into my time and energy. Then the inevitable happened: I fell ill with influenza. The bad air of the libraries and other public places was one of the things that was sure to give me respiratory troubles. I became so sick, indeed, that not only did I have to give up my studying but I had to give up Paris. I sought relief in balmier Italy, but there I would be better one day and worse the next. I traveled around a bit and saw old friends, but I could not get to feeling so that I could get back to work. Finally, I decided to return to the farm, where I believed that I could take better care of myself. This return did not work out as I had hoped. My wife remained in Italy to pursue her work and I was left alone to cope with my health problem as best I could.

Unfortunately I did not get well under my own care, for I had too much housekeeping to do; and the various jobs around the farm, which were being left undone, kept me on edge. At last I convinced my doctor that he should put me in a hospital where I could get the rest and care I needed to get well. There I did show improvement, partly because I shared a room with a country clown (also a band leader and electrical company worker) who kept me royally entertained. Finally I recovered to a point where I thought that I could take care of myself at the farm and returned to Peacham.

My wife ultimately came back from Italy and began her last year at Finch, while I remained at Peacham to continue my book on France. That task went very slowly and I champed at the bit most of the time. I realized, as my elder son was forever telling me, that I was wrapped up in the Calvinist syndrome and simply could not think of doing nothing.

Eventually, I finished a piece, which was to have been the first chapter of my book, on the economic consequences of the French Revolution and the Napoleonic Period. I submitted it to *French Historical Studies*, a review of the Society of French Historical Studies, which seemed to me to be the logical place for it. I had been a founder of the review, took great pride in it, and had been president of the Society. In addition, the editor, David Pinkney was a friend of mine, for whom I had done many favors. As was his practice, he sent my article for review to one of his advisers and eventually wrote me that this scholar thought that I said nothing new. I was crestfallen. I thought that I had considerable standing in the community of scholars of French history in this country and that I should not have been brushed off so lightly. I was convinced that after a year of concentration on my theme, I had indeed a lot of things to say.

There was, of course, nothing I could do about the matter. Consequently I published my piece in an Italian journal; it won very favorable critical acclaim; and it was one of the articles chosen for inclusion in a very selective series of articles published in a German work on the French Revolution. I felt vindicated, but I cite the case to illustrate the foibles of scholarship and disappointments in old age.

The episode did much to bring me to a decision regarding my French economic history project. I was at last willing to concede that the likelihood of my mobilizing the resources and energy to conclude the work were very slight. So, with great reluctance, I "folded my tent," so far as my French study was concerned. I found some solace in an aphorism of William Westermann that "the sensible scholar knows when to hang up his typewriter."

I did hanker, however, for some activity that would not be very burdensome and that could be combined with my life at Peacham. I did a certain amount of traveling to meetings of the executive committee of the International Economic History Association; I attended annual meetings of professional societies;

and I did some lecturing including a stay at the Center of Historical Studies at Budapest, Hungary. I discovered also that reviewing books and reading manuscripts for the *Journal of European Economic History* gave me some of the activity which I craved. Yet, I needed a little bit more work than I had, and the search for a "little bit more" led me to the writing of this autobiography.

A short time before I decided to abandon my French study, an event took place which was to make a marked change in my remaining years. During my wife's Christmas vacation from Finch College (1970) she did not consider joining me at the farm but, as was her wont, took off with a friend for Florida. While she was there, she found a house for sale which she thought I should buy. She liked Florida because it made her think of Italy and because she believed the Floridian climate was good for her arthritis. I felt, also, that it might not be a bad idea to have a place in a warm clime so that I could avoid the rigors of Vermont winters and, in addition, have a refuge to which I could retreat in my later years if I could not live alone at the farm. I had a sum of money from the sale of my professional library, which I was willing to use for the purpose. Finally, I had a concern for my wife's brother, who had lived with us for several years and who was so failing in health that he needed our supervision. He was, however, very trying, so we wanted a property with a "garage apartment," or something of the kind, so that he could be near us and yet not in our house. The place which my wife had located had such a second house.

The upshot was that I decided (February, 1971) to go to Florida to look at this find. I took along my trusted friend, Ben Berwick, and his wife,with the thought that he could help with the driving and that we could work on the place, if I decided to purchase it. I was planning to go to Europe a little later to meetings of the International Commission of Economic History, so I knew that I would have to get my friends back to Peacham within a month's time. I also took my sister with me. She had not been to her place at West Palm Beach since her husband had died a couple of years earlier and now wanted to spend her winters there.

The trip down went well. Ben, who had never been

south of New York, was a great help and a general delight. The routes about New York were a maze to him and after I had driven through them and was out in "open country" at New Brunswick, N.J., he said, "Shep, how in the hell do you know your way through all them overpasses, underpasses, turnoffs, tunnels, and bridges?" My reply was simple: "The first time you took me to the Peacham Bog (an area about seven miles by five miles without any roads) I asked you how you found your way through it and you said, 'If you had been there as many times as I have, you'd know where to go!' " He always drove after lunch, unless we were in a city, for I was sleepy then from being accustomed to a siesta. One day while I was half-dozing, I heard my sister remark, "Ben, don't you think that 95 is rather fast through here?"

In spite of such speeds, we arrived at West Palm Beach quite safely. After looking at many houses, I decided to buy the place which my wife had found. Unfortunately the laws are such that I could not do any work on my place until title had been transferred and that was going to take some time. So I went back to Peacham with Ben and his wife. Then to Europe for my meeting, which was held at the Villa Serbelloni on beautiful Lake Como. Thence I returned to Peacham, where I spent the summer alone, again.

In the fall of 1971, I repaired to West Palm Beach and the new houses. My wife had moved our belongings from New York there and had the house all organized by the time I arrived. The place was very beautiful. She was an excellant decorator, so far as esthetics were concerned. She gave very little consideration, however, to livability. She placed the T.V. set, for example, in the "Florida Room," where she could watch it from a couch, but where there was then no place for me in an easy chair. Also, in the living room there was no place where I could read in comfort. And in the breakfast nook we had to move the table so far to my side, so she could get in hers, that I could scarely get in at all.

I did, however, take much pride in my new possession and worked hard all winter to improve it and the grounds. I repaired what needed to be fixed, including ravages by termites in the little house; I set up an outdoor laundry; I painted the buildings; I pruned the shrubs, hedges, mangoes, and citrus trees; I set out new fruit trees, such as avocados and figs; and I built up the lawns. For the most part, I enjoyed the hours spent in home improvements.

Yet, I realized that all was not well—that my marriage was becoming very shaky. During the last several years, my wife and I had spent little time together, except for the stay in Paris. In New York, she had her work and I had mine, she had one set of social activities and I had another; and she had one group of friends and I a different one. On weekends, when we might have been together, she worked on some writing project, while I went to the country for some exercise and fresh air. In periods of vacations, she went to Florida, Europe, or Middlebury, and I went to the farm.

When we began to spend all our time under one roof, we got into each other's hair. If we had no large concerns to divide us, we made mountains out of molehills. Then there was her brother, whom I found very difficult as he grew older.

As I have said, many things annoyed one or the other of us, but no useful purpose will be served by relating them here. I can say, however, that after the first winter together in our new Florida home my wife decided to remain there during the summer and not accompany me to the farm. When I left West Palm, she did not get up to bid me farewell; she did not inform me of the death of her brother during the summer; she did not communicate with me; and when I returned to Florida in the fall, she had changed the locks on the house so that I could not get in. At that point, I decided that to live under the tensions which were aroused by being with my wife was not what I wanted for the rest of my days. None of my efforts at reconciliation was of any avail. Divorce seemed the only remedy. As a matter of fact, she had invited me many times "to get out, if I were not happy around here."

I do not need to carry the reader through the details of the divorce process. Yet, I learned from my experience things which may be of profit to my readers. In the first place, I engaged a lawyer from a list that had been provided to me by a judge whom I knew. The person whom I selected was a gentleman and a scholar, but he was interminably slow. Fortunately, I made an arrangement whereby I was to pay him a fixed fee. If I had paid him by the hour, my bill would have been astronomical. My wife, on the other hand, hired a lawyer who was reputed to be the meanest member of the bar in all the state—and his reputation was fully deserved. His strategy was to try get everything out of me which he could and his technique was to threaten the worst in hope that I would make all manner of concessions. In one of the hearings before the judge, he tried to intimidate me by stating that he would get for his client what I cherished the most—the farm. His tactic only served to get my back up.

My lawyer's strategy was, on the contrary, quite different from that of my wife's counsel. He proposed that we make a fair and equitable offer, which was not only what I wanted, but what would win the judge to our side and would prevent my being "taken to the cleaners," as the saying goes. We offered an equal division of all my property. My stocks would be divided equally between us; she would get the place in Florida and I would get the farm; and I would pay a certain alimony.

No settlement was reached that winter of 1972-73. Fortunately, I was able to spend those months with my elder sister, who had, as I have written above, a house in West Palm which had been in the family for years.

One of the reasons for not coming to a settlement was that the judge who sat on our case kept prodding the lawyers to effect an arrangement which would be satisfactory for both of us. This they failed to do. I went back to the farm, alone, for the summer of 1973. Finally in September I received a call that the case was on the court's docket for trial within two weeks. This was bad for me because of harvests, but I hurried to the southland. When I arrived, I learned that the lawyers had still not agreed on a settlement. I learned, too, that my wife had fired her counsel (the fifth whom she had employed to work me over) and had engaged another. Her new man kept making demands for more and more until finally I instructed my lawyer to let the case go to trial. This threat, together with a concession of a little land at the farm, brought the whole matter to a conclusion. I was soon a single man again.

I returned to Peacham after these events, but once there realized more than ever that living alone, even though I was free, was not what I wanted for the long haul. My children and grandchildren, who lived in Boston and New York, came to see me but never remained for any length of time. I spent the winter after the divorce in West Palm with my sister, then in the summer of 1974 I went back to Peacham. The sense of loneliness returned with a vengeance, especially at mealtime. Although my eldest grandson worked for a neighboring farmer, he was so busy that I saw little of him. I had, of course, many local friends, but I saw them mainly when they invited me for a meal or I invited them. I found solace in cutting firewood with my friend Ben Berwick. We took the work slowly, with many a bottle of beer between felling, limbing, skidding, and "cutting-up." I was also helped by the fact that my elder sister, a widow, came to the farm during strawberry and raspberry harvesting and my other sister and brother came for Thanksgiving.

From time to time, I went to Boston or New York to see my children and grandchildren and perchance to take in theater and concerts. My sons and their families led very busy lives and could not relieve my pangs of loneliness for very long; and I found both cities, particularly Morningside Heights in New York, so deteriorated or downright repulsive that I gave up going to them.

Although I made a serious effort to refrain from being depressed or bored, I am sure that it became apparent that I was not content to continue the life of a single man. Some of my friends tried to lend me a hand in finding a mate, but as so frequently happens in such circumstances, the mere thought of what they were attempting to do turned me off.

Perhaps I was not doing my looking in the right areas or the right age groups. I had long been impressed with the advice given to men in my circumstances by Benjamin Franklin: If a man is to remarry, he should always choose a lady of a certain age, because she will be so grateful. Such counsel seemed logical and sound, but it is advice that is neither "bull high nor hog tight." There are so many factors involved in mating that they cannot be reduced to gratitude based on age.

As time went on, it became more and more evident to me that I was not going to have an easy time in finding a person who would share the rest of my days with me. More and more I began to think of myself as not a very good catch.

I did, however, discover a person whom I found very compatible and very attractive. She was assistant to an opthalmologist to whom I had been going for several years and who lived in a town not far from Peacham. I began to take her out for dinner, for she was so very busy she had little free time except for meals.

Upon one of these occasions, which became more and more frequent, I found her reading in the lounge of one of the country inns which we frequented a book of the "Dear Abby' or Ann Landers variety. As I glanced over her shoulder, I noticed that the book was open to a chapter entitled, "How to Catch a Man." That gave me some hope, but when I first broached the subject of matrimony to her, I received little encouragement. She expressed a very strong loyalty toward her employer with whom she had been for twenty-three years. My friends who knew about my interest thought that I would never win this fair lady, no matter how hard I tried. I did, however, continue to see her fairly often during the summers, but I made, so far as I could ascertain, little headway.

I do not know even to this day what happened to change her mind. Perhaps as much as any one thing was a letter which I wrote her from Florida in the spring of 1976 saying in effect that I would never return to the South again without her. In any case, when I was driving north, I phoned her to let her know when I was arriving, and in the ensuing conversation she intimated that she was beginning to change her mind. That news sped me home and she finally said "yes."

The ensuing three months were exceedingly busy ones. We decided that we should be married as soon as was practicable, and fixed the date for the middle of June. There were, of course, innumerable arrangements which had to be made. There was, for instance, the problem of finding a replacement for my fiancée in the job as assistant to the opthalmologist. That was ultimately resolved and the training of the new person begun. Then my future wife had to give up her apartment and her belongings moved out. Finally, she started to make arrangements for the wedding. We planned to be married at the home of the bride's sister, which involved having the ceremony in a garden. This meant that a tent had to be erected in case of rain, wind, or even snow (this was, after all, Vermont). If one has never tried to hire a tent and have it put up in a small town, one cannot imagine the trouble and turmoil involved in doing so.

Although the preparations for the wedding fell largely on my bride, I had plenty with which to be concerned. As was my practice, I had my annual physical as soon as it could be arranged after my return from Florida. This examination I began with some trepidation, for I had had two operations for cancer of the skin before I left the South and just before I took off a new growth was discovered. I was to have this removed in conjunction with a complete examination. Unfortunately in the examination the doctors discovered that I had a physical disability of a certain gravity. I was, of course, very upset and thought that I should refrain from inflicting myself in my condition on the lady I loved. I discussed my doubts in great detail with the brother of my fiancée, who is a surgeon and professor at the University of Vermont Medical School. He is a very level-headed person and counseled us to go ahead with our plans. His opinion was that my trouble could be controlled with medical treatment. Besides, he said, life is a long series of taking risks and the one that I had just come to know about was no worse that lots of others.

I also talked the whole thing out with my bride-to-be and she concurred completely with her brother in whom she had the utmost confidence—a confidence bordering on worship. So we went ahead with our plans. This meant some rearranging of things at the farm and the construction of storage facilities to house many of my bride's belongings. She is an inveterate collector of antiques and a saver of everything. I doubt that she has discarded a single dress since she was in kindergarten. Fortunately, I was able to engage my faithful friend, Merle Jones, Jr., whom I had "brought up" from childhood to be a first-rate carpenter, electrician, plumber, and jack of all trades. He built just what I wanted, but as things turned out the storage space he constructed was not large enough!

The happy day finally dawned, and dawned cold, windy, and rainy. My brother and sisters were there, as well as my two sons and their families, including two darling granddaughters, who were to be the flower girls. They stole the show. Then, there were all of Marion's friends and relatives, who were very numerous inasmuch as the ceremony was taking place on her home grounds. Everything was all set by the appointed time. The portable organ was in place; the weather had turned out to be bright and warm; the tent heater had made things confortable; and even the minister was there.

On this last subject there had been some confusion, for he came from Chicago where he was on the staff of a theological seminary. He was a summer resident in Peacham and had become a friend of both of us. He had been held up by graduating ceremonies at his institution, by a mix-up in air reservations, by bad weather, and at the last minute by being informed that he was not licensed to marry people in Vermont. How he managed to get squared away with the law or how he obtained special dispensation, I do not know. He finagled it somehow, for red tape can be cut through and the wiles of Vermont politicians and licensors are marvels to behold. At all events, he performed the ceremony in a beautiful manner and so far as I know and, so far as any body seems to care, Marion and I were legally joined in holy matrimony.

Following a lavish buffet, Marion's nephew brought out his antique motor-driven fire engine (vintage of 1910) and much to the delight of the children, both young and old, paraded everyone who was so inclined up and down the driveway. I am certain that my young flower-girl granddaughters attached more importance to the rides which they had and to the sirens which they manipulated than they did to the marriage ceremonies.

In the small towns of northern New England a tradition persists of making the getaway of the bride and groom on their honeymoon a difficult and even at times dangerous excercise. I thought that the tradition had disappeared, but to take no chances we had hidden our car in a neighbor's driveway which was so located that we could get to it by slipping through a hedge. We were, as a consequence, on our way before we were spotted and we escaped with only a feeble blowing of horns behind us. We went to the Sunset Hill House in the White Mountains for our first night and I can recommend the place to anyone who is looking for a quaint, quiet spot with beautiful surroundings and excellent food. The next day we took off for the Boston area where we spent the next week at the College Club of Wellesley College. Then back to Peacham and the farm.

This was a period of "getting to know you, getting to know all about you," as the song goes in *The King and I.* It was a happy time. The adjustments were easier that I had imagined that they would be, which I attribute to the fact that Marion has a very sweet disposition.

She fitted extremely well into my life in Peacham. She was accepted joyously by members of my circle, by both local people, and by people from "away." She knew much less about farm life than I had expected and I was really astounded at how urbanized a person living in a town of 10,000 can be. Soon she learned the difference between an open heifer and a closed door, between a cant hook and a headland, and between distributor points and spark plugs. She liked most of my exotic dishes like brains, snails, and frog legs, but she never did develop any enthusiasm for kidneys. On the other hand, she rapidly got into the cooking act and after one lesson made better bread that I did and several other dishes as well.

When fall arrived and the beautiful foliage had passed, we began to discuss whether or not we should go to Florida for the winter, or to Europe or to stay in Peacham. I had been invited to read a paper in Rome on the subject of inflation, but for various reasons the meeting which I was to address kept being put off and then was canceled altogether. The indecision over this matter resulted in making our plans for the winter more difficult than they otherwise would have been. Also I was not certain that I should absent myself from my doctors until we were sure that the therapy which I was undergoing was effective. Lastly, I love my place, the people who are my neighbors, and the beauty of the snow with the crunchy sound as one walks on it when the temperature is at zero. I even had visions of taking up skiing again, although I doubted that I would make it.

At all events, we finally decided to remain on the farm for the winter. We got along well, although we had such annoyances as having the oil furnace clog up and cover the downstairs with soot, as getting stuck in snow banks, and as getting up in the night to stoke the fires with wood. I personally never suffered from cabin fever, but I think that Marion had touches of it along in March. Just at the crucial moment, however, as is usual, the sun began to warm things up, the maple sugaring began, thoughts of planting became uppermost in my mind, and then the flowers began to bloom. It was summer again.

The summer and fall following our full winter in Peacham (in which, incidentally, I did not take up serious skiing again) passed happily and smoothly. My ailment responded to treatment and my doctor assured me that, although I would die some time of something, it would not be from *that* particular problem. Our friendships in Peacham deepened with closer associations and our circle was somewhat extended. I managed to keep exceedingly busy with one thing and another.

The following summer was also busy. The vegetable garden required much of my time and the amount of effort which can be expended on flowers and fruit trees is only limited by the number of daylight hours. In addition, the summer always brings my sons and their families to our place for holidays or ritualistic visits. Moreover, friends came from far and wide to share a few days with us.

When the harvests had been completed in the fall and we had experienced another "festival of foliage" colors, and when the winter winds again whistled overhead and, for that matter, through the house, we began once more the debate over whether or not we should remain in Peacham or seek warmer climes. We both wanted to be at the farm for Thanksgiving and Christmas, family days best spent at home, and so we celebrated them at Peacham.

Subsequently, we both had bouts with the flu and these set-backs decided us to turn our footsteps southward. By the middle of January, we had snow up to our windowsills and had burned most of our firewood, which I had so laboriously cut during the summer. So at the end of the first month of the new year, we took off for Florida.

Originally I had hoped that, if we did go to the south, I would visit friends along the way as one method of making the hard trip easier and more agreeable. When we came to go,however, we were not feeling up to seeing friends, so we went slowly by doing some sight-seeing and by not driving far in any one day. Of the cities which we visited and which we did not know, we were very favorably impressed with Savannah. The town is laid out geometrically and has a wonderful waterfront. We hope to go there again.

By stages we got to Florida and tried out several areas new to us, but we found none to suit us. By default we finally wound up in West Palm Beach. The place was so crowded, however, that we had to take quarters which were not satisfactory and this fact did much to make us leery about seeking refuge there in the future.

From what has preceded, one can gather that my professional life continued to be pushed into the background. Inasmuch as that was the case, I was surprised to receive, shortly after we were settled in West Palm, an invitation to give some lectures at the University of California at Santa Barbara. Then, not long after this opportunity presented itself, I was invited to go to the European University Institute at Fiesole, Italy, just outside Florence, as a visiting lecturer for two months. This establishment had been created by the Common Market countries to train international civil servants. It had attracted many distinguished professors and paid them some of the highest academic salaries in the world. I decided to accept both invitations. I wanted to go to southern California, to see La Jolla, where I had once considered accepting a post, and to Riverside, where one of my former students was a teacher. I wanted also to go to Italy in order to show it to Marion, to visit friends, and to improve my bank balances.

The visits to both California and Europe were delightful. The person who invited me to Santa Barbara had taken his Ph. D. with me at Columbia and he had written an excellent dissertation on the spread of French culture to Senegal. He, with others, had developed at Santa Barbara courses to train historians for other employment than teaching. I had had considerable experience in activity of this kind, for I had been in charge of placement for our department for a long enough period and had had to find openings for our people in non-academic walks of life as well as in academic ones. I had much to say to Johnson's students, which made me feel that the trip was worthwhile. Our greatest satisfaction came, however, from getting to know Johnson's wonderful family.

Our trip to Europe was, for the most part, equally enjoyable, except for the weather. Our first stop was Paris, where we visited old friends and, of course, the city. Unfortunately Paris, plus its suburbs, has grown so fast that every public place was crowded. Much of the new architecture, especially Le Centre Pompidou, is not pleasing and the city has become a "gas chamber" with the high-rise buildings of the suburbs holding the smoke from Paris within the city limits.

Our stay in Florence provided a great opportunity for Marion to become acquainted with one of the artistic centers of the world. I was able to meet many old friends there and my teaching was so light that I could indulge in sight-seeing with my wife and in sampling the gastronomic delights of the city.

From Florence, we went to Rome to visit more friends, especially Rosario Romeo and Salvatore Villari and their wives; and I had a chance to show Marion that city. We were there, unfortunately, just after the Aldo Moro murder, which cast a pall over the city and over us. After Rome, we went to Madrid and Toledo for a week, again to take in one of my favorite places—El Prado. Thence we turned toward home via Lisbon and the Azores. In retrospect, we may say that Marion and I took our European Grand Tour as a kind of valedictory. We are glad that we went, but travel is to me neither so pleasant nor so thrilling as it once was.

Our return to Peacham (June, 1978) was timed in such a way that once at home, we had to scurry to do all the essential chores—cleaning, planting, and generally getting back into our normal routines.[3] Ever since, I have been less and less active professionally, but I do remain a member of the editorial board of the *Journal of European Economic History*; I continue to write reviews for learned journals; and I maintain a large correspondence, largely with students. They still seek my assistance in getting fellowships or in advancing themselves professionally. Many of them have made their marks in the world. I also maintain close relations with many friends: Ben Hunningher, professor of Netherlandish history and literature in my time at Columbia; Jean Fourastié, a French economic historian; Rosario Romeo, of Rome; Paul Sutorius, the only one of my college days whom I continue to see; and a host of others. I have been able to keep up my large correspondence because I am fortunate enough to have a neighbor, Lorna Quimby, who serves with great efficiency as a secretary. She comes to the house once a week and in brief order deals with a multitude of things, including keeping me posted on events in town.

Another of my activities is to reflect upon the changes in America during my lifetime. In more than three-quarters of a century I have seen our economy move from a predominantly agricultural one to an industrial one, and with this change the gradual disappearance of the small, one-man family farm with its partial self-sufficiency and the growth of large units producing products for an impersonal, money-oriented market. In this same period, I have witnessed the wonders, and horrors, created by the internal combustion engine. In fact, my life has spanned the "gasoline age," or at least it has covered this age from its beginning to its maturity. I have observed the aging of our population with the expectation of life at birth rising from 47.3 in 1900 to 74 in 1980 and I have seen the aged become a unique problem in our society. I have seen a decline in the family as an institution for guiding our behavior, as a unified economic unit, and as a place where the youth receives much of its education. I have seen a decline in the role of the church in our society, a revolution in our sex mores, and an enormous

---

[3] Upon our return, we discovered that one of our freezers had ceased to function and that all the meat from a large steer had rotted! May it be said to the credit of my wife that she cleaned up this mess with not much help from me!

extension of education for the masses. I have observed the shift of our population from one composed predominantly of Northern Europeans and their descendants to one that is a composite of many peoples, with newcomers especially from Southern Europe, Latin America, and Asia. I have beheld the growing importance of "minority" groups in our domestic politics, the disappearance of isolationism in international affairs, and the increase in our power status in the world with all its attendant responsibilities.

These changes, not to mention a host of others, constitute a real revolution in our ways of making a living, in our social behavior, in our thinking, and in how we govern ourselves. As I reflect upon what has happened during my days on earth, I am forced to wonder to what extent our life as human beings has been improved or worsened. We certainly have more comfortable, healthier, and longer existences, but I am not sure that we are happier. I plan to put some of my thoughts in this regard on paper as I approach my next project—a study of the changes which have taken place in my Vermont town of Peacham since I have known it.

It is obvious that no autobiography can ever be complete—one has to stop writing before one stops breathing. The point at which I now am seems to be a reasonable place to conclude my tale. I do not want to take my fingers from the keys of my typewriter, however, without expressing some of my views on old age. In sum, I have little good to say for it. I advise my readers to avoid it. Believe me, the aphorism that "one is only so old as one thinks one is" borders on the ridiculous. In my opinion, Shakespeare gave a true-to-life view of old age in the "seven stages of life" from *As You Like It:*

> This sixth age shifts
> Into the lean and slippered pantaloon,
> With spectacles on nose and pouch on side,
> His youthful hose, well saved, a world too wide
> For his shrunk shank; and his big manly voice
> Turning again toward childish treble, pipes
> And whistles in his sound. Last scene of all,

That ends this strange eventful history,
Is second childishness, and mere oblivion,
Sans teeth, sans eyes, sans taste, sans everything.

Some there have been who have sung the praise of old age. Cicero in his *De Senectute* could say that, "Old age, especially an honored old age, has so great authority, that this is of more value than all the pleasures of youth." Maybe this was true in Ancient Rome, but it is hardly the case in America, 1979. Nicholas Murrary Butler did not begin to laud old age until he wanted to advance the time of mandatory retirement in order to retain the presidency of Columbia University. And if one takes seriously Browning's words, put in the mouth of *Rabbi Ben Ezra,* that

"The best is yet to be
The last of life for which the first was made"

one may wonder about the earlier part of Browning's life.

As I have said, I cannot find much to say in favor of old age. The old man begins his day by reading the obituary page, and then, if his name is not there, has breakfast. After a few years, he hardly bothers with death notices, for all of his friends have passed through newsprint to the grave—only he is left. In any case, after breakfast (or before) he checks his weight, and curses. He then considers his ailments, phones his physician, takes his pills, unless he is so absent-minded he does not remember where he put them, and gets his new prescription filled. He eats his meals, taking care to have nothing which will upset his fragile digestive system, does those few chores of which he is still capable, looks at some unfinished work (maybe a manuscript), or desultorily reads a book, or, "God forbid," looks at television. Finally, he creeps arthritically to bed, perchance to dream about life in the nursing home he had just visited, or to wake up with cramps or the itch.

Although I have little good to say of the last stage of life, particularly compared with that of the fifth of Shakespeare's seven stages, I cannot pretend that my later years have not been happy ones. I have been thrice blessed for not having taken the advice of Ben Franklin in the selection of a wife. Fortunately, I did not choose an elderly person, but one younger than myself. She has been an excellent companion to me and watches out for my well-being as attentively as a mother duck looks after her ducklings. She shares many of my interests at Peacham and partakes of many of my concerns and duties.

If I have a final counsel to give to those who are entering later maturity, as it is now called, it would be this: continue to lead the kind of life which you enjoy the most; take the best possible care of your body that you can; and keep busy doing something. When the grim reaper appears to perform that most democratic act of all, do not resent his coming. Be able to say that you have had a good life—that you have fought the good fight—that you are leaving the world no worse for having been in it.

PRINCIPAL BOOKS AND ARTICLES

by

Shepard B. Clough

With Herbert W. Schneider, *Making Fascists.* Chicago: Chicago University Press, 1929.

*History of the Flemish Movement in Belgium.*New York: Richard R. Smith, 1930. Revised Edition. New York: Octagon Books, 1968.

"The Evolution of Fascist Economic Theory and Practice." *Harvard Business Review,* April, 1932.

"The Objectives of Education in Fascist Italy." in Rexford G. Tugwell and L. H. Keyserling, *Redirecting Education,* New York: Columbia University Press, 1935.

France, a Study in National Economics. New York: Scribner's Sons, 1939.

With Charles W. Cole, *An Economic Hisory of Europe.* Boston: Heath, 1939 and several re-editions.

"What About Reparation This Time?" *Political Science Quarterly,* Vol. lix, 1944, pp. 220-226.

"The House that Pétain Built." *Political Science Quarterly,* Vol. lix, pp. 30-39.

"The Flemish Movement." in J. A. Goris, *Belgium.* Berkeley: University of California Press, 1945.

"Retardative Factors in French Economic Development in the Nineteenth and Twentieth Centuries." *Journal of Economic History,* 1946, pp. 91-102.

"Crisis in French Economy at the Beginning of the Revolution." *Journal of Economic History,* November, 1946, pp. 191-196.

A History of American Life Insurance. New York: Columbia University Press, 1946.

The Rise and Fall of Civilization. New York: McGraw-Hill, 1951 with French, German, Spanish, and English editions.

"Presentation d'une théorie des transformations sociales." *Revue économique,* November, 1952.

The American Way. New York: Thomas Y. Crowell, 1953. With translations in some ten foreign languages.

Histoire Economique des Etats-Unis. Paris: Presses Universitaires, 1954.

With Carlo Livi, "Economic Growth in Italy: An Analysis of the Uneven Development of North and South." *Journal of Economic History*, September, 1956.

"The Diffusion of Industry in the Last Half Century." *Studi in Onore di Armando Sapori*. Milan: Cisalpino, 1957, vol.ii.

The Economic Development of Western Civilization. New York: McGraw-Hill, 1959.

Basic Values in Western Civilization. New York: Columbia University Press, 1960.

"Philanthropy and the Welfare State in Europe." *Political Science Quarterly*, March, 1960.

An Economic History of Modern Italy, 1861-1963. New York: Columbia University Press, 1964.

With Peter Gay and Charles K. Warner, *The European Past, Reappraisals in History from the Renaissance*. New York: Macmillan, 1964. 2 vols.

With several collaborators, *A History of the Western World*. Boston: D. C. Heath, 1964.

With Carol Gayle Moodie, *European Economic History, Documents and Readings*. Princeton: Van Nostrand, 1965.

Storia dell'economia Italiana dal 1861 ad oggi. Bologna: Cappelli, 1965. Translation of *An Economic History of Modern Italy, 1861-1963*. New York: Columbia University Press, 1964.

"The Economic History of the Fascist Period." *Il Nuovo Osservatore*, January, 1966.

"French Social Structure, Social Values, and Economic Growth." In Acomb, Evelyn M. and Brown, Marvin L., Jr., *French Society and Culture since the Old Regime*. New York: Holt, Rinehart, and Winston, 1966.

European Economic History. Economic Development of Western Civilization. New York: McGraw-Hill, 1968. Revised edition of: *The Economic Development of Western Civilization*. New York: McGraw-Hill, 1959.

With Salvatore Saladino, *A History of Modern Italy in Readings and Documents*. New York: Columbia University Press, 1968.

With Theodore F. Marburg, *The Economic Basis of American Civilization*. New York: Thomas Crowell, 1968. Revised edition of *The American Way*. New York: Thomas Crowell, 1953.

With Thomas and Carol Moodie, *European Economic History in the Twentieth Century in Documents*. New York: Harper & Row, 1968.

"Loria Achille." *International Encyclopedia of the Social Sciences*, 1968,

"The Industrial Revolution." in Peter Gay and Jack Garraty, *Columbia University History of the World*. New York: Harper & Row, 1968.

Storia della civiltà e sviluppo economico. Naples: Giannini, 1969.

With Peter Gay, Charles K. Warner, and John M. Cammett, *The European Past*. 2nd edition, New York: Macmillan, 1970, 2 vols.

With Antonio di Vittorio, "Nuove ricerche e nuovi punti di vista sui fattori di ritardo nello sviluppo economico francese durante la rivoluzione e il periodo napoleonico." *La Rassegna.* March-April, pp. 281-305, 1971.

"Taxation and Capital Formation since 1870 in France and the United States." *Ricerche storiche ed economiche in memoria di Carrado Barbagallo a cura di Luigi de Rosa.* Naples: Edizioni Scientifiche Italiane, 1970, vol. lll, pp.135, 156.

"American Textbooks in European Economic History during the Last Fifty Years." *Journal of European Economic History,* Vol. 1, No. 2—Fall, 1972. Banco di Roma.

"The Social Sciences in Historical Studies in the United States." *Mélange en l'honneur de Fernand Braudel,* Private Edition, 1973.

"Retardative Factors in French Economic Growth at the end of the Ancien Regime and during the French Revolutionary and Napoleonic Period." In *Studies in Economics and Economic History.* New York: Macmillan, 1972. Trans. in German: *Die Französische Revolution.* von Eberhard Schmitt, Cologne: Kiepenheuer & Witsch, 1976.

With Luigi de Rosa, *Storia dell'economia Italiana dal 1861 ad oggi.* Bologna: Cappelli, 1974. Translation of *An Economic History of Modern Italy.* New York: Columbia University Press, 1964.

With others, *European History in a World Perspective.* 2nd Edition. Boston: D. C. Heath, 1975.

With Richard T. Rapp, *European Economic History,* 3rd Edition. New York: McGraw-Hill, 1975.